Gett

"There is a vast gulf between making music for pleasure and making music for money. David Arditi's *Getting Signed* intelligently and compellingly captures the difficulty, frustration, and hope felt by musicians as they attempt to enter the realm of the music industry and make money at music."

—Timothy D. Taylor, *Professor of Ethnomusicology, University of California, Los Angeles, USA*

"Even in our digitized era of streaming media and DIY culture, the seductions of landing a record deal with a cash advance have never been stronger for musicians, singers, rockers, and rappers. But in *Getting Signed*, sociologist David Arditi shines his well-honed critical gaze on the venality of the pop music industry, showing how even a record contract struck in good faith can be a dream-killing Faustian bargain for most musical artists."

—David Grazian, *Associate Professor of Sociology and Communication and Faculty Director of Urban Studies, University of Pennsylvania, USA*

"In *Getting Signed*, Arditi deftly cuts through the fog of mythology, wishful thinking, and industry propaganda surrounding artist-label relations. As his exhaustive research shows, the recording industry is both fundamentally exploitative and still profoundly necessary, even as the technology, economics, and culture of the broader music industry continue to transform drastically in the wake of new, digital technologies. A must-read for aspiring musicians and scholars of the industry alike."

—Aram Sinnreich, *author of* The Essential Guide to Intellectual Property *(2019)*

"*Getting Signed* is a timely and trenchant reconsideration of the economics of the recording industry, and how it relies on ideology to convince musicians not only that they have to play by its rules, but also that they desperately want to. You won't think about the music business in the same way after reading it."

—Brian L. Frye, *Spears-Gilbert Associate Professor of Law, University of Kentucky, USA*

David Arditi

Getting Signed

Record Contracts, Musicians, and Power in Society

David Arditi
The University of Texas at Arlington
Arlington, TX, USA

ISBN 978-3-030-44586-7 ISBN 978-3-030-44587-4 (eBook)
https://doi.org/10.1007/978-3-030-44587-4

This Palgrave Macmillan imprint is published by the registered company Springer Nature Switzerland AG
The registered company address is: Gewerbestrasse 11, 6330 Cham, Switzerland

Acknowledgments

The ideology of getting signed is something that I know intimately from my own early dreams to those of my friends. I spent 10 years actively gigging and teaching drums. During that time, I went from dreaming of making it big to recognizing musician celebrity is a pipe dream. I'd like to thank the musicians I gigged with the most for setting me on the path to this book. Thank you, Cameron McLaughlin, Gjergji Theka, Karanja Burke, Wayne Hancock, Genesis Osagboro, K.C. Moyer, Keith Thomas, Richard Jesse, Mike Orlando, Scott Orlando, Myra Gourley, Chris Tansey, Francis Dayton, Dani Rosner, Chas Hill, Matt McCarthy, Mike Jones, Chris Mullins, and many others.

While the idea for this book worked alongside my years gigging, one conversation began the research. In 2012, I spoke with my colleague James Welch about his experience as a musician in Austin, TX. He told me the worst part was South-by-Southwest (SXSW) where all the musicians would posture and claim that they were about to be signed. Of course, getting signed is the explicit goal of performing at SXSW because there are so many label representatives in Austin for the occasion. James' discussion of the musicians brought me back to my early days gigging in Virginia and inspired me to take on this project a couple years later. Even though I never made it to SXSW because of the excessive cost, I visited Austin several times to observe musicians there and musicians readily displayed this desire to me.

A special thanks goes to colleagues who read early drafts of some of the chapters: Brian Connor, Mary Ann Clawson, Dan Cornfield, Timothy Luke, Rachel Skaggs, and William "Bill" Roy. Your feedback helped the project, and I am indebted to you for your help. Also, thanks to friends and colleagues who provided me with great conversations about this project (even when it was me prattling on about it). Thank you, Jason Shelton, Patrick Burkart, Michan Connor, Kelly Bergstrand, August Woerner, Heather Jacobson, Amy Speier, Bob Young, Beth Anne Shelton, Anthony Kwame Harrison, Timothy Dowd, Massimo Airoldi, Liliana Pérez-Nordtvedt, Michael Palm, and Dan Cavanagh. I also presented several of these chapters at conferences and benefited greatly from feedback from audience members.

I'd like to thank Jennifer Miller for your support throughout the process of this book. No one heard me discuss these ideas more than you. You provided incredible feedback on every chapter. And allowed me the opportunity to go out and work on a musician's schedule late at night. This book would not be possible without you. And finally, I'd like to thank Owen Arditi who challenges me to dream and cast aside my own cynicism.

Contents

1

Introduction

In 2004, my band, Ethnic Detour, played a gig at Latitudes, a small music venue at the Sheraton Four Points in Blacksburg, VA. While the show itself was otherwise ordinary, an experience speaking with the other band playing that night planted the germ in my head for this project. My band co-headlined[1] this gig with a band from out-of-town. When the other band arrived, they pulled-up in a commercial van towing a trailer with their equipment. They displayed no interest in speaking with my band. As a drummer, I offered for their drummer to use my drum kit—a common courtesy to reduce time between acts—but he insisted on using his own kit; of course, the band's name was printed on his bass drum. From the moment they arrived, they started demanding the manager change the agreed upon co-headliner arrangement so they could headline.[2] The other band insisted on headlining because they were in discussions with multiple labels. They were touring the East Coast to build their credibility for a better deal. My band agreed to play first, since we would still split the door; however, since the crowd showed up to see my band, most left after we finished our set.

Although the band was unremarkable, they probably signed a record contract with a label. Assuming they did, they most likely recorded an

D. Arditi, *Getting Signed*,
https://doi.org/10.1007/978-3-030-44587-4_1

album, at which point they would be lucky to have the label pay enough attention to their project to promote and market it. They would be even luckier if they recouped their advance.

Record contracts are notoriously exploitative of artists who sign away their copyrights in exchange for the potential to make it big. Although it is widely acknowledged that record contracts only on rare occasions equal big-time monetary success, the desire remains strong among bands and recording artists to sign unequitable record contracts. This project addresses the following questions. In what way does the desire to sign record contracts change the way labels treat musicians? How pervasive is the ideology of getting signed? Why are musicians willing to sell the rights to their music in exchange for an advance to record an album? Why do they desire a record contract? How does signing a record contract materially affect the parties in the agreement? This band is one example of a widespread desire in the American cultural imaginary wherein a record contract signifies great achievement (Celebrity? Wealth? Status?).

Dozens of authors and musicians have detailed the inequity that originates from signing major record label contracts, most notably describing the relationship, however hyperbolically, as like slavery. For instance, Prince wrote the word "SLAVE" on his face to characterize his relationship with Warner Brothers.[3] Around the time, Prince's struggle with his record label resulted in him abandoning his name to become a sign. In another example, George Michael described his record contract as "professional slavery."[4] Additionally, in separate instances Courtney Love and Semisonic drummer Jacob Slichter both characterized a record contract as that of a sharecropper.[5] These celebrities share their own experiences with record contracts, which demonstrate that no one is immune and that celebrity isn't a way to more equitable relations.

Along with comparisons to slavery and sharecropping, industry insiders have often described the one-sided nature of record contracts. In an op-ed written for *Billboard*, Jeff Berke, an attorney who represented musicians in contract negotiations, admonished the contemporary record contract as "an instrument of torture and oppression" in 1988.[6] Berke explains that through these contracts, a label has the "right to do anything it wants with [artist's recordings] (including nothing)."[7] Berke wrote this over 30 years ago, and the only thing to change with these record deals is that they have become more exploitative. Record labels use their power to negotiate one-sided deals with emerging artists who do not have the power to forge a strong position—labels will just move to the next musician. The more musicians who believe in the ideology of getting signed, the less bargaining power any given musician holds to negotiate with a label. Popular music scholars almost universally describe how difficult it is to succeed at earning a living from a record contract. Yet the belief on the part of musicians persists to the detriment of music, musicians, and culture.

While musicians sign record contracts for a multitude of reasons and record labels cite specific business rationale for them, in this book I argue these contracts create the fundamental mechanism with which to exploit musicians. Exploitation occurs any time that workers are underpaid for the labor that they perform.[8] Instead of providing musicians with material resources, record contracts reinforce the power held by major record labels, and create the means through which record labels can generate profits. Aspiring musicians grow up hoping they will one day sign a record contract and become a star. Since the belief is widespread among musicians and non-musicians, there are always more people desiring a contract than the industry can sustain, this depresses wages for most recording artists while simultaneously obscuring the realistic outcomes of signing a contract by foregrounding the less likely experience of "big" stars. At the same time, record contracts are the only viable path to success in the recording industry, but the model works for very few people.

Today, viral music sensations are signing multi-million dollar record deals without ever having performed to a live audience. Each year, thousands of aspiring singers audition for *The Voice* and *Idol* brands worldwide for the goal of winning and landing a record contract. Thousands more pay to perform at record label showcases in large and small cities everywhere for the hope of signing a record deal. Record contracts have been the goal of aspiring musicians since Ralph Peer started signing blues and country artists in the 1920s. Many people think that the core logics of recording contracts are no longer important because of alternative distribution forms. This book intervenes in this narrative by demonstrating that musicians believe that record contracts still represent and mark success.

The Ideology of Getting Signed

My object of study is the ideology of getting signed. The ideology of getting signed is a social phenomenon that exists outside individuals and persists across time. Regardless of genre, aspiring musicians often dream of signing a record contract, which represents financial security, potential stardom, and is a clear marker of legitimacy. While this may have different meanings across class, race, and gender, the musicians possess the prevalent feeling that a record contract is an end in itself in addition to a means to greater things. Musicians don't sign record contracts as a back-up plan; it is their goal. Ideology is an expression of the world around us that helps produce the idea of that world. It is an upside picture of reality that helps obscure the real relations of production (more on this in Chapter 2). Furthermore, the ideology exists throughout society as the major aspirational achievement that non-musicians expect musicians to pursue. There is a widespread belief among musicians and non-musicians that these record contracts bring incredible wealth to anyone who signs one because of the large sums of money earned by a few artists.[9] In numerous conversations I had with friends, family members, colleagues, and strangers, people often emphasized to me that so-and-so on the radio is rich. Non-musicians and musicians, alike, internalize the model of success through record contracts; non-musicians encourage musicians to pursue these contracts, and musicians oblige, often believing that record contracts will bring them wealth and fame.

Aspiring musicians have desired to sign record contracts across the world beginning early in the twentieth century and continuing in the twenty-first century. The desire existed in the early days of country music when Ralph Peer began signing blues and country singers in the South.[10] Tin Pan Alley brought young crooners in New York City to national fame around early record contracts. When record labels began signing British acts in the so-called British Invasion in the 1960s, those artists believed they could make it big with a record contract. The ideology existed when Barry Gordy churned out records in a factory-style production line at Motown Records.[11] And the ideology existed when Island Records mined the Carribean for reggae acts in the 1970s and 1980s. During the heyday of rock 'n' roll, bands aspired to sign record contracts with major labels memorialized in popular entertainment such as movies *Almost Famous* and *This Is Spinal Tap*, and the current list of movie biopics or television series that focus on the music industry (*Nashville*, *Atlanta*, and *Empire*). It existed even when punk and later grunge rock derided major record label deals in favor of small independent labels.[12] It exists among aspiring emcees in LA trying to "blow up."[13] It exists when aspiring singers watch talent search game shows with the ultimate goal of signing a major record label contract.

Nashville Dream

The writers of *Nashville* saturated the popular television drama with dreams of signing a record contract. Not only are the main protagonists, Rayna Jayne and Juliette Barnes, world famous singers, almost everyone on the show is involved in pursuing a contract in one way or another. At the Bluebird Café, a real venue and Nashville institution, singer-songwriter fictional characters hope to be noticed. At least six characters sign record contracts through the course of the show. Rayna's own daughters pursue a record contract with her oldest daughter, Maddie, signing to her mom's rival label. After Rayna ends the deal by claiming that Maddie, as a minor, cannot sign a contract, she never gives up the dream of signing a contract. In the final season of Nashville, Maddie even competes on the fictional music competition television show, *Nashville's Next*. While Maddie ultimately loses the competition, she signs with her (then deceased) mother's former label Highway 65.

At the same time, most of the singers on the show end up having their own music careers. Lennon Stella, the actress who plays Maddie, had the real life opportunity to sign a record contract. One blog described her signing thusly: "After seasons of trying to land a record deal as the character of Maddie on *Nashville*, Lennon Stella finally signed to her own dream as a new recording artist for RECORDS." Not only does Nashville hype the idea of signing record contracts, but quotes like this emphasize the pursuit of a record contract as a "dream."[14]

However, the ideology of getting signed exists outside of popular entertainment and in the everyday lives of musicians pursuing their dreams. Record label showcases occur across the United States to attract potential talent to perform for Artist & Repertoire (A&R) staff at the same time that A&R staff scour the bar/club scene to find new talent. Musicians distribute their recording demos to labels and invite A&R staff to their shows. People perform at open mics and battle of the bands in the hope of being "discovered." These individual phenomena vary as to why people may pursue a record contract, but the fact remains that they have this common desire to sign a contract. This project scrutinizes that idea; however, I do not analyze it to understand the motivations of individuals, groups, or communities, but rather to understand cultural hegemony.

By exploring cultural hegemony, I hope to move beyond a purely political or coercive conception of the means of domination and exploitation because the desire to sign record contracts is not forced upon anyone. The key to cultural hegemony for Antonio Gramsci is the act of consent; subordinated classes of people consent to the dominant class.[15] Cultural hegemony is "an inclusive social and cultural formation which indeed to be effective has to extend to and include, indeed form and be formed from, this whole area of lived experience."[16] For Gramsci, liberalism's division between the state and civil society creates the room for subordinate classes to consent to their domination by accepting the cultural order. The free association of labor is one area that we consent to our domination, Americans believe that people have the ability to turn down employment in one place and find it elsewhere. Not only is this not the case, but its emphasis on autonomy (the ability for individuals to act) allows everyone else in society to blame the person's decision. The liberal ideology of free association of labor does not emanate from the coercive arm of the state, but emerges all around us. Culture informs the way that we interpret and experience the world, so we must look at culture to understand systems of domination.

Musicians sign contracts on their own fruition. This is the position many label apologists and advocates fall back to in which they expound neoliberal ideology—the idea that we are free individuals that must be unencumbered by the state. Label apologists contend that musicians have the liberty as free labor to enter into contracts of their choosing, and if the details of a contract are disadvantageous, then they can walk away from the contract. However, this is a shortsighted view that ignores just how powerful the pull toward record contracts is for aspiring musicians. While it is easy to ignore the desires and interests of musicians, understanding the ideology of getting signed helps to explain the broader political, economic, social, and cultural milieu that exists in everyday life.

The ideology of getting signed applies beyond the music industry whenever people dream of making it big and lifting themselves out of their present condition. These dynamics materially reshape comparable moments in other areas of endeavor where "getting signed" is a big deal, especially for young talent. Signing a contract happens during the NFL and NBA draft spectacles where ESPN covers signing. The spectacle of signing with a pro-sports team leads kids to pursue college sports with the only aim of making it to the pros, but very few college athletes make it to the pros or last long in them.[17] The dream exists with PGA winners capturing endorsements, or Olympians desiring pro contracts, commercial careers, and coaching gigs. Landing a film or TV gig is an ongoing trope in television shows because so many people move to Hollywood or New York City to try to become actors. Similarly, I observed it in Washington, DC as recent college graduates acquire internships on Capitol Hill in the hope of working in government. These dreams propel people to pursue careers that won't likely be fulfilled.

***Avery and Earl: iPhone BOGO* (Verizon Commercial)**

Earl (the Dad): So recently my son's band was signed by a record label ...

Earl (interjects from another shot): A record deal ... unbelievable!

Avery (holding an iPhone): Whenever we're about to on stage for a huge audience. I always give my Dad like a FaceTime kinda moment.

Earl: You see the crowd, you see the emotion.

Avery: You know he has that experience for the first time with me, and it's really important to me.

Earl: I created a rock star!

Avery: [laughs]

The point of the commercial is for Verizon to sell the idea that they are "there for you when it matters most" while selling iPhones and Verizon coverage. But this is not the only message sent by Verizon because the whole commercial is about record contracts. Earl sees his son's success crystallized in signing a record contract. This and the crowd, he says, makes him feel like he brought the world a rock star. The viewer at home sees the importance of a record contract anchored in the joy that it brings both Earl and Avery.

At the same time, we accept the power of a record contract as a force to make someone a rock star. We do not find out any details about the contract that Avery, and his band, signed. In my surface search of data from Spotify, YouTube, Twitter, Instagram, and Facebook, the band does not seem to have hit rock star status. More than likely, they are struggling through a tour as an opening act and have not come close to recouping their contract's advance. If they signed a 360 record contract (discussed below), the label likely profits from Avery's appearance. These details are unimportant to Verizon's goal of selling their capacity to connect family members. However, these details are quintessential to selling the ideology of getting signed.[18]

My Approach

To analyze the ideology of getting signed, I deploy several methods, but my guiding methodology is in the critical theoretical tradition. In that tradition, I view "political behaviors, social forces, institutional structures, and cultural activities as densely encoded but largely decodable *texts*."[19] As such, I use what Robert Antonio describes as "immanent critique"—"a means of detecting the societal contradictions which offer the most determinate possibilities for emancipatory change."[20] Ideological formations present themselves as natural, but underlying their presentation lies a hidden reality that seeks to strengthen the political economic system. This is my attempt to peel back some of the layers that obscure the ideology of getting signed.

The project stems partly from ethnographic observations[21] in several settings where I was a participant observer who occasionally interviewed other participants. Over three years, I attended local shows in more than 20 cities, went to musicians' meet-ups in the Dallas–Fort Worth region, sought people who have varying contacts with the recording industry, and experienced the music scene in whatever city my academic and personal travels guided me to (Atlanta, Quebec, Boston, Baltimore, Philadelphia, New York, Nashville, Seattle, Austin, Dallas, Fort Worth, San Antonio, Chicago, Washington, DC, Richmond, Williamsburg, VA, and Arlington, TX). Several times, I attended musician showcases and competitions; these were frenzied occasions where I received a heavy dose of the ideology. At shows, I observed the performers and the crowd, spoke to people working at the venue, the musicians, their management, and listeners. I also met with museum curators of music exhibits, family of signed acts, musicians themselves, label executives, venue executives, and everyone in between. These conversations ranged from brief encounters to 3-hour interviews. Furthermore, I am a product of the music scene as a musician who gigged for more than 10 years, and I have many friends who perform and work in different parts of the music industry to this day. Therefore, my own personal history has given me insight into the hopes, dreams, and processes people follow to "make it" in the recording industry.

However, my ethnographic approach does not posit that research subjects provide eternal truths. Rather, I view ethnography through a critical theoretical lens—as "a way of seeing and a form of knowing that employs historical knowledge, reflexive reasoning, and ironic awareness to give people some tools to realize new potentials for the emancipation and enlightenment of ordinary individuals today."[22] In other words, I read ethnographic texts with the same skeptical eye that I use to read any other texts. My position as an insider provides me with the unique ability to decode these texts. This process is both textual and interpretive. It is a textual approach because I analyze discourse about the ideology of getting signed. This process is interpretive because I inform the discussion from my own positionality and read representations based on my own cultural context. For this reason, a different researcher may take different interpretations from the same texts. By interpreting the texts in everyday life, critical theory aims to disturb power and domination. My interrogation of the ideology of getting signed will illuminate how the everyday taken-for-granted use of record contracts creates the space for, allows for and perpetuates the exploitation of musicians.

Record Contracts

"Record labels are legitimate loansharking companies"—Bond, a Folk Singer-Songwriter.

Throughout my research, people often thought I was writing a "how-to" guide to record contracts. In this section, I outline some of the important features of legal contracts and record contracts in particular, but keep in mind that my goal is not to provide an exhaustive description of record contracts. While my object of analysis is the ideology behind signing record contracts, contracts themselves are important social artifacts. And "contracts also have cultural meanings, and contract provisions sometimes act not as technologies but as symbols."[23] The fact that contracts come to signify something to social actors opens them up to gaining ideological meaning, interpretation, and concealing power. People do not only interact to construct record contracts; they construct the desire for others to participate in their meaning. Record contracts are cultural and therefore contain public meaning.[24]

In an economic system with a complex division of labor, Émile Durkheim explains that contracts allow society to function, and that "the contract is the symbol of exchange,"[25] and the "legal expression of cooperation."[26] People cooperate in a complex division of labor because contracts and the law stipulate that people behave a specific way. The most important contract for the division of labor, in Durkheimian terms, is the guarantee that people will pay for a service. If a worker fulfills their end of a contract, they expect the employer to pay them for their labor; similarly, Durkheim is aware of the legal gray area between the time someone takes possession of a good in a store and the moment when they pay for it. The western legal tradition places contracts above most other legal documents.

As with any contract, a record contract presents two sides with legal precedent to exchange something. Specifically, "a recording agreement between an artist and a label is a contractual arrangement between two parties based on the exchange of promises. The artist promises to make recordings for this label, and for no other (an exclusive agreement), in exchange for the label's promise to pay the artist royalties based on the sale and use of those recordings, when and if they occur."[27] Record labels provide the artists with the means to record, distribute, and market a recording in exchange for the rights to the recording through an advance (a prepayment of cash on potential royalties). This is possible because copyright is transferable. "Only the creator of a work is entitled to copyright at the moment of creation, but the creator can sell, trade, or give the copyright in whole or in part to another party at any point after that."[28] As a result of this trade, artists typically take the advance while thinking the dollar amount of that advance is their money. However, it remains the recording company's money, and the label continues to make decisions about how the money will be and can be spent.[29] Before an artist receives any royalties, they must recoup (i.e., repay) their advance on their part of the royalties. In simplest terms, if a band has a $500,000 advance and makes $1 from the sale of an album, they would need to sell 500,000 albums (the RIAA certification for a gold album) before they earn any royalties. Meanwhile, if a label makes $1 in royalties for every album sold, they would recoup at 250,000 albums (the label's dollar plus the band's dollar), profiting $500,000 at the point when the band recoups. These are approximations, but they provide a useful explanation.[30] Contracts allow musicians to give up their copyrights in exchange for a promise of future money while they remain deeply indebted to a company that exploits their labor.

Crucially, contracts can supersede of the law (except in cases where the contract would be to violate the law—e.g., a contract murder wouldn't supersede any criminal laws). Within the recording industry, record contracts take precedent over labor law, so musicians forfeit more rights than just copyrights. While federal and state laws stipulate how much a person can work and how much companies must pay them (i.e., minimum wage), musicians signed to a record contract do not fall under these laws because they are considered independent contractors. Everyone working full time at the major record labels must be paid and they receive benefits (major labels are large enough companies that they are required to provide health insurance under the Affordable Care Act). That means everyone from top executives to janitors, and marketers to administrative assistants must be paid and receive benefits, but not musicians—i.e., the employees who create the most value at record labels. In the act of signing a record contract, recording artists become positioned as a business that labels contract with to complete a task thereby giving up their labor rights.

With the development of digital technology, a perspective developed that record contracts were no longer as important for musicians to record, distribute, and promote an album. This perspective, mainly among technology enthusiasts, does not hold water when viewed through the perspective of both young aspiring musicians and the mechanics of the recording industry's dominant business model. While digital technology (especially file-sharing, and later, streaming) has upended the recording industry, it has done so at the hands of the major record labels, and they have worked to use technology to benefit their bottom line.[31] Instead of decreasing the number and size of recording contracts, streaming caused what *Rolling Stone* magazine describes as a "bidding war."[32] Record labels increasingly sign new talent when they hear that other labels have interest in an artist. The bidding war centers around musicians who self-release music on SoundCloud, a popular music platform that allows users to upload their own music. Since record labels can observe the number of streams that an artist receives on online platforms, they have a good estimate of how they will perform for a label. Now labels eagerly sign these acts because digital technology provides so much data. What I observed is that streaming has not decreased the need or desire for recording contracts, but rather digital technology fundamentally altered the way people obtain record contracts. Whereas aspiring musicians had to play the bar or college fraternity circuit nationally and regionally to gain the attention of record labels in the past, today Artist & Repertoire (A&R) staff pay attention to "the numbers"—an act's social media following, streams on SoundCloud, etc. This data becomes the prerequisite for signing artists. Today, viral content and social media "reach" substitute for what used to count as a demonstrable following (size of shows and sales of CDs/Records/Merchandise). In Chapter 4, I discuss the importance of viral content in obtaining a record contract.

Furthermore, record contracts possess power beyond the contractual arrangements because people believe in the ideology of getting signed. By claiming "Poverty made me sign in the end," Fetty Luciano, a rapper signed to Def Jam Records, highlights this ideology as if signing a record contract is a way out of poverty.[33] This is similar to what Sarah Cohen observed in Liverpool where "being in a band was seen by many, whether employed or unemployed, to be a 'way out' of their current situation, 'a way out of the jungle,' as some phrased it."[34] While the hard facts about record contracts guarantee that most signees will not make money,[35] the dream remains. Furthermore, the contracts bring other tangible benefits to artists, for instance in Chapter 6, I describe the way contracts create cohesion in bands. However, even if record contracts provide tangible benefits, their overall affects result in the exploitation of recording artists.

Making It, Breaking In, Blowin' Up: The Ideology Is Everywhere

Nearly every time I read *Billboard*, *Rolling Stone*, *XXL*, or *Spin*, I'm confronted by the ideology of getting signed. Not only do musicians dream about signing record contracts, but the music press helps naturalize this desire. Throughout this book, I provide critical readings of these positions, but I am not alone analyzing the ideology of getting signed. While the dream to sign a record contract is still strong in the popular press, scholars have been critical about the dream to be a "rock star." By looking at the everyday lives of musicians and the political economy of music industry, we can begin to peel back the grip that the ideology of getting signed has on society.

An early critic of the recording industry was social theorist Theodor Adorno. In his work, Adorno demonstrates that the recording of music fundamentally changes the music written, performed, and recorded. For instance, he contends that "The only thing that can characterize gramophone music is the inevitable brevity dictated by the size of the shellac plate."[36] In other words, music could not exceed three minutes because one side of a 78-rpm record could only hold three minutes. This changes what we hear and it changes how we approach music. Furthermore, he argues that the Fordist logics of recorded music closes critical thinking. To demonstrate the industrial production logic of the entertainment business, Adorno and Max Horkheimer deployed the term "Culture Industry." By labeling it an "industry," Adorno and Horkheimer placed making profit as the core interest of cultural producers. Furthermore, they did so to reverse the tendency to assume that "mass culture" is of the "masses."[37] Their theoretical framework attempts to separate pop from mass culture. Adorno and Horkheimer's "The Culture Industry" essay points to the star system as a way for the industry to obscure the relations of production. They argue that instead of viewing the Culture Industry as an industrialized production system no different from Ford's factories, people assume that there is something special about celebrities. At the moment that we assume celebrities are different from the rest of us, it obscures their labor. In *Getting Signed*, I show that the recording industry's obfuscation of musician labor allows everyone to dream about how great it is to be a star.

There has been a long history of scholars who love popular music but critique the scheme major record labels deploy to profit from music. Steve Chapple and Reebee Garofalo wrote the definitive book about the political economy of rock music, *Rock 'n' Roll Is Here to Pay*, in 1977.[38] Since rock music is so entwined with industry, Chapple and Garofalo take "a view that links the music to the lives of the musicians and the history of the musicians to the economics and politics of the music industry. And it is an industry."[39] They argue that it is difficult to separate the recording industry from rock music because rock is a product of the recording industry. Trying to study rock music without studying the recording industry fails to understand that rock is "part of an ever-growing and highly profitable cultural industry"[40] (Chapple and Garofalo 1977, p. xii). With street cred as rock fans, Chapple and Garofalo wrote an excoriating book that demonstrates how capitalist and exploitative the industry is toward musicians and fans. This mode of criticism provides the ground on which I wrote this book because they opened up popular music to an analysis from the inside.

In *Music and Capitalism*, Timothy Taylor identifies the relative dearth of studies that address the production and distribution of music in terms of capitalism (excepting Jacques Attali, whose work has had a profound impact on my own). Taylor contends that studies of music "ought to have something to do with capitalism, not in an economistic sense, but with the understanding that capitalism as a social form profoundly shapes people's relationships to each other, and their relationships to cultural forms such as music."[41] *Getting Signed* focuses on this absence. Not only do I address the ways that music production and distribution exploit workers (i.e., musicians), but I also demonstrate that the desire to join this political economic system is reproduced by society. While the recording industry benefits from the organization of the means of production, musicians help create the conditions through which labels exploit them. Musicians produce the ideology of getting signed in their interactions and relationships with other musicians; they see people signed to record contracts on TV and on stage, and they idolize their every move.

A number of sociologists have explored the micro-social level of the dreams of aspiring musicians. In *Rock Culture in Liverpool*, Sarah Cohen follows the everyday life of several rock bands in Liverpool, England. Through this ethnography, Cohen traces what it means to be in a local unsigned rock band. She studied two bands, the Jactars and Crickey It's the Cromptons!, for whom music was their life—the band members socialized with each other, learned to play their respective instruments together, and shared common dreams. There is a strong commonality between what Cohen observed in these bands' everyday life and my own experiences and observations, especially among punk (and other lifestyle) bands. Cohen's "making it" is equivalent to what I call the ideology of getting signed that focuses on earning a living through playing music. When the possibility existed for these rock musicians in Liverpool, "the quest for success became a major motivation and preoccupation, a ray of hope in a grim reality, and band members were drawn into all kinds of plans, strategies, and activities designed to achieve that success."[42] Musicians view music as a way to succeed in life.

In *Destined for Greatness*, Michael Ramirez explores the lives and aspirations of rock musicians in Athens, Georgia—a town known for both the University of Georgia and its vibrant independent rock music scene. Ramirez discusses "the intersections of musical careers, gender, and adulthood among musicians active in the local music scene."[43] Musicians during the period of emerging adulthood, he argues, are not different from other people in this life phase. Increasingly, middle-class whites experience their 20s as a period of experimentation as they prepare themselves for adulthood. This is prevalent for musicians, who face great uncertainty over whether or not they can make a career through music. Ramirez finds that many musicians negotiate their identities as musicians and college students in Athens in a way that non-college students cannot inhabit. College becomes the perfect time to pursue a music career because these emerging adults do not have family and other commitments beyond school. As a result, these musicians experiment with their identities as musicians away from the negative influence of their parents, who tend to encourage them that they need a college education to get a "real" job. Ramirez's overarching question is "Why, then, do some men and women in early adulthood decide to proceed with their musical dreams"[44] despite the economic insecurity of being a musician? In contrast to Ramirez I ask, why do people possess these musical dreams in the first place?

While relatively few aspiring rappers sign major record label contracts, Jooyoung Lee demonstrates, in *Blowin' Up*, that pursuing a career in music provides tangible benefits for young working-class black men in Los Angeles. As part of his research, Lee became a regular at Project Blowed, a hip-hop venue started with the intent to provide an environment that gives young black working-class men something to do outside of gang activity, and it acts as a creative space for these men to harness their creative energy. Lee found that many emcees relentlessly practiced their craft by writing music, practicing, recording, and participating in freestyle ciphers, rap battles, and open mic nights. Lee develops the concept "blowin' up" to describe the aspirations of emcees; it signifies a desire to sign a major record contract and earn "enough money to move out of the 'hood.'"[45] Few of the aspiring artists featured in his study come close to blowin' up, but the pursuit of their dreams provided tangible benefits, such as learning to use social media marketing—skills they could apply in other career pursuits. Whereas Lee looks at the unfolding lives of aspiring rap artists and the way the dream develops other skills, *Getting Signed* explores the ideology itself.

The ideology of getting signed comes in a variety of places among musicians in varying genres. Lee and Cohen discuss many of the same trials that bands/artists/musicians face across genres, time, and place from having last minute out of town gigs postponed to traveling to that gig with friends and family to generate an audience. Both rock musicians in Liverpool, England in the 1980s and hip-hop emcees in Los Angeles, California in the 2000s share the desire to sign record contracts at the same time that they face structural barriers. Different barriers may exist that further contextualize the individual struggles among these populations, but the similarities in the desire to sign a record contract and the experiences that make this so difficult are quite similar. Outside of popular music, Robert Faulkner analyzes the career goals and trajectories of orchestral musicians. Once again, this feeling of making it comes up. "In making sense out of and assessing whether they are getting ahead or, colloquially put, 'making it,' players can look at *where* they are located, *how long* it took them to make each upward move, and what the next move might be."[46] In a study about songwriters "breaking in" to writing for the country music industry, Richard Peterson and John Ryan identify:

> Aspiring contemporary American commercial musicians, actors, painters, writers, and the like have to learn how to 'break in to' their chosen line of work. 'Breaking in,' 'getting a break,' and similar oft-repeated phrases suggest a pattern of career entry which mixes aggressive self-assertion, luck, and probably failure. The terms also suggest that the rewards are rich and career success assured once one has broken through the initial barrier.[47]

To their terminology, we can add for performers "getting signed" as the ultimate moment of "breaking in." David Grazian discusses a parallel dream for blues musicians in Chicago of achieving financial stability and recognition by other playing the blues. Grazian tells a story about Greg an aspiring musician who moved to Chicago to play the Blues. Interesting to think about financial instability.

> In actuality, Greg recognizes the hardscrabble difficulties inherent in pursuing a career in music and realizes that, in all likelihood, he will eventually have to seek out an occupational life elsewhere. After sharing

> his dreams about achieving status as a bluesman, he acknowledges that he lacks alternative career goals and fears the uncertainty of his future. Meanwhile, Greg finds the financial instability of the musician's life unsatisfying and frightening, and he clearly dislikes his present blue-collar job working for the city.[48]

While musicians like Greg do not see immediate monetary rewards from performing, they cling to the idea that earning a living from music is possible. Regardless of genre, musicians often believe that one day they will be able to support themselves from playing music.

Positioning musicians as workers is important regardless of whether they earn much from the endeavor because they see themselves as earning a living through music. In *Unfree Masters*, Matt Stahl wrestles with the contradictory position of musicians in the labor market.[49] On the one hand, musicians experience a degree of autonomy unheard of for most workers under late capitalism. Record labels use recording artists' autonomy to admonish musicians as akin to owners who operate as independent contractors. On the other hand, unless a recording artist is one of the few successful acts, record labels control most decisions that their artists make. In one of the most fundamental contradictions, Stahl contends that record labels enforce contracts to disallow musicians from signing to other record labels. Record contracts stipulate that signed artists provide a definite amount of records, but record labels do not need to allow them to record those records; if recording artists try to free themselves of the contracts, record labels force them to pay for unrecorded albums.

The Book Going Forward

I structured *Getting Signed* in two parts. Part I emphasizes the theoretical underpinnings of the ideology of getting signed. In Part II, I build my argument by presenting cases that I observed through my ethnographic work. While Part I provides a rich description of how the ideology of getting signed works, Part II provides the reader with specific places where the ideology becomes observable.

To begin Part I, I provide the theoretical groundwork on ideology that propels my interpretations of the ideology of getting signed. Critique of ideology has been an underlying theme in critical theory dating back to Marx. Ideology helps to reproduce the dominant material relations in society. In Chapter 2, "Record Contracts: Ideology in Action," I theorize ideology. Because most people are unaware of how record contracts operate at the same time they see celebrity musicians living lavish lifestyles, they believe record contracts result in wealth—this is a product of alienation. Alienation between different musicians, musicians and fans, and musicians and the recorded product allows this ideology to function. Part of the functioning of the ideology of record contracts is that musicians possess a different relationship with the product of their labor. I demonstrate that ideology obscures the lived reality of recording artists and it motivates aspiring musicians to sign record contracts.

Record contracts deploy copyright as the means through which record labels turn musicians into workers. In Chapter 3, "Copyright Enclosure," I discuss Karl Marx's analysis of England's land enclosure acts. Then I demonstrate the parallels between the process of land enclosure, and what I call copyright enclosure. English land enclosures created property rights that kicked serfs off the land thereby forcing them into a wage relation under capitalism. Similarly, copyright creates what many describe as an intellectual property right, but it is not property in the traditional sense. Rather, law creates a set of statutory rights that some describe using an analogy to property. In turn, copyright law allows record labels to profit from musician labor similar to how land enclosure allowed landowners to profit from farmworkers' labor. This chapter highlights the institutional incentive to sign a record contract under the current political economy of the recording industry.

While the recording industry changed dramatically over the past twenty years, much of the underlying business structure remains the same. In Chapter 4, "The Digital Turn: Music Business as Usual," I take the rhetoric about change seriously, but find that the main change to the ideology of getting signed lies in the way record labels find new talent. There is a new bidding war for record label signees, according to *Billboard* magazine, the trade magazine for the recording industry. Whereas the route to a record contract used to be through bars/small venues on regional and national tours, now record labels sign young artists who are viral sensations as a result of their social media reach. Simply put, streaming platforms favor social media reach over everything else. This chapter explores the changes that streaming brings to the recording industry at the same time that the logics of the recording industry remain fundamentally unchanged. Finally, this chapter looks at the alternatives to the major record labels, but I demonstrate that those musicians who find alternative ways of surviving in the music industry cling to the more conventional paths to success.

When musicians begin playing music, a constant aspect of performance involves competition. Chapter 5, "On Competition in Music," rounds out Part I of the book. I show how competition not only leads musicians to covet record contracts, but also how this competition reinforces the need for a contract. The ideology of getting signed develops from the American capitalist ethos of competition: eat or be eaten. Free enterprise in the liberal economic tradition espouses a type of economic Darwinism that contends that businesses succeed through survival of the fittest. Neoliberalism is the current stage of capitalism that views competition as the crucial characteristic of society. In effect, music (and the arts) are hyper-illustrative of the neoliberal ideal of free market competition because musicians compete for gigs and contracts in the open; where most job interviews are at least somewhat private. This chapter presents competition in music as a visible expression of this neoliberal ideal. I trace it through inter- and intra-school band competitions to the number of views that astounding musicians receive on Instagram. I describe several ethnographic experiences that I had during the research of this book. One was an experience at a music showcase. Another involved local band competitions in two major cities in Texas. While these are limited events, I demonstrate how competition permeates musicians' demeanor. The ultimate way to win the competition is to sign a record contract.

Part II of the book begins with Chapter 6, "We're Getting the Band Back Together." When a band forms, several factors determine its success. One over-determining factor relates to the commitment that individual members possess to play in their band, along with the degree to which they want to make a living from it. This chapter addresses one of the motivations behind signing a record contract: the cohesiveness of bands. I focus on the following questions. Does an individual band member see himself or herself as a musician or as a band member? How does this affect the desire for a record contract? How does it influence cohesion? Band members have varying reasons for performing in a band. My research demonstrates that one factor that leads to the potential for a band to sign a contract relates to their organizational structure. I argue that when musicians view their performance identity strongly linked to their band's identity, the band has greater solidarity, and will be more likely to last longer through more contractual arrangements.

Since *American Idol*, aspiring singers have viewed television singing competitions as a way to bypass playing in bars to achieve success in the music industry. Many musicians define success in the music industry as obtaining a record contract. Chapter 7, "*The Voice*: Popular Culture and the Perpetuation of Ideology," explores how music competition shows shape the ideology of getting signed. As the reigning singing competition on television, NBC's *The Voice* positions itself to "coach" singers to become celebrities. Through a cultural study of the show, legal documents, and news reports, I argue the show advances ideology about record contracts while it exploits contestants. While contestants labor for up to eight months without pay, show executives and coaches earn millions each season. Meanwhile, the show seduces viewers at home who come to believe the show provides a pathway to musical success. This affects the attitudes viewers and aspiring musicians have about the recording industry, allowing industry executives to perpetuate the exploitation of musicians.

In Chapter 8, "Buying the Dream," I contend that not all strategies that appeal to the ideology of getting signed have the same effects on artists. Some strategies that target aspiring musicians are confidence games that charge musicians exorbitant fees to participate for the chance to be seen. This chapter looks at a case study of Coast 2 Coast LIVE—an artist showcase that travels and charges participants for the chance to compete in future showcase competitions. This is one scheme, among dozens, that targets young musicians with the chance to be discovered by Artist & Repertoire staff.

To conclude the book, I try to end a dark book by bringing some light to the ideology of getting signed. Signing a record contract is not only an ideological dream, but also something that many musicians receive benefits from signing. While most musicians will never be a wealthy celebrity, signing a record contract does allow them to live the "rockstar" dream. This section of the conclusion will demonstrate seductive forces exist to sign a record contract that benefits musicians. By exploring some of the benefits of signing a record contract, I demonstrate that musicians are not just dupes. Finally, I discuss alternatives to the current recording industry structure. By seeking alternatives, I hope to expand the conversation about copyrights, record contracts, and musician labor.

While reasons vary among musicians for signing a contract and labels think contracts help musicians, record contracts establish the fundamental mechanism with which to exploit musicians. Instead of providing musicians with material resources, record contracts reinforce the power held by major record labels and create the means through which record labels can generate profits. Aspiring musicians hope that one day they will sign a record contract and become a star. Since the belief is pervasive among musicians and non-musicians, there are always more people desiring a contract than the industry can sustain, this depresses wages for most recording artists while simultaneously obscuring the realistic outcomes of signing a contract by foregrounding the less likely experience of "big" stars. At the same time, record contracts are the only viable path to success in the recording industry, but the model works for very few people. To live the ideology of getting signed is to live the broader ideology of capitalism.

Notes

1. A number of arrangements exist for how venues pay and list bands for a gig. Co-headlining means that while one band may perform before another band, there is not an opening act; the venue pays both bands equally.
2. Conflict over the order bands will perform is a fairly common occurrence at smaller local venues when there is not an established headliner. Sarah Cohen observed the situation in Liverpool, England: "The order in which

bands performed was, however, important at most gigs besides those of the more famous bands, and bands often argued over it, firstly because it supposedly reflected the popularity of each band, but also because audiences usually increased in size as the evening progressed so the last band was likely to play to more people." (*Rock Culture in Liverpool*, 84.) In addition to carrying more prestige and a larger audience, the headliner receives better sound. In my experience, the headliner has the sound system set to their needs. One guitarist once observed to me that major headliners purposefully give the opener worse sound to make the headliner's performance sound and appear better than the opener. I have experienced this at concerts where I was in the audience as well—most annoyingly when I saw The Roots open for Erykah Badu. There are stakes to perform last for a concert.

3. Norment, "The Artist Formerly Known As Prince."
4. Stevenson, "George Michael Loses Lawsuit Against Sony."
5. Slichter, *So You Wanna Be a Rock & Roll Star: How I Machine-Gunned a Roomful of Record Executives and Other True Tales from a Drummer's Life*; Love, "Courtney Love Does the Math."
6. Berke, "The Problem with Record Contracts."
7. Berke.
8. Marx, *Capital*, 320–28.
9. Lena, *Banding Together*, 42.
10. Peterson, *Creating Country Music: Fabricating Authenticity*.
11. Smith, *Dancing in the Street*.
12. Thompson, *Punk Productions*.
13. Lee, *Blowin' Up*.
14. Brickey, "Lennon Stella of 'Nashville' Signs Record Deal."
15. Gramsci, *Selections from the Prison Notebooks of Antonio Gramsci*.
16. Williams, *Marxism and Literature*, 111.
17. Beamon, *The Enduring Color Line in U.S. Athletics*.
18. Even though I did not interview the participants in this advertisement, I changed their names to soften my critique of the band.
19. Luke, *Screens of Power: Ideology, Domination, and Resistance in Informational Society*, 7.
20. Antonio, "Immanent Critique as the Core of Critical Theory," 332.
21. Everyone who I spoke with during the course of this project remains anonymous here. To do this, I use pseudonyms for both individuals and groups and I change locations and times of occurrences. In some instances,

I even change names of people who I did not speak with if I thought that my work could in some way interfere with their careers.
22. Luke, *Screens of Power: Ideology, Domination, and Resistance in Informational Society*, 8.
23. Suchman, "The Contract as Social Artifact," 92.
24. Geertz, "Thick Description: Toward an Interpretative Theory of Culture."
25. Durkheim, *The Division of Labor in Society*, 98.
26. Durkheim, 97.
27. Hull, Hutchison, and Strasser, *The Music Business and Recording Industry: Delivering Music in the 21st Century*, 198.
28. Sinnreich, *The Essential Guide to Intellectual Property*, 8.
29. Slichter, *So You Wanna Be a Rock & Roll Star: How I Machine-Gunned a Roomful of Record Executives and Other True Tales from a Drummer's Life.*
30. For a useful breakdown of this type of accounting, see Hull, Hutchison, and Strasser, *The Music Business and Recording Industry: Delivering Music in the 21st Century*, 202; Vito, *The Values of Independent Hip-Hop in the Post-Golden Era*, 79.
31. Arditi, *ITake-Over.*
32. Wang, "'F-ck It, We'll Take the Bet.'"
33. Buerger, "The New Style," 49.
34. Cohen, *Rock Culture in Liverpool*, 3.
35. Fewer than 5% of signed recording artists will recoup their advance and turn a profit from their music. Vito, *The Values of Independent Hip-Hop in the Post-Golden Era*, 78.
36. Adorno, "The Curves of the Needle," 271.
37. Horkheimer and Adorno, "The Culture Industry: Enlightenment as Mass Deception."
38. Chapple and Garofalo, *Rock "n" Roll Is Here to Pay.*
39. Chapple and Garofalo, xii.
40. Chapple and Garofalo, xii.
41. Taylor, *Music and Capitalism.*
42. Cohen, *Rock Culture in Liverpool*, 3.
43. Ramirez, *Destined for Greatness*, 6.
44. Ramirez, 16.
45. Lee, *Blowin' Up*, 6.
46. Faulkner, "Career Concerns and Mobility Motivations of Orchestra Musicians," 337.

47. Peterson and Ryan, "Success, Failure, and Anomie in Arts and Crafts Work: Breaking into Commercial Country Music Songwriting," 301.
48. Grazian, *Blue Chicago*, 110.
49. Stahl, *Unfree Masters*.

Bibliography

Adorno, Theodor W. "The Curves of the Needle." In *Essays on Music/Theodor W. Adorno*, edited by Theodor W. Adorno, Richard D. Leppert, and Susan H. Gillespie, 271–76. Berkeley, CA.: University of California Press, 2002.

Antonio, Robert J. "Immanent Critique as the Core of Critical Theory: Its Origins and Developments in Hegel, Marx and Contemporary Thought." *The British Journal of Sociology* 32, no. 3 (September 1, 1981): 330–45.

Arditi, David. *ITake-Over: The Recording Industry in the Digital Era*. Lanham, MD: Rowman & Littlefield Publishers, 2014.

Beamon, Krystal. *The Enduring Color Line in U.S. Athletics*. 1st ed. New York and London: Routledge, 2013.

Berke, Jeff. "The Problem with Record Contracts." *Billboard; New York* 100, no. 23 (June 4, 1988): 9.

Brickey, Kelly. "Lennon Stella of 'Nashville' Signs Record Deal." *Sounds Like Nashville* (blog), January 18, 2018. https://www.soundslikenashville.com/news/lennon-stella-record-deal/.

Buerger, Megan. "The New Style." *Billboard*, March 2, 2019.

Chapple, Steve, and Reebee Garofalo. *Rock "n" Roll Is Here to Pay: The History and Politics of the Music Industry*. Chicago, IL: Nelson-Hall, 1977.

Cohen, Sara. *Rock Culture in Liverpool: Popular Music in the Making*. New York: Oxford University Press, 1991.

Durkheim, Emile. *The Division of Labor in Society*. Edited by Steven Lukes. New York: Free Press, 2014.

Faulkner, Robert R. "Career Concerns and Mobility Motivations of Orchestra Musicians." *The Sociological Quarterly* 14, no. 3 (1973): 334–49.

Geertz, Clifford. "Thick Description: Toward an Interpretative Theory of Culture." In *The Interpretation of Cultures*, 3–30. New York, NY: Basic Books, 1973.

Gramsci, Antonio. *Selections from the Prison Notebooks of Antonio Gramsci*. Edited by Quintin Hoare and Geoffrey Nowell-Smith. London: Lawrence & Wishart, 1971.

Grazian, David. *Blue Chicago: The Search for Authenticity in Urban Blues Clubs*. Chicago, IL: University of Chicago Press, 2003.

Horkheimer, Max, and Theodor W. Adorno. "The Culture Industry: Enlightenment as Mass Deception." In *Dialectic of Enlightenment*, xvii, 258 pp. New York: Herder and Herder, 1972.

Hull, Geoffrey P., Thomas W. Hutchison, and Richard Strasser. *The Music Business and Recording Industry: Delivering Music in the 21st Century*. 3rd ed. New York, NY: Routledge, 2011.

Lee, Jooyoung. *Blowin' Up: Rap Dreams in South Central*. Chicago: University Of Chicago Press, 2016.

Lena, Jennifer C. *Banding Together: How Communities Create Genres in Popular Music*. Princeton, NJ: Princeton University Press, 2014.

Love, Courtney. "Courtney Love Does the Math." *Salon*, June 14, 2000, Online edition, sec. Entertainment News. http://www.salon.com/2000/06/14/love_7/.

Luke, Timothy W. *Screens of Power: Ideology, Domination, and Resistance in Informational Society*. Urbana: University of Illinois Press, 1989.

Marx, Karl. *Capital: Volume 1: A Critique of Political Economy*. New York, NY: Penguin Classics, 1992.

Norment, Lynn. "The Artist Formerly Known As Prince." *Ebony*, January 1997.

Peterson, Richard A. *Creating Country Music: Fabricating Authenticity*. Chicago: University of Chicago Press, 1997.

Peterson, Richard A., and John Ryan. "Success, Failure, and Anomie in Arts and Crafts Work: Breaking into Commercial Country Music Songwriting." *Research in the Sociology of Work* 2 (January 1983): 301–23.

Ramirez, Michael. *Destined for Greatness: Passions, Dreams, and Aspirations in a College Music Town*. New Brunswick, NJ: Rutgers University Press, 2018. https://www.jstor.org/stable/j.ctt1vgw7xj.

Sinnreich, Aram. *The Essential Guide to Intellectual Property*. New Haven, CT: Yale University Press, 2019. https://www.worldcat.org/title/essential-guide-to-intellectual-property/oclc/1055252885.

Slichter, Jacob. *So You Wanna Be a Rock & Roll Star: How I Machine-Gunned a Roomful of Record Executives and Other True Tales from a Drummer's Life*. New York: Broadway Books, 2004.

Smith, Suzanne E. *Dancing in the Street: Motown and the Cultural Politics of Detroit*. Cambridge, MA: Harvard University Press, 2001.

Stahl, Matt. *Unfree Masters: Popular Music and the Politics of Work*. Durham, NC: Duke University Press Books, 2012.

Stevenson, Richard W. "George Michael Loses Lawsuit Against Sony." *The New York Times*, June 22, 1994. http://www.nytimes.com/1994/06/22/arts/george-michael-loses-lawsuit-against-sony.html.

Suchman, Mark C. "The Contract as Social Artifact." *Law & Society Review* 37, no. 1 (2003): 91–142.

Taylor, Timothy D. *Music and Capitalism: A History of the Present*. Chicago, IL: University of Chicago Press, 2015.

Thompson, Stacy. *Punk Productions: Unfinished Business*. Albany, NY: SUNY Press, 2004.

Vito, Christopher. *The Values of Independent Hip-Hop in the Post-Golden Era: Hip-Hop's Rebels*. Palgrave Pivot, 2019. https://doi.org/10.1007/978-3-030-02481-9.

Wang, Amy X. "'F-ck It, We'll Take the Bet': The Gold Rush to Sign the Next Rap God." *Rolling Stone*, July 18, 2018. https://www.rollingstone.com/music/music-features/f-ck-it-well-take-the-bet-the-gold-rush-to-sign-the-next-rap-god-699707/.

Williams, Raymond. *Marxism and Literature*. Marxist Introductions. New York: Oxford University Press, 1977.

Part I

2

Record Contracts: Ideology in Action

The ultimate goal of most aspiring recording artists, whether individuals or bands, is a record contract. Signing a record contract represents success to these musicians. However, by signing a record contract, musicians become a part of an inequitable relationship that supports their exploitation. Ideology is the "ideal expression of the dominant material relationships, the dominant material relationships grasped as ideas."[1] Ideology obscures the real relations of production by making workers think that they control the conditions in which they live.[2] To that end, record contracts construct the idea that musicians (i.e., recording artists) are independent contractors who own their means of production. These contracts create the mechanism for musicians to sign away their copyrights and labor as workers while believing they are owners. Record contracts are ideology because they represent success at the same time that they limit the vast majority of signees' capacity to earn a living.

Record contracts are ideology in action; they do not convince people of an ordered world, but rather they create the order—they make the social relations of production in the recording industry. These contracts create a system of exploitation because without them there is no way for record labels to expropriate value from musicians' performances.

D. Arditi, *Getting Signed*,
https://doi.org/10.1007/978-3-030-44587-4_2

The ideology of getting signed convinces people of the order; it gives musicians a reason to sign record contracts. "Power works through a logic of coercive detainment and continuous indoctrination, which finds expression in elaborate, extended narratives."[3] Musicians experience this continuous indoctrination through their everyday lives and interactions with music, friends, colleagues, and recording industry businesspeople. Whereas record labels and their lawyers produce record contracts, the ideology of getting signed operates through a dispersed hegemony bolstered by social and cultural institutions throughout society.

In this chapter, I theorize ideology as both the active construction by musicians and entertainment workers and the inactive absorption by everyday consumers of popular culture. First, I demonstrate a key to the ideology of getting signed is alienation. The commodified nature of recorded music means that music fans and musicians lack unmediated contact with each other creating estrangement. This alienation leads to a misrecognition of the material relations of production. Second, I develop a theory of ideology as action, which includes a dialectical relationship between action, inaction, and reaction. Next, I theorize the way ideology manifests in the material relations of production in the recording industry through the conventions of the broader music industry. Finally, I discuss the GRAMMYs as an institutional apparatus that produces and disseminates ideology.

Alienation and Ideology

In "The Culture Industry: Enlightenment as mass deception," Max Horkheimer and Theodor Adorno demonstrate that companies produce mass culture as a way to distract workers from the mundaneness of industrial labor.[4] We go to work and suffer through hours of tedious labor that our employers underpay us to do for the reward of going home to watch television shows, listen to music, go to a movie on the weekend, or go on a vacation trip during our "free time." Horkheimer and Adorno theorize that these entertainment goods provide enough reward to allow workers to go begrudgingly back to work the next day because if we work hard, we can save money for entertainment. However, in this context, the entertainment becomes part of the drudgery. The more we desire entertainment goods, or Culture Industry commodities, the more we are willing to work through these conditions. As the consumption of Culture Industry commodities increases, capitalism expands the means of consumption.[5] "Essentially, the planned productivity of corporate capital needs more and more people to need more and more products … to maintain its programs for economic growth."[6] Entertainment goods were the easiest types of commodities to expand with the rise of mass media in the early twentieth century, and they have expanded ever since. The key to understanding the status of workers lies in the status of these goods as commodities. Musicians, actors, directors, writers, etc., are workers no different from industrial labor at a Ford factory. However, Horkheimer and Adorno contend that society idolizes these workers for their celebrity status. In the process of idolizing these people, we ignore their status as industrialized workers whose exploitation is embedded in the production of commodities for mass consumption.

As with all labor under capitalism, the problem is alienation: alienation between workers; alienation between worker and product; and alienation between worker and consumer.[7] The ideology of getting signed is especially acute in the latter case because the manufacture of celebrity leads consumers to believe the ideological trappings of the Culture Industry. However, what consumers do not see is the day-to-day labor of the celebrity or the Culture Industry workers who never rise to the level of celebrity. (In a later chapter, I discuss the process through which *The Voice* pretends to give a behind-the-scenes view of the production process, while actually obscuring it further.) Adorno claims musical reproduction is by definition alienation.[8] Musical reproduction removes the production of music from the consumer. This begins with early musical annotation, accelerates with the printing press' capacity to produce high volumes of musical scores, and crystallizes in the mechanical (and later digital) reproduction of sound.[9] Our regular contact with recording artists consists of the top 1% of artists who achieve celebrity, and that contact is highly mediated. We do not see celebrities' daily lives, but occasionally we see a representation. For instance, *MTV Cribs* created the air of *Lifestyles of the Rich and Famous* for 2000s era popular culture, especially music celebrities, but producers often rented the cars and houses displayed on the show.[10] The viewer does not see the business managers, promoters, publicists, booking agents, etc., who the artists use to manage their celebrity, but viewers see them perform live, on television, or in other highly scripted scenarios. Now their lives become open books for us to consume via social media, but that too is highly managed. These media spectacles "embody contemporary society's basic values, serve to initiate individuals into its way of life, and dramatize its controversies and struggles, as well as its modes of conflict resolution."[11] Douglas Kellner's definition of media spectacle places the role of celebrity spectacle in line with the reproduction of values already embodied in society. Alienation is the key mechanism that enables this distortion of reality.

Through alienation, corporate record labels deceive the public about the role of an autonomous artist. Labels rely on a romantic notion of an artist working on music through their own independent creativity. Lee Marshall traces the history of this romantic notion back to the Romantic Era in *Bootlegging*.[12] During the Romantic Era of art in the nineteenth century, ideas about authorship arose next to copyright. "The elevation of the author, however, was also reliant upon the developments in copyright. If Romanticism is understood to have emerged as a result of the changing material circumstances of artists themselves, one of the most significant of the changes was the possibility of them being the owners of cultural property through copyright."[13] At the center of this romanticism is the "expression of individual human dynamics and private animation which it, of course, no longer is."[14] The work of the artist has to appear as the creation of the individual because the individual is the center of bourgeois ideology. Adorno places the rationalization of music production as "highly useful in the ideological concealment of the monopoly capitalist development of society."[15] Corporations work to sell individual creativity because capitalism rests on the ideology of the individual fighting against nature and succeeding against other individuals in a competitive market—an idea closely linked to the Romantic Era. This not only obscures the collective nature of music production, but also more importantly, conceals the industrial apparatus that creates music.

The consumer and aspiring performer believe in the apparition of individual music production while the songwriting process remains alienated from its audience.

In the initial phases of most musicians' careers, the alienation between musicians obscures their views of success because it is so rare for most musicians to interact with musicians who have record contracts. Musicians tend to perform and interact with other musicians at the same level of performance as themselves. Since most early career musicians do not have experience with record labels, they do not hear stories about negotiating contracts, recording and promoting albums, and recouping advances. Instead, the everyday struggle for gigs and recognition become the most common problems that musicians pass on to each other. When they do have the chance to speak with signed artists, they do not discuss business as such. As is often the case in American culture, we do not discuss salaries with each other. Most signed acts do not want to admit in conversation that even though they signed a record contract, they are broke. This would be a strange conversation to have after meeting someone for the first time. Instead, musicians put on airs to demonstrate their careers are about to take off (as I discuss in the Introduction). Over time, aspiring musicians realize the realities of the working conditions in the Culture Industry, but only after they internalize the dream of signing a record contract. When everyone identifies record contracts as the key indicator of success, musicians internalize the same model even when they face a rather different reality.

Copyright allows artists to become alienated from the product of their labor because record contracts allow artists to sign their copyrights to third parties (i.e., record labels). "The existence of copyright creates a valuable 'property' that can be commodified and alienated that is not the work itself. The key source of value within copyright is not the work itself (which is easily copied) but the legal rights which prevent copying."[16] When musicians sign away these rights, their creative works become removed from them as an alien object. Record labels can then deploy these rights, however they see fit. Musicians lose all control of the product of their labor, but they continue to believe that it is their inalienable property.

Furthermore, record contracts allow the contemporary Culture Industry to alienate musicians from the music they purportedly create through the production process. When musicians sign record contracts, they not only sign away their copyrights, but also relinquish creative control to record labels. Ultimately, a signed artist can ignore recommendations from industry executives, but labels can decide to sit on the album or "shelve" (i.e., refuse to release) after production is complete. A manager who I spoke with described two instances when the artists' labels refused to release albums because executives did not like the creative decisions made on the album. Independent musicians often complain about the practice of labels sitting on albums.[17] If an artist agrees to a label's demands, they hand over creative control to A&R (Artist & Repertoire) staff at the record label and music producers. In the process, A&R staff and producers can select songwriters, change compositions, alter instrumentation, and even change the pitch of a vocalist. In a 2006 documentary entitled *Before the Music Dies*, Andrew Shapter reveals the artifice of the industry in a potent segment in which a teenage model, with subpar vocal skills, transforms into a popular music phenomenon.[18] The segment of the documentary highlights the use of production software such as auto-tune and the over-reliance of appearance over music. This demonstrates a shift that places "an increased emphasis on the computer itself as the primary tool of contemporary sound recording."[19] The process of shifting to computers is visible in the instrumentation with drum programming and quantization (realigning the timing of notes to a grid) occurring in the hands of the producer.[20] These techniques take control further from the musicians and act to alienate them from their music.

In the Frankfurt School's construction of alienation, capital alienates workers not only to create working conditions favorable for capitalism, but also to promulgate the ideology that workers receive something for working hard. Since reproduction separates musicians from the product, consumers, and each other, individual musicians do not recognize the pervasive exploitation in the recording industry. In its place, they see popularized representations of record contract successes. Part of what the Culture Industry produces is its own image of success.

Consumers only see what the Culture Industry promotes. The construction of the recording artist as celebrity is a spectacle that produces itself by convincing aspiring musicians that record contracts are the measure of success. This ideology stirs them to action. In appearance, the recording industry advances people who work hard, while the recording artists who do not succeed are blamed for their failures. Instead, we need to see personal troubles rooted in public issues.[21]

Ideology as Action

Ideology is not only the production of ideas, but also the social context in which people function. Ideology motivates people to maintain the hegemonic power structure in three ways: action, inaction, and reaction. First, ideology is action. People act to maintain hegemony. They feel as if they act for personal benefit, but they perform for the system. Second, ideology is inaction. In this case, they maintain hegemony through stasis. Instead of protesting, they accept. Third, ideology is reaction. When people feel that the system leaves them behind, they do something to keep things the way they were in a bygone era—an era that never existed. We observe this in the rise of the global-right. Alternatively, they seek to build an alternative to the system, which often remains firmly imbedded in it. Record contracts exercise hegemonic power through all three ways, but the primary force of record contracts is through action.

Record contracts as ideological constructions incite people to action. Aspiring recording artists understand that the goal of performing music is to sign a major record contract, so they pursue their dreams by pursuing a record contract. As they turn their consumption of ideology into the action of pursuing a record contract, they enact the ideology. Believing the record contract is the model of a successful career as a musician is pervasive in American society, but it cannot sustain itself because people need to see it. However, when musicians pursue that dream, ultimately, some receive contracts, and a few of those recording artists experience monumental success. Because people at home then see very wealthy recording artists, they internalize the dream and pursue record deals—the cycle continues. Music fans do not see the countless musicians who, while spectacular musicians, never receive a contract. Furthermore, they do not realize that most of the recording artists who sign record contracts never earn paychecks from their recordings, and many file bankruptcy because they too believe that a record contract will bring them incredible wealth.

Musicians put ideology to action whenever they make commonsense decisions about performance as they pursue their careers. However, common sense is not good sense.[22] Common sense is that which is held in common among a group of people, which enables hegemony to function. These commonsense decisions start when bands begin to imagine the audience for which they will perform.[23] The basic formulas that serve as the foundation of popular music styles ultimately derive from commonsense decisions, but point to broader considerations of industry and technology.[24] Furthermore, the common sense of musical performance in popular music assumes the recording of music,[25] and recordings are always-already commodities; to perform popular music is to record music for sale. These are commonsense decisions made by musicians that are deeply embedded within the logic of music performance itself. Few people become rock guitarists or hip-hop emcees without the desire to record an album to sell. Whenever musicians begin playing music, they do so enacting ideology.

Moreover, the more they perform, the more they begin to ascribe and enact other elements of this ideology. A friend that I used to play in a band with once described making it in the recording industry as a business transaction. He said in order to garner the interest of a record label, musicians need to demonstrate that they already sell music. In other words, musicians need to record, perform, and sell records to demonstrate to a label that they have a following and are willing to hustle. Alternatively, as Horkheimer and Adorno explain, "Talented performers belong to the industry long before it displays them; otherwise they would not be so eager to fit in."[26] Record label A&R staff do not peruse bars looking for talent, but rather, they receive word from band managers about sales data from an act and then follow up with bands who they see as containing the potential to enact a business plan. In this understanding of the recording industry (which I think is accurate), musicians need to set themselves up as a business, demonstrate their profitability, and hope that a larger business (i.e., record label) buys them out (i.e., signs them). This is not different from mergers and acquisitions in the business world. Of course, the record contract resembles a subcontracting contract instead of a buy out; the artist remains an independent business. As Jay-Z puts it "I sold kilos of coke, I'm guessin' I can sell CD's/I'm not a businessman; I'm a business, man!"[27] In these two lines, Jay-Z sums up my friend's point—being a successful musician is no different from any other business, whether that business sells drugs, CDs, cars, or vacuums. Furthermore, musicians have to sell themselves—Jay-Z is a brand, and CDs are his commodities—no different from his clothing line. However, the quote's importance lies in the fact that it is on a popular Kanye West album heard by millions of people. Jay-Z enacts the ideology of what success in the music industry looks like for aspiring hip-hop artists. In order to sign a record contract, musicians must provide action on the ideology to which they subscribe; they must set themselves up as a business.

When music listeners accept the rhetoric offered by the recording industry, they contribute to ideology as inaction. The act of consumption results in the slow, passive, and banal acceptance of the ideological frame. We listen to music produced by the recording industry because we think we like it.[28] The recording industry produces this music through a system where only the most profitable performers have their music circulated (playlists, radio, Walmart/Best Buy/Target, etc.). Popular recording artists accede to the logic of the system to become famous while those who oppose it toil in obscurity. In turn, we only see those musicians who submit entirely to the recording industry, so "the deceived masses are today captivated by the myth of success even more than the successful are. Immovably, they insist on the very ideology which enslaves them."[29] Music listeners consume not only music, but also the ideology of success. Audiences think that signing record contracts results in fame and wealth, but they also apply a normative value judgment that identifies this with the good life. To live the good life, musicians must sign record contracts while holding the paths of Jay-Z, Taylor Swift, Michael Jackson, and Britney Spears as virtuous. Accepting this ideology takes nothing on the part of music consumers because they only see it without alternatives.

Ideology as inaction is a form of consent; it demonstrates that subordinated groups consent to the will of the dominant group to reproduce hegemony.[30] The recording industry co-opts any alternative message to feed the ideology of success.

Many musicians actively work against the recording industry because they recognize the exploitation inherent in record contracts. However, these musicians participate in the ideology as reaction instead of emancipation. Ideology as reaction recognizes the problems contained in an ideology, but aims to reconfigure the ideology to be beneficial to another population; emancipation moves beyond the rhetorical playing field of the ideology and attempts to establish a new order. While proffering a critique of ideology, ideology as reaction becomes an accommodationist strategy by agreeing to the norms of the system with a slightly different power center. For hegemony to exist, it "has continually to be renewed, recreated, defended, and modified."[31] Modification happens from both inside and outside because the dominant order must continue to make cultural sense. On the one hand, the industry tries to remake what is old seem new; on the other hand, those excluded from the recording industry attempt to create their own positions. Independent labels serve the recording industry by offering an outlet for opposition to the status quo, but they do so through the social construction of labels themselves.

Independent artists often sign contracts with independent labels or create their own labels because they recognize the weaknesses in the current recording industry or that there is no place for them within it. "Alternative" music as a genre category follows neatly Raymond Williams' theorization of "alternative hegemony." For Williams, the dominant hegemonic order must "control or transform or even incorporate" alternatives.[32] For instance, grunge music, the first labeled "alternative" music emerging out of Seattle, WA, not only developed a different sound, but it did so with rhetoric in opposition to the recording industry's major labels. Nirvana actively rejected corporate greed most famously embodied in the shirt Curt Cobain wore on a *Rolling Stone* cover that read "Corporate Magazines Still Suck."[33] Major record labels co-opted these rejections of the recording industry throughout the 1990s. At first, these oppositional messages found a place in independent labels. Eventually, major record labels purchased independent labels, and let the labels retain their brand. Then, the industry applied the label "Indie" music or "Indie" rock to this music to signify the music's independence from the uncool corporate monsters. However, these corporate behemoths pulled the levers in the background of this music. By the 2000s, "Indie" rock became a shorthand for pop punk in such a way that "Indie" could mean "industry" just as easily as "independent." A similar pattern emerged with independent hip-hop artists around the same time.[34] Whereas emancipation would involve the radical reconfiguration of recorded music, these musicians create music in the image of major labels. By signing a contract with an independent label, these musicians seek an alternative that major labels always-already dominate.

To sign a contract with an independent label reifies the value of record contracts even when they have decidedly different terms that benefit recording artists because the fundamental idea (1) commodifies music, (2) trades copyrights for material resources, and (3) places musicians in a prone position to larger business interests. Artists signed to independent labels submit themselves to the system that perpetuates profit for record labels. Signing with an independent record label commodifies the musician's music by placing value on the recorded product. A record contract, whether it is with a major or an independent label, trades an agreed upon package of copyrights for the means to record an album (and likely subsequent albums). In order to fulfill their terms of the contract, the musician must sell their music. By participating in the system, independent musicians hope to compete with major labels on equal ground. However, major labels (and their aligned "independent" labels) have insurmountable resources, which are important for placing music on the radio, distributing to retailers, and cracking the front page of iTunes or Spotify.[35] While independent labels advance a counter ideology to the corporate interests of major record labels, their position in the broader music industry constructs ideology as reaction because it reinforces the value of record contracts.

Emancipatory ideology is the only way to restructure the music industry, and this is only possible by rejecting the premise of record contracts. Gramscian hegemony operates as a totality, and the only way to create emancipation is through the wholesale reconfiguration of hegemony.[36] To develop a new hegemonic system, there must be a new ideology that no longer rests upon the premise of exchanging copyrights for the resources to sell the recorded commodity (or worse one's own image). However, the capitalist system entrenches the ideology of getting signed through the material relations of production. In order to recognize the pervasiveness of this ideology, I next turn to the material needs of people and the organization through which people meet those needs.

Material Relations of Production in the Recording Industry

Ideological constructions do not develop based only on the whims and rhetoric of a small cadre of powerful people, but rather, ideology emerges from the material relations of production of a given society. Popular music exists within the conventions of the production of popular music that possesses a logic emerging from previous technological and economic formations of music with a firm link to the overarching economic structure. Howard Becker analyzes the conventions of what he calls "art worlds,"[37] and claims that the structure of these conventions plays a determining role in the creation of art. Becker goes as far as to claim that "[n]o art has sufficient resources to support economically or give sympathetic attention to all or any substantial proportion of those trainees in the way customary in the art worlds for which they are being trained… If the arts were organized differently—less professional, less star-oriented, less centralized—that support might be available."[38] People need to be trained to work within the material conditions of production for a given art world. The art world creates the norms, desires, and practices of people within it. In this case, the music industry organizes music in a way that not everyone can "make it" because some must fail. And yet, the system does not have to exist in this way because music and the music industry are social constructions. Social organization, Becker explains, is the product of social behavior. However, the social organization of the music industry is also reflective of the social organization of society at a given moment—i.e., the social relations of production.

According to Becker, the art worlds in the United States are organized around three characteristics: professional, star-oriented, and centralized.[39] More importantly, he discusses the fact that art requires "sufficient resources to support economically" people who want to practice the art.[40] However, Becker stops short of discussing Karl Marx's contributions to sociology where he describes how the economy serves as a way to construct the social world. Marx is quite clear that the material relations of society produce the mechanisms that allow that society to function. According to Marx:

> The social structure and the State are continually evolving out of the life-process of definite individuals, but of individuals, not as they may appear in their own or other people's imagination, but as they really are; i.e., as they operate, produce materially, and hence as they work under definite material limits, presuppositions and conditions independent of their will.[41]

For Marx, capitalism is the base of the society and structures all social organization. Music is an art world partly because of capitalism, but we can also see that the economic structure of society helps to determine the organization of the musical art world. In other words, generally people don't play music purely for enjoyment. If a person wants to be good at music, they have to dedicate a lot of time to their craft. If they dedicate a lot of time to practicing their musical skills, that is time that they won't spend doing other productive activities. Under capitalism, people need to meet their material and social needs. To meet those needs, people need to work to earn a wage. If someone wants to dedicate their time to performing music, they need to do it at a sufficient level that will meet their material and social needs. Becker's description of the basic organization of art worlds describes some of the key tenants of capitalism. We often overlook the fact that people produce music (even to think of music as being produced denotes capitalism) under the material circumstances of capitalism—we need money to meet our needs. Since we do not tend to connect these dots in our everyday lives, the circumstances under which people work in art worlds are ideological. We think primarily about how we make art, but Marx says this is an upside-down picture of the world because we must first conceive of the material conditions underlying that organization.

Under capitalism, people play music to make money. This statement does not seem ideological because capitalism has an over determining effect on the popular music world's organizational conventions. From the instrumental composition of a band to a record label's hierarchy, these conventions allow the industry to commodify and mass market music for sale. However, the conventions appear natural to musicians and music listeners alike. In order for record labels to extract profit from the sale of music, they need to have musicians work in some sort of wage relation (in the next chapter, I discuss how copyright creates this wage relation). Ideology obscures the wage relation by leading people to believe that musicians live to perform when in reality they perform to live; their labor is a means to meeting their needs. As I discussed earlier, we do not question the commodity logic of recorded music even though the commodification is anything but an inherent characteristic of music. There is a material need for musicians to earn income from performing music if they want to spend a significant amount of their time playing music in a capitalist system. Record contracts represent the means through which many musicians establish their professional careers as musicians. They *represent* the means, rather than *being* the means, because they create a false reality in which musicians will achieve success beyond measure. Instead, record contracts are an ideological mechanism that allows musicians' exploitation.

Not everyone who plays music does so to earn a living; rather, the way musicians meet their needs is as varied as the genres of music they play. Few people actually earn a living from performing music alone. The typical gigging musician has a "day job," which enables them to pay bills; many musicians who earn a living from music do so through teaching music lessons on their instrument instead of through performance. Whether or not someone aims to perform music full time reflects their relations to the means of production. Pierre Bourdieu conceptualizes the class position of different types of music performers through his analysis of the field of cultural production.[42] This class-based approach helps think through how one specific musician may navigate their decisions about what type of music to play. According to Bourdieu's analysis, members of the dominant fraction of the dominant class (i.e., those with both economic and social capital) are freed from market considerations "because economic capital provides the conditions for freedom from economic necessity, a private income [*la rente*] being one of the best substitutes for sales [*la vente*]."[43] In other words, those people who do not need to concern themselves with meeting their needs can perform music for music's sake, whereas people from modest means internalize the logic of the market in the production of their music. Furthermore, Bourdieu adds that people with economic capital also possess "self-assurance, audacity and indifference to profit,"[44] which allows them to play avant-garde music. Only in special circumstances, i.e., where a person's class status permits it, can people dedicate their lives to music without concern with conventions. These exceptions to the norm stand out as further ideological embodiments of the romantic ideal—where the creative artist is free to create their own music—instead of highlighting the farce that they must operate within a system that motivates profit above all else.[45]

Additionally, the popular music world's conventions serve to maintain the music industry status quo beyond record contracts. Conventions create an entire bureaucratic structure that ensures the hegemony of major record labels by forcing everyone through a few conduits to produce, market, and distribute music. To gain access to these conduits, it is easier to be a major label artist. Whether that is having an album distributed to Walmart stores or having one's music featured on iTunes, major record labels have the staff, technical expertise, and social capital to funnel their artists through these channels. In a way, Napster and the digital threat represented the potential to destabilize the gatekeepers and distribution nodes the recording industry relies on to eliminate competitors. The trick of free market rhetoric is to tout competition while doing everything to eliminate competition through non-competitive means. Independent artists cannot compete with major labels, or their independent imprints, because they lack access to the means of distribution and promotion. When an opportunity arises to subvert that system, major labels use their resources to end the potential for greater competition. Furthermore, the organization of the labels gains their own inertia as people with jobs attempt to maintain their jobs. For instance, the conventions of popular music may include hiring a band manager because labels, booking agents, etc., begin to expect to interact with a manager. If a band does not have a manager, these gatekeepers do not view them as professionals. The professional conventions then stipulate that a band hires a manager. Labels have divisions meant to manage artists, distribute recorded music, promote new products, etc.; each division has employees who, again, work a job to earn a wage, which allows them to meet their needs. Fundamental change to the conventions of the popular music industry wouldn't only affect the status quo, it would threaten these people's livelihood.

Often, the result is strange political bedfellows in the production and dissemination of ideology for policy purposes. For instance, the Institute for Policy Innovation (IIP), a think tank founded by former Republican Congressman Dick Armey (TX) and funded by the Koch brothers, produced a series of reports contending that intellectual property theft hurts workers in the entertainment industries.[46] The AFL-CIO's Department for Professional Employees then cited these reports in a report arguing for the protection of copyright in order to protect entertainment industry jobs.[47] As a result, union-loathing Armey became a propagator of ideology at the service of a union. Using IIP's report, the AFL-CIO claims, "The broad reach of the entertainment and copyright industries means that digital theft and counterfeiting hurt average American workers and the U.S. government."[48] Violations of intellectual property law hurt not only large corporations, but also the workers at those companies. Then, musicians lobby congress to support legislation that fits these ideological positions. This is a clear example of Marx's discussion of how the ruling class used its control of material production to control mental production. Billionaire capitalists (i.e., the Koch Brothers) use their capital to fund organizations (think tanks like IIP) to produce ideology. Meanwhile, musicians and other members of the music industry's working class become pawns as they deploy the ideology for what they perceive to be their interests, but what really expands capital's power at their expense.

The lived experiences of both musicians and industry workers are the result of the ideological production and material relations of production in society. While record labels exploit their workers, popular music's conventions are a product of the material relations of production in society, which means that they do stand to benefit from the strengthening of the ideology. This is not simply false class-consciousness, but rather the effective deployment of ideology that allows workers to recognize that they are in the same boat as the capitalists. Despite the exploitation of workers, they meet their needs through the same pathways that benefit capital. Ideology obscures exploitation at the same time that it lubricates the conventions within the popular music art world.

Institutions

Ideology only succeeds in affecting how people think when institutions exist that reproduce the relations of production. In recent years, the Recording Academy's GRAMMYs have been exemplary of the production of the ideology of getting signed. First, the 2015 GRAMMY Awards show concluded with a lobbying effort to create tougher copyright laws. By starting the Creators' Alliance, the Recording Academy placed itself strongly on the side of major record labels against the recording artists who constitute the bulk of the Recording Academy members. Second, the Recording Academy operates a summer camp for aspiring musicians and industry workers called GRAMMY Camp. These two programs provide examples of Louis Althusser's "Ideological State Apparatus," (ISA) "a certain number of realities which present themselves to the immediate observer in the form of distinct and specialized institutions."[49] For Althusser, ISAs reproduce the relations of production by developing specific skills for the workforce and disseminating messages about the social relations of production. Both ideology as action and ideology as inaction are visible through these two apparatuses because the GRAMMY Awards show demonstrates success in the recording industry to the average viewer while GRAMMY Camp involves musicians pursuing their dreams. The GRAMMYs and GRAMMY Camp work to reproduce the ideology of getting signed through ISAs by creating the dream, desire, and necessity to sign record contracts at the same time that they call people to action to defend the system.

The Creators' Alliance, which is an arm of the Recording Artists' Alliance, claims to represent recording artists' interests to counter the Recording Industry Association of America (RIAA). Countering the power of the RIAA is something that needs to be done. However, organizations exist already that do so for musicians such as the American Federation of Musicians (AFM). There needs to be a viable counter to the power of major record labels, but GRAMMY winners are hardly the best ambassadors for such a movement because their interests are the most aligned with the labels themselves. Here, a class alliance is visible where exploited musicians ascribe their interests as aligned with the top 1% of musicians. Whereas popular GRAMMY winners sell millions and make millions through record contracts, most recording artists do not recoup the advance for their contracts because of the exploitative character of record contracts. However, this is not the story the Recording Academy told in announcing its Creators' Alliance. Rather, the Recording Academy repeated the decade and a half old piracy panic narrative.[50] They said file sharing is piracy; piracy is stealing; and stealing hurts the artists that you love. Ultimately, they argue, this will kill music. Recording Academy President Neil Portnow follows this logic by asking, "What if we're all watching the Grammys a few years from now and there's no Best New Artist award because there aren't enough talented artists and songwriters who are actually able to make a living from their craft?"[51] Portnow's claim is a perfect example of ideology. First, by contending that there will be no Best New Artist, he ignores there will always be new musicians creating new music. Second, there will always be an award show to give those people awards because it is such an important ISA. But most importantly, Portnow implies that people create music (1) to make money and (2) that labels pay them for their work! The industry-driven ideology in support of copyright (and other intellectual property) sets forth that people would not be creative without compensation for their creativity. This flies in the face of reality because most musicians struggle to earn a living from their craft, but they make music anyway. Most visual artists do the same thing. Even people in software development and scientific research make these types of ideological arguments, but open source software, such as Firefox and OpenOffice, demonstrates that this argument is false because people consistently create things without compensation.

To develop an ideology, Althusser explains that the educational ISA is the most important institution under the capitalist system. GRAMMY Camp is a division of GRAMMY in the Schools, which has the mission of creating "opportunities for high school students to work with music professionals to get real-world experience and advice about how to have a career in music." The mission is benevolent and reasonable because GRAMMY in the Schools demonstrates to students what it takes to make it in the music industry. This is a realistic vision of the recording industry that disillusions the fantasy many people have about how to sign a record contract. However, embodied in this lesson is the perpetuation of the status quo, i.e., the ideology of getting signed. GRAMMY Camp is a five-day non-residential summer camp developed to expose students to "music professionals as well as guest industry professionals [who] provide valuable insight to give the campers the best chance at achieving success in their chosen career." In other words, students can meet people who work in the industry to receive insight about how to be successful in the recording industry. Those same professionals who navigated the recording industry define success for the students. Since the camp is $1500 less room and board and travel to the camp, aspiring industry workers must be of a class background sufficient to make the trip. Therefore, the camp opens a realistic vision of the recording industry, along with the social capital accrued from contact with industry professionals only to those able to afford it, while the recording industry sells the opportunity to make it to everyone, regardless of class.

The GRAMMY ISAs came full circle in 2017 when the winner of the Best Solo Country Performance GRAMMY was a former camper at the very first GRAMMY Camp in 2005. Neil Portnow consistently touts the fact when he promotes GRAMMY Camp. Furthermore, very few awards make the final cut for the GRAMMY Awards show—always Best New Artist, Album of the Year, Song of the Year, and Recording of the year—but genre-based awards rarely make prime time. At the 2017 GRAMMY Awards, they made sure to announce the award for Best Solo Country Performance, and the winner started her acceptance speech by acknowledging her attendance at the first GRAMMY Camp.

The not-so-hidden subtext here is that if you attend GRAMMY Camp, you too could one day win a GRAMMY Award. Many people watching the GRAMMYs at home desire to one day win a GRAMMY. On the one hand, the 2017 awards show gave these viewers a viable path to win a GRAMMY. On the other hand, it took over a decade for an artist to go from camper to award winner, and even among that small population, she remains the sole winner, which demonstrates the implausibility of winning a GRAMMY. However, the individuals watching the GRAMMYs at home each recognize themselves as the eventual winner of an award. The aspiring musician watching at home "is interpellated as a (free) subject in order that he shall submit freely to the commandments of the Subject, i.e., in order that he shall (freely) accept his subjection."[52] The concept of the individual itself is an ideology only conceived in the capitalist system where the division of labor permits people to believe only they can fulfill a specific task in society.[53] By targeting this sense of individuality, the awards show allows musicians to undergo subjugation of themselves. Ensconced in the national broadcast of the awards show is the ideology of getting signed even though the Recording Academy never intends to broadcast it as ideology.

Institutions create ideology, and ideology is institutional. No person or group alone creates ideology, but rather ideology is the product of a number of institutions working simultaneously and autonomously. ISAs reproduce the relations of production without consciously doing so because ideology exists everywhere, and these institutions cannot help but articulate it. The Recording Academy provides examples of this ideological work, but it does not do so with intention. ISAs produce ideology and reproduce the relations of production without intent. The ideology of getting signed saturates everyone working within the recording industry. Musicians and industry workers accept and embody the ideology, and with their acceptance, they perpetuate the ideology.

Conclusion

As I write, the only conceivable way to be a star in the recording industry involves signing a record contract, but this conception is ideological. We are the products of the world around us, and the world around us is a social construction that existed long before us. Our desires don't emerge from some inner inertia that compels us as individuals, but rather, we interface and interact with a set of relations that are outside of our control. Under capitalism, we must work a job that pays a wage in order to meet our basic needs; however, our day-to-day activities obscure this relation with an artifice that we want to work a job (or at least certain jobs). People want to find "careers" instead of "jobs"—a career being something that provides us fulfillment in itself whereas a job is a means to an end (i.e., pay bills). The ideology consists of believing that there can be fulfillment in any type of work. Within the recording industry, the way for musicians to have a career involves signing a record contract. While record contracts provide major record labels with the means to exploit musicians, musicians view contracts as the fulfillment of their dreams.

Aspiring musicians subscribe to the ideology of getting signed because it is common sense to sign a record contract. When people decide to pick up an instrument and play popular music, they likely do so because of the influence of the seduction of this ideology. In other words, at the point when they begin playing music, musicians always-already succumb to the ideology of getting signed long before they recognize the scope of it. Ideology as action, inaction, and reaction exists all around musicians before they are musicians. The art world of the music industry requires the ideology to enlist workers throughout the industry at the same time that the industry's conventions reinforce the strength and longevity of the ideology. By infecting our everyday consciousness, ideology changes a world of exploitation into the means to dream fulfillment.

Notes

1. Marx, "The German Ideology," 172.
2. Marx, "The German Ideology."
3. Luke, *Screens of Power: Ideology, Domination, and Resistance in Informational Society*, 46–47.
4. Horkheimer and Adorno, *Dialectic of Enlightenment.*
5. Aglietta, *A Theory of Capitalist Regulation.*

6. Luke, *Screens of Power: Ideology, Domination, and Resistance in Informational Society*, 100.
7. Marx, "Economic and Philosophical Manuscripts."
8. Adorno, "On the Social Situation of Music," 412.
9. Jacques Attali follows a similar relationship between economic class power and the stages of music. Attali, *Noise: The Political Economy of Music.*
10. Brucculieri, "JoJo Talks Making a Comeback, 'Cribs' and Battling Her Record Label."
11. Kellner, *Media Spectacle*, 2.
12. Marshall, *Bootlegging*.
13. Marshall, 54.
14. Adorno, "On the Social Situation of Music," 416.
15. Adorno, 415.
16. Marshall, *Bootlegging*, 77.
17. Vito, *The Values of Independent Hip-Hop in the Post-Golden Era*, 53.
18. Shapter, *Before the Music Dies.*
19. Théberge, "The End of the World as We Know It: The Changing Role of the Studio in the Age of the Internet," 82.
20. Arditi, "Digital Downsizing."
21. Mills, *The Sociological Imagination.*
22. Gramsci, *Selections from the Prison Notebooks of Antonio Gramsci.*
23. Lena, *Banding Together*; Cohen, *Rock Culture in Liverpool*; Negus, *Music Genres and Corporate Cultures*; and Frith, *Performing Rites: On the Value of Popular Music.*
24. Adorno, "The Curves of the Needle"; Adorno, "On Popular Music"; Adorno, "The Form of the Phonograph Record"; and Horkheimer and Adorno, *Dialectic of Enlightenment*.
25. Frith, "The Industrialization of Popular Music."
26. Horkheimer and Adorno, *Dialectic of Enlightenment*, 122.
27. Jay-Z and West, *Diamonds from Sierra Leone.*
28. Horkheimer and Adorno, *Dialectic of Enlightenment*.
29. Horkheimer and Adorno, 133–34.
30. Gramsci, "Hegemony, Relations of Force, Historical Bloc," 205.
31. Williams, *Marxism and Literature*, 112.
32. Williams, 113.
33. *Nirvana: Taking Punk to the Masses.*
34. Vito, *The Values of Independent Hip-Hop in the Post-Golden Era.*
35. Arditi, "ITunes"; Arditi, "Digital Subscriptions: The Unending Consumption of Music in the Digital Era."

36. Laclau and Mouffe, *Hegemony and Socialist Strategy: Towards a Radical Democratic Politics.*
37. *Art Worlds.*
38. Becker, 52.
39. Becker, 52.
40. Becker, 52.
41. Marx, "The German Ideology," 154.
42. Bourdieu, *The Field of Cultural Production: Essays on Art and Literature.*
43. Bourdieu, 68.
44. Bourdieu, 68.
45. Marshall, *Bootlegging.*
46. Siweck, "The True Cost of Sound Recording Piracy on the U.S. Economy"; Siweck, "Copyright Industries in the U.S. Economy: The 2006 Report."
47. "Intellectual Property Theft."
48. "Intellectual Property Theft," 3.
49. Althusser, "Ideology and Ideological State Apparatuses."
50. Arditi, "Downloading Is Killing Music."
51. "57th Annual Grammy Awards."
52. Althusser, "Ideology and Ideological State Apparatuses."
53. Durkheim, *The Division of Labor in Society.*

Bibliography

"57th Annual Grammy Awards." *Grammy Awards*. Los Angeles: CBS, February 8, 2015.

Adorno, Theodor W. "On Popular Music." In *Essays on Music/Theodor W. Adorno*, edited by Theodor W. Adorno, Richard D. Leppert, and Susan H. Gillespie, xvii, 743 pp. Berkeley, CA: University of California Press, 2002.

———. "On the Social Situation of Music." In *Essays on Music/Theodor W. Adorno*, edited by Theodor W. Adorno, Richard D. Leppert, and Susan H. Gillespie, 391–433. Berkeley, CA: University of California Press, 2002.

———. "The Curves of the Needle." In *Essays on Music/Theodor W. Adorno*, edited by Theodor W. Adorno, Richard D. Leppert, and Susan H. Gillespie, 271–76. Berkeley, CA: University of California Press, 2002.

———. "The Form of the Phonograph Record." In *Essays on Music/Theodor W. Adorno*, edited by Theodor W. Adorno, Richard D. Leppert, and Susan H. Gillespie, 277–80. Berkeley, CA: University of California Press, 2002.

Aglietta, Michel. *A Theory of Capitalist Regulation: The US Experience*. Translated by David Fernbach. New Edition. New York, NY: Verso, 2001.

Althusser, Louis. "Ideology and Ideological State Apparatuses." In *Lenin and Philosophy, and Other Essays*, edited by Ben Brewster, 229 pp. London: New Left Books, 1971.

Arditi, David. "Digital Downsizing: The Effects of Digital Music Production on Labor." *Journal of Popular Music Studies* 26, no. 4 (December 2014): 503–20.

———. "Digital Subscriptions: The Unending Consumption of Music in the Digital Era." In *Annual Meeting of the American Sociological Association*. Seattle, WA, 2016.

———. "Downloading Is Killing Music: The Recording Industry's Piracy Panic Narrative." Edited by Victor Sarafian and Rosemary Findley. *Civilisations*, The State of the Music Industry 63, no. 1 (July 2014): 13–32.

———. "ITunes: Breaking Barriers and Building Walls." *Popular Music and Society* 37, no. 4 (2014): 408–24.

Attali, Jacques. *Noise: The Political Economy of Music*. Theory and History of Literature. Minneapolis: University of Minnesota Press, 1985.

Becker, Howard Saul. *Art Worlds*. 1st ed. Berkeley, CA: University of California Press, 1984.

Bourdieu, Pierre. *The Field of Cultural Production: Essays on Art and Literature*. Edited by Randal Johnson. New York: Columbia University Press, 1993.

Brucculieri, Julia. "JoJo Talks Making a Comeback, 'Cribs' and Battling Her Record Label." *Huffington Post*, October 6, 2015, sec. Entertainment. https://www.huffingtonpost.com/entry/jojo-interview-comeback_us_5612df41e4b022a4ce5f1618.

Cohen, Sara. *Rock Culture in Liverpool: Popular Music in the Making*. New York: Oxford University Press, 1991.

Durkheim, Emile. *The Division of Labor in Society*. Edited by Steven Lukes. New York: Free Press, 2014.

Frith, Simon. *Performing Rites: On the Value of Popular Music*. Cambridge, MA: Harvard University Press, 1996.

———. "The Industrialization of Popular Music." In *Popular Music and Communication*, edited by James Lull, 2nd ed., 53–79. Newbury Park, CA: Sage, 1992.

Gramsci, Antonio. "Hegemony, Relations of Force, Historical Bloc." In *Antonio Gramsci Reader*, 189–221. New York: Schocken Books, 1988.
———. *Selections from the Prison Notebooks of Antonio Gramsci.* Edited by Quintin Hoare and Geoffrey Nowell-Smith. London: Lawrence & Wishart, 1971.
Horkheimer, Max, and Theodor W. Adorno. *Dialectic of Enlightenment*. New York: Herder and Herder, 1972.
"Intellectual Property Theft: A Threat to U.S. Workers, Industries, and Our Economy." Fact Sheet. Washington, DC: AFL-CIO, Department for Professional Employees, August 2010.
Jay-Z, and Kanye West. *Diamonds from Sierra Leone*. Late Registration. United States: Roc-A-Fella: Made available through Hoopla, 2005.
Kellner, Douglas. *Media Spectacle*. 1st ed. London and New York: Routledge, 2003.
Laclau, Ernesto, and Chantal Mouffe. *Hegemony and Socialist Strategy: Towards a Radical Democratic Politics*. Vol. 2. London and New York: Verso, 2001.
Lena, Jennifer C. *Banding Together: How Communities Create Genres in Popular Music*. Princeton, NJ: Princeton University Press, 2014.
Luke, Timothy W. *Screens of Power: Ideology, Domination, and Resistance in Informational Society*. Urbana: University of Illinois Press, 1989.
Marshall, Lee. *Bootlegging: Romanticism and Copyright in the Music Industry*. 1st ed. Thousand Oaks, CA: Sage, 2005.
Marx, Karl. "Economic and Philosophical Manuscripts." In *Selected Writings*, edited by David McLellan, 2nd ed., 83–121. Oxford and New York: Oxford University Press, 2000.
———. "The German Ideology." In *The Marx-Engels Reader*, edited by Robert C. Tucker, 2nd ed., 146–200. New York: Norton, 1978.
Mills, C. Wright. *The Sociological Imagination.* 40th anniversary edition. Oxford, UK and New York: Oxford University Press, 2000.
Negus, Keith. *Music Genres and Corporate Cultures.* New York: Routledge, 1999.
Nirvana: Taking Punk to the Masses. Seattle, WA: Experience Music Project, 2016.
Shapter, Andrew. *Before the Music Dies*, 2006.
Siweck, Stephen. "Copyright Industries in the U.S. Economy: The 2006 Report." International Intellectual Property Alliance, November 2006.
———. "The True Cost of Sound Recording Piracy on the U.S. Economy." Institute for Policy Innovation, August 2007.

Théberge, Paul. "The End of the World as We Know It: The Changing Role of the Studio in the Age of the Internet." In *The Art of Record Production: An Introductory Reader for a New Academic Field*, edited by Simon Frith and Simon Zagorski-Thomas, 77–90. London: Ashgate, 2012.

Vito, Christopher. *The Values of Independent Hip-Hop in the Post-Golden Era: Hip-Hop's Rebels*. Palgrave Pivot, 2019. https://doi.org/10.1007/978-3-030-02481-9.

Williams, Raymond. *Marxism and Literature*. Marxist Introductions. New York: Oxford University Press, 1977.

3
Copyright Enclosure

"Music rights (copyrights, performing rights) are the basic pop commodity"—Simon Frith.[1]

In 2016, I founded a digital music archive (MusicDetour) to preserve and promote local music in the Dallas–Fort Worth metropolitan area. The idea is to provide a nonprofit platform for musicians to distribute music to audiences free of charge while at the same time preserving their music for generations to come. While my intentions for the archive align with the subject of this book, musicians continually demonstrate concern about relinquishing their copyrights to the website. They do not show much concern for me exploiting them, but rather, concern that their music has a monetary value. One bass player expressed to me, "why would anyone want to give their music away for free? They should just use CD Baby to get digital distribution." Contrary to his point, most musicians who sign up for CD Baby find it difficult to make their $30 investment back. When I spoke with one group at a battle of the bands, they did not want to contribute because they wanted to sell their music for money—the band broke up 2 months later. Many musicians expressed the desire to have a link to their Bandcamp[2] page where people could purchase their music. Inevitably, I notice musicians make music

D. Arditi, *Getting Signed*,
https://doi.org/10.1007/978-3-030-44587-4_3

available on Bandcamp that they did not authorize for my archive. For instance, they provide the archive with live albums and reserve the studio albums for Bandcamp. Other times, musicians expressed that I may have some ulterior motive to profit from their work. Dirty Dusters asked, "We just want to be absolutely sure we're not giving you the right to sell our intellectual property from your site or any other place on the web. This has happened to us before, and we'd prefer to not let that happen again."

At their core, musicians believe recorded music is a commodity through which they can generate money. They recognize that if they want to earn a living from their music, they have to sell their recordings (even if the sale of recordings is one prong in a broader strategy that includes performance, merchandise, etc.). The tool that these musicians use to monetize their recorded product is copyright because as Frith claims, copyrights are the commodity. However, copyright is also the means through which the music industry can exploit a musician's labor.

Everyone has an idea about the fundamental moral principle that supports copyright. The problem is that no fundamental moral, ethical, or even juridical principle that supports copyright exists. "There is, after all, no Platonic copyright against which we can match the ideal form of copyright."[3] Record labels exploit the fact that copyright does not exist in simple terms, but our brains seek to operate in simple moral terms. This is ideology. The artifice enables the economic organization of society. We can examine how the economic system creates the foundation of such a configuration, but without the legal apparatus in place, it does not work. Record labels depend on the ideology of getting signed to convince unsuspecting musicians that the way to support themselves is through record contracts, which sign away their copyrights to the record label in return for an advance on their royalties.

Musicians want to be compensated for their creative labor for writing, producing, performing, and recording music. Since music is always-already commodified, this makes perfect sense. Under capitalism, the only way for musicians to meet their basic and social needs—if their primary productive activity is playing music—is by turning their labor into money. There are two ways that musicians can do this. First, they can sell their labor to produce music for a wage. Second, they can attempt to sell the commodity (recorded or performed music) for a price.

In the former, the musician guarantees some type of compensation for work performed, but in the latter, their income depends on someone else's decision to buy their commodity. Again, in the first form, the musician is a worker, but in the second form, the musician engages in a capitalist enterprise that resembles a small business owner. The trick of the major record labels involves convincing musicians that they are the latter, while exploiting them as the former. However, musicians would be unable to sell music without copyright, and major record labels would be unable to exploit a musician's copyrights without record contracts. By signing away their copyrights on future royalties, musicians believe that their value derives from being little capitalists instead of as workers.

In order to understand the central role that copyright plays in the exploitation of musicians, first we must recognize the social constructed nature of these laws. "Statute law and government regulation shape the financial and aesthetic conditions within which popular culture develops. For example, copyright law transforms whole classes of creative activity into property that can be bought, sold, stolen and litigated about much like other goods."[4] Without copyright law, music would not be a commodity and musicians would not be labor. "Without capitalism, after all, most of what we think about music wouldn't be possible. Indeed, most music wouldn't be possible, since most of the music most people hear is industrially produced as a commodity, mass distributed as a commodity, and widely consumed as a commodity."[5] With the commodification of music, there is a parallel process of commodification of the worker. The alienation of music "involved, of course, the objectification and rationalization of music, its separation from the simple immediacy of use which had once defined it as art and granted it permanence in contrast to its definition in terms of mere ephemeral sound."[6] Music becomes alienated from the musician when it becomes commodified. "When the market lays siege to and invests in music, it reduces the musician to a consumer good, an inoffensive show of submission and subversion, the first product of mass production and mass sale, with rebellion as its raw material."[7] The musician is both a consumer good as the congealed labor contained in the recorded commodity and as a worker. Jacques Attali sees the musician's commodification as a form of subversion, but the act of submission tends to be stronger in the music industry as it becomes self-reproductive; that is, the ideology of getting signed helps diminish acts of subversion as musicians become more readily exploitable.

Copyright comes to hold significance to musicians as the means to subsistence. They view copyright as their intellectual property. As owners of copyright, musicians conceive of themselves as owners, as capitalists; record contracts reify this relationship because musicians enter these contracts as contractors. However, record contracts are ideology: they provide musicians with an upside-down vision of the world.[8] In this chapter, I start by explaining the cost and existence of the means of musical production. Second, I apply the labor theory of value to the contemporary recording industry. Next, I explore the process of land enclosure, and I argue that copyright is a form of land enclosure. Finally, I present record contracts as the means for separating musicians from their copyrights.

Musical Instruments and the Means of Musical Production

For my 13th birthday, my parents gave me my first drum set. It was a five-piece New Sound drum set that included two cymbals and a set of hi-hats. They purchased it used for $200 through a classified ad in the *Daily Press*—the daily newspaper for Hampton Roads Virginia. The instrument was not great, but it did the job. For the price, it was a great first kit for me to learn to play the drums. Later on, I purchased a nicer kit with money from my first job. This second kit was a five-piece Tama shell-kit (i.e., no hardware or cymbals) and cost about $1000. Ultimately, I bought a used eight-piece Yamaha kit with hardware and a double pedal for $300 from the local music store where I taught drum lessons while I was in college. A straight edge punk drummer previously owned the drum kit, and he had placed anti-smoking and anti-drinking stickers all over the kit along with poems to/from his girlfriend—it was very beat-up and missing parts. I had a friend artistically paint the kit, and I gigged regularly with this kit for 10 years. This $300 kit and some cymbals were all I needed to play music for years. Most musicians own their musical instruments outright at an accessible cost to most people. As the means of musical production, musical instruments do not create an insurmountable entrance cost for people to produce their own music. Furthermore, most anyone who plays an instrument owns their instrument outright.

Capitalism only works because workers do not own the means of production and therefore have to sell their labor-power to someone else in order to earn a wage to meet their needs. The means of production are both the tools/equipment and raw material used to produce commodities. While the means of musical production include musical instruments (and their accessories), sound systems, mixers, microphones, computers, studio facilities, etc., the primary means of musical production are musical instruments. Since most musicians own their musical instruments, they own their means of musical production.

The barriers to purchase musical instruments are relatively low. Running a search on Guitar Center's website, used guitars are available for as low as $30 and new guitars for $60 (though the $120 models are of decent quality); for most instruments, there are beginner instruments available under $200. According to the National Association of Music Merchants (NAMM), in 2009, 58% of households had at least one musical instrument player and 43% had two or more players.[9] In homes with less than $46,000/year income, 49% had a musical instrument player, while 66% of homes with more than $46,000/year income had at least one player.[10] In my discussions with musicians for this project, everyone I spoke with owned their instruments, and they owned an instrument ever since they began playing music.

Of course, owning a musical instrument is not the only means of musical production. From cymbals and drumsticks to guitar amps and effects pedals, musicians are notorious consumers, but most of this is for personal obsession, not sonic requirements. Most of my guitarist friends, from when I was a gigging drummer, owned multiple guitars and amps, and had assorted effects pedals. Other drummer friends of mine possessed collections of cymbals and many had multiple drum sets. Keyboard players usually own and perform with multiple electric pianos or synthesizers. In other words, contemporary musicians have a strong consumerist obsession for musical equipment, especially those who play instruments typically associated with rock music. However, the act of performance often requires more equipment than just a musical instrument and its accessories. For many music performances in twenty-first-century America, musicians need a PA system to project sound. Without going too far into the political economy of music performance, a venue often provides the PA system. If a PA system is not available, musicians need to bring their own sound system—musicians can buy a low-end PA system for around $120 new and under $100 used—but most musical instrument stores also rent this equipment for a low price.

With the commodification of recorded music, making recordings becomes an additional cost in the means of musical production. If musicians want to make a recording, they need to either purchase additional equipment or hire someone to record them. Fortunately, since the 1990s, the cost of recording equipment has fallen through the basement. The deployment of digital technology in the recording process accelerated the declining cost of recording equipment. Digital Audio Workstations (DAWs) are available for most computer systems: Apple's GarageBand is available free of charge for Mac computers, and people can purchase Pro Tools for as little as $100. Musicians do need some hardware to interface with their computers, but Amazon sells small USB mixers for as low as $25. By creating cheap computer software, every personal computer can become a home recording studio.[11] There has been a steep drop in price to record an album from the 1990s when a state-of-the-art mixer sold for $400,000 and studio rental cost $2,000/day.[12] Furthermore, as I argue elsewhere,[13] the drop in price of recording technology parallels the deployment of flexible labor relations in the recording process whereby producers open their home studios and shoulder the costs of recording. In turn, this generates cheaper recording facilities for those who do not own recording equipment or lack the skills to record themselves. However, at the point when musicians decide to record, they see value in recorded music as a commodity.

Since musicians own their means of musical production, capital has struggled to find a way to turn musicians into productive labor. If the cost of the musical means of production is so low, why do musicians become laborers? How does the system of musical production encourage musicians to sell their labor-power? The simple answer is copyright and the recorded commodity. I discuss below that copyright is the mechanism that changes the relationship between capital and labor or label and musician.

Labor Theory of Value

One musician who I spoke with summed up the disposition of people across the music industry by stating, "Austin wants people to play for free." The Blues/Country singer, Evette, expresses this in her struggle to make a living. She works four jobs and plays music, but still struggles to pay her bills in Austin, TX. Her critique is just as valid for Nashville where live musicians usually play for tips. A rather cavalier booking agent who I spoke with, Immanuel, expressed that acts such as Evette should take the opportunity to play in venues with ready-made audiences for $0–100 and tips because it gives them the opportunity to sell their recorded music and gain fans. At the same time, Evette reified the value of recording by stating that she wants to sell records and stop playing live. While she said she does not need a record label to make this happen, they would help her with distributing her music to a larger audience. People in the music industry devalue the labor performed by musicians at the same time that musicians split their labor between recording and performing music. Since the acts of recording and performing music are separate activities, it deceives musicians into believing that these spaces have different values (composition represents a third area of musical production). By creating the boundaries between performance, recording, and composition, copyright allows for value to be produced as it creates a division of labor between musicians.

However, musicians expend similar labor activities when they record and perform music. Through years of practice and performance, musicians develop the skill to perform music. When musicians record, they record a musical performance, but if we do recognize these as different zones of musical performance, similarities remain. The unique circumstances in the live venue and the studio change the way that musicians receive compensation. When a musician performs at a venue, they (should) receive a wage. For live performances, the people in the audience who hear the performance generally pay for the performance in one way or another (whether they pay a cover/buy tickets, purchase drinks, or give a tip to the band), and musicians earn a wage from this payment. In the recording studio, studio/session musicians receive a wage for hours they perform in the studio from whomever funds the recording session.[14] However, a distinction exists between recording artists and recording session musicians. Labels don't pay recording artists for their performances in the studio; rather, labels pay royalties for the sale of the recorded commodity later on. Musicians earn money through different mechanisms in these similar positions because of the intervention of copyright and the existing political economy of music.

In order to think about the role that copyright plays in a musician's life, we first need to look at the way musicians earn a wage, and how they create value. Marx's labor theory of value helps to explore the conditions in which musicians earn money from their music. Simply, the labor theory of value is the idea that labor creates all value. More specifically, the value equals the socially necessary labor-time needed to produce the commodity. The socially necessary labor-time is the time on average that it takes to produce a given commodity. For instance, car repair shops use manuals to estimate the average labor-time needed to fix a specific mechanical problem. Any given car mechanic could take more or less time to complete the job, but the shops use the average. This average is the socially necessary labor-time to complete a car repair. By using the average, it disincentives workers from working slower because slow workers will do the same task in a longer time earning them less money per hour. Since labor-power is a commodity (i.e., labor's commodity), it too has a value. In the case of labor-power, the socially necessary labor-time equals the cost to produce and reproduce the worker.

Applying the labor theory of value to music, two important factors contribute to the monetary cost of reproducing the labor of musicians. First, there is the cost to meet the worker's material needs (i.e., food, clothes, and shelter) so that they can labor again the next day.[15] For musicians, this cost in labor is relatively high because their paid working day tends to be very short but their wage has to cover what a different worker may earn in eight hours (a session drummer may charge between

$50 and 150/hour). Second, there is the cost to reproduce the worker in the sense of what it costs to train a new worker.[16] Since musicians perform a highly specialized function in the division of labor, new workers need to have years of practice and training (i.e., skilled work) to replace old workers. When musicians practice their instruments and rehearse with their bands, they engage in unpaid activity that increases the value of their labor. Without time practicing and rehearsing, musicians would have a low degree of skill and people wouldn't want to hear them perform. However, the time they spent practicing is time they could spend selling their labor-power or learning a different skill. A musician's wages therefore include the cost of training, time lost to practice, and the cost for them to meet their basic needs.

Marx himself says little about music. In one often-cited note in the *Grundrisse*, Marx disparages the productivity of musicians.[17] He makes the claim that people who make pianos are productive labor, but pianists are unproductive labor. Marx's point here is that while piano making can produce surplus value, piano playing cannot produce surplus value. It is difficult to see how piano playing could be productive in this sense using the labor theory of value in Marx's time. However, in the interceding years, recorded music upended Marx's formulation as it allowed pianists the ability to commodify their craft. Assuming that a piano maker does not own the means of production, they must work for a piano manufacturing company. The piano maker sells their labor-power for a wage to turn material into a piano, but the owner of the piano manufacturing company underpays the piano maker for their labor-power. Piano makers earn a wage that is equivalent to the socially necessary labor-time to make pianos, but they produce more value than they earn in wages. The difference between a piano maker's wage and the value they produce is surplus value. Marx defines productive labor as labor that produces surplus value for capital. On the other hand, for a piano player in Marx's time, there wasn't a way to produce surplus value because musicians owned their means of production and they didn't produce a commodity. Music is fleeting and exists outside of the commodity form when musicians perform it, and most pianists didn't charge people to listen to them play in the mid-nineteenth century. This changed with the introduction of recording technology at the end of the nineteenth century; with it, musicians could produce a commodity and sell it on the market.

Recording developed and accelerated the commodification of music as it created new means of musical production. In an economy where recordings are commodities, the means of musical production multiply. For a musician to earn revenue from an album, they have to record, produce, distribute, and promote the album. Each stage in the production of a recording is expensive. As I mentioned above, studio time and/or recording technologies can cost hundreds of thousands of dollars. Mixing an album requires paying highly skilled engineers and producers who understand how to manipulate recorded sound. Once a master copy of the recording is completed, the actual recorded commodity must be made and distributed. When recordings took a primarily physical form, this required not only gaining access to printing plants, but also being able to tap into distribution networks. No one person could contact all mom and pop record stores throughout the United States in the 1980s and earlier. With the rise of chain record stores and big box stores in the 1990s, distribution became easier because there were fewer retailers to contact, but these stores limited their shelf space to major record distributors. While digital recording and distribution have reduced some of the costs associated with the commodification of recordings, costs associated with the promotion of recordings remain high. Furthermore, the influence that major record labels and their affiliates have within the music industry makes it exceedingly difficult for independent artists to promote their music. While anyone can upload a YouTube video of their music, it is difficult to compete with the hundreds of thousands of other aspiring artists doing the same thing. This makes it so that musicians need to do something in order to make their labor-power valuable enough to earn a living from making music.

However, the transformation of music to a commodity does not fully explain the transition of music making from unproductive to productive labor. Since the means of production in the music industry are minimal, capital required other mechanisms to expropriate musician labor. Here, we see a parallel process in the expropriation of farm labor during the English land enclosures and the application of copyright law to recorded music.

Land Enclosures

When the King of England accelerated land enclosure in the fifteenth century, it forced people to adopt a new mode of production (i.e., capitalism). With the enclosure of land, England created private property. Under feudalism, serfs worked land as rentiers for their feudal lords. Serfs did not own land, nor did they rent it in the sense that we rent property today, but rather, they lived on land that they farmed for their lord (hence the name "landlord"). In return for living and farming the land, Serfs gave a percentage of their crop to the lord who controlled their land. An important distinction here is that they did not earn a wage for their crop, nor did they own it. The aristocracy owned all the land, but not in the sense that property works today. Land enclosure brought about the violent beginning of capitalism that Marx terms primitive accumulation. According to David Harvey, primitive accumulation "is about the violent dispossession of a whole class of people from control over the means of production, at first through illegal acts, but ultimately, as in the enclosure legislation in Britain, through actions of the state."[18] These violent fits of capitalism echo through different aspects of the economy through the dispossession of the means of production. A strong parallel exists between the development of land enclosure and the establishment of copyright legislation. Both enclose rights for people that did not exist previously, and in the process allowed capitalism into different aspects of the economy.

With the land enclosure acts, the English government enclosed parcels of land (i.e., drew property lines) and assigned deeds to individual parcels. At that moment, Marx illustrates how the new property owners gave the former serfs an option.[19] Either serfs could continue to work the land for a wage and rent property using that wage from the owner of the property or they would face expulsion from the land because they possessed no "right" to the land. Because of these acts, the government of England forced people into the capitalist mode of production. A mode of production is the conditions under which people live and the way people meet their needs in that system. Under feudalism, people met their needs by farming the land for the aristocracy and using their percentage of the crops to trade (usually using money as an intermediary) for other needs not immediately met through growing crops. When the property relation began through land enclosure, former serfs began working for a wage as either farmworkers or elsewhere, but in both cases, they worked for a wage and met their needs with that wage. Those new farmworkers produced higher yields of crops, so there was no longer a need for many of the former serfs even if they chose to continue farming—ultimately property owners evicted this excess labor. In turn, a mass migration proceeded from rural farms to urban centers in England. Ultimately, most of the people who moved from farms to cities could not find work, so the English government classified them as vagabonds—people who wander without a home or a job.[20] In fact, King Henry the VIII committed a form of genocide when he had 72,000 vagabonds executed even though their vagrancy was a direct result of the King's land enclosure acts.[21] The system forced people into the capitalist economy even though it did not have room for many of them.

Because of enclosure, two forces disturbed the feudal economic system in Europe. First, enclosure is a process that creates property where none exists. Whereas lords controlled land and allocated it to peasants through a rentier system, land deeds as such did not exist. By drawing lines around land and awarding deeds to that land, real property developed. At the same time that some people received property, the land enclosures displaced many peasants from the land they lived on and had farmed for generations. Second, it constitutes "the rearrangement of labor relations by separating workers from the land."[22] As the peasants left the land, they sought different forms of labor to meet their needs, all of which required exchanging labor-power for a wage. Those who remained on the land began selling their labor-power to work on farms for a wage. The upheaval created by the land enclosure acts changed the social relations of production dramatically by forcing a large segment of the population into wage labor. An influx of peasants into urban areas and towns provided the bourgeois with an oversupply of labor, which caused wages to decrease with every new wave of dispossessed peasants. Primitive accumulation in the form of land enclosure was a state-sponsored program to change the economic system from top to bottom. However, land is not the only area where enclosure created property rights and changed the social relations of production.

Creating Intellectual Property

Two hundred years after the land enclosure acts created property, forced feudal peasants from the land, and helped change the economic mode of production to capitalism, the British government established an additional form of property enclosure: intellectual property. Any discussion about intellectual property rights, as Sean Johnson Andrews asserts, "is really more about the history of property rights."[23] Here, I'm concerned with one specific type of intellectual property right: copyright. Passed by the British Parliament in 1709, the Statue of Anne granted two types of copyright. First, it gave authors a copyright for their books. Second, it reinforced existing copyright statutes that gave a printer exclusive rights to print copyrighted books.[24] "In the beginning, the purpose of copyright was not to defend artists' rights, but rather to serve as a tool of capitalism in its fight against feudalism."[25] By securing rights for the author, the Statute of Anne established the first legal justification that ideas could be considered a type of property.

Publishers of books and other published texts were the original recipients of copyrights. In France and England, "the first true copyright legislation, the regulation of publishing was through a set of 'privileges' given to printers, not rights given to authors."[26] In *The Music Industry: Music in the Cloud*, Patrik Wikstrom provides a lucid explanation of copyright. The British Statute of Anne, Wikstrom explains, "marks a shift from a system where printers were able to print books without compensating authors for their creative labor to a system where *authors* would have the exclusive right to reproduce books."[27] While Wikstrom focuses on the author as the intended beneficiary of early copyright legislation, the true beneficiary was the publisher. Book publishers did not want to produce a text (which involved paying the author) only to have another publisher copy the book without having to pay for the text's development. The idea that this was about "authorial right grew as an afterthought."[28] This change in perspective is significant because it demonstrates that from early on, copyright developed to enable capitalist imperatives.

Copyright's relationship with music began first with publishing long before the advent of sound recording. Therefore, in order to understand the transition to the copyright system, we must begin with music composers as the first musicians to have copyright enclosed. Timothy Taylor traces the first commodification of music back to the fifteenth century when Italian printer Ottaviano Petrucci used movable type to reproduce sheet music using a printing press.[29] Next, Beethoven, Taylor contends, "articulated the notion that his published music wasn't simply for consumption by contemporaries but, as a commodity, could have a life beyond him, a new idea at the time."[30] It was not until after Beethoven's death that the United States government gave automatic statutory protection to music through the Copyright Act of 1831. Through this copyright act, the composer became the source of musical commodification. Tin Pan Alley later became the quintessential industrialized manufacture of musical compositions in the form of sheet music.[31] While the relationship between copyright and music extends to the late eighteenth century, Tin Pan Alley in New York City in the early twentieth century established copyrights as a primary commodity of exchange. "The rise of the ideology of exchangeability meant that composers, and everyone else, could begin to conceptualize other cultural forms, other things, more and more in terms of their exchangeability."[32] Taylor suggests Tin Pan Alley created music in "song factories" to make sheet music eminently commodified.[33] Publishers in the sheet music industry rationalized song production in a way to make songs appealing to a broad range of voices that created earworms. When people want to play a composition, they pay for the rights by purchasing the sheet music. Performing musicians have paid composers for the right to perform musical works since copyright began applying to music.

What I hope is evident to this point is that the commodification of music is only possible by securing the materiality of music—the musical idea needs to be solidified as a "property" right. However, copyright is not a property right, it is a regulatory privilege granted by Congress. "By describing copyright as a private property right, proponents of the description hope to get policy makers and courts to believe that only private, and not public rights are implicated."[34] While I agree with William Patry's position that copyright proponents use metaphorical language to strengthen their position, I contend that the overall point of copyright as intellectual property provides businesses with a way to bring musical production (and all intellectual creations) into the capitalist fold. This is why the idea of copyright as property enclosure is so important. "Copyright legislation is what makes it possible to commodify a musical work, be it a song, an arrangement, a recording, etc."[35] Intellectual property supports the concept that monetary value exists in the creative process of songwriting and individual recorded performances. In order "to be able to license the use of that content … to consumers and businesses they need to be protected by copyright legislation."[36] Copyright is important in this process because it limits the ability of others to reproduce copyrighted material.

Primitive accumulation can help to explain how enclosure in other sectors changed the relations of production to bring other sites of production into the capitalist economy. For instance, Mark Andrejevic describes the recent "digital enclosure" as a process whereby we generate capital through surveillance by providing massive amounts of data about our online usage to companies.[37] When the Internet developed, no apparent form existed for companies to generate revenue from the Internet apart from charging for access to the network. However, Andrejevic argues that the Internet was enclosed through surveillance technologies that track our every move on the World Wide Web. The enclosure of digital networks parallels copyright enclosure as a process of primitive accumulation because it creates exchange value where none existed previously. Copyright enclosure is not entirely different from land enclosure.

The first commonality is the thought that copyright is "intellectual property." John Locke's "'labor theory' of property, which conceived the fruits of one's labor as one's own property" established the idea that creators conduct labor and own the rights of what they produce.[38] In other words, that which people create is their property.[39] James Boyle discusses "an intellectual land grab" brought about by new technologies.[40] While Boyle explains that intellectual property is not a property right, the term remains useful for analyzing copyright, trademarks, and patents. Furthermore, the analogy to property rights proves useful for thinking about copyright as enclosure. The analogy between intellectual property and land enclosure appears in other works. For instance, "Intellectual property laws, which create private property rights in cultural forms, afford fertile fields of inquiry for considering social intersections of law, culture, and interpretive agency."[41] Rosemary Coombe alludes not only to the creation of private property, but also to the idea of "fertile fields." These connections are not accidental, as property possesses this long tradition connected to labor in the fields.

Second, copyright expropriates the labor of a group of people, and forces them into a capitalist economy. "The existence of copyright creates a valuable 'property' that can be commodified and alienated that is not the work itself."[42] Musicians, who want to earn a living performing music, need to participate in the economy through recording, performing, and publishing music. These three areas of activity in which musicians participate require musicians to have some relationship to copyright because copyright encloses the production of music. For musicians to perform or record a song, they must secure the right to perform a song. If the musician composed the song, then they can perform it, unless they have a publishing deal—in which case they still need permission from the publisher. Without this permission, musicians violate copyright law. "Copyright thus established a monopoly over reproduction, not protection for the composition or control over representations of it."[43] Whether or not musicians want to participate in the copyright system, the law already establishes the order, so they must participate in it if they want to earn a living through music.

Finally, there is not enough room for everyone who hopes to earn a living from making music. If everyone could produce, record, distribute, promote, and sell music, music would be overproduced driving the value of each recording down in a capitalist economy. Therefore, most people who produce copyrighted material will not be able to meet their needs through this system. Just like land enclosure, copyright enclosure creates a reserve army of labor[44] because those who control the copyrights limit who they record, promote, and distribute. When landowners forced feudal serfs from the land, they flocked to the towns and cities in England in search of work. However, there weren't enough jobs for the emigrating masses to fill; this drove down the cost of labor. Musicians want to play music to earn a living despite the lack of opportunities for them to work, and this creates a reserve army of labor. If one musician is not willing or able to take a gig, another musician can easily take their place. This has the general effect of driving down wages across the music industry. Whether that means a session musician may be willing to take a gig for less money or a band is willing to play at a bar for tips. To return to Immanuel, the booking agent from Nashville, he insisted that his bars fill in Nashville regardless of who performs. Immanuel uses that knowledge to drive wages down for the bands because he knows he can always find a band willing to play for what he will offer them.

Despite the surplus of people who desire to earn a living through making music, no mechanism exists to dissuade people from this desire. In the contemporary American economy, the division of labor arises organically, not through a managed economy where an outside entity forces people to do a specific type of labor.[45] "There are plenty of musicians who want their music to be commodified simply so they can make a living, and it would be difficult for someone with a stable job to criticize them for that."[46] How does someone go about selling his or her labor-power for a wage? There are a number of ways to earn a wage through the performance of music, but signing record contracts makes sense as a means to commodify one's labor in a system whereby one must labor to earn a wage to pay for one's means of subsistence. In one discussion I had with a lap steel guitarist, she described a record contract as an opportunity "to create – not to have to work a day job to pay your bills." Despite our conversation touching the exploitative practices of record contracts, she still felt that contracts allow musicians to dedicate their full time to playing music.

Earning income through the performance of music is the dominant ideology behind the commodification of music. In fact, there is a strong feeling among musicians and music industry workers and executives that economic incentive must exist for musicians to create music. "The utilitarian/consequentialist origin story is based on the assertion that only by providing copyright protection will there be sufficient incentives for authors to distribute their works to the public. The public will then benefit from having available works that would not have been produced but for copyright."[47] This is evident when Neil Portnow ask the question, "What if we're all watching the Grammys a few years from now and there's no Best New Artist award because there aren't enough talented artists and songwriters who are actually able to make a living from their craft?" at the 2015 GRAMMYs.[48] This is also the myth that Tom Phillips and John Street analyze when they surveyed musicians' attitudes about copyright.[49]

> Put simply, we might expect musicians to think differently about music if they conceive of themselves as 'artists' or as 'craftsmen/women' or as 'entrepreneurs'.... the role of copyright, and the business model which underpins it, assumes that musicians will be 'incentivized' by the revenue they receive from their music.[50]

However, from Street and Phillips' interviews and my own observations, this is not the case. People write and perform music for a variety of reasons, but since very few make money through its production and performance, those who argue that copyright is an incentive to make music operate from purely a rational business perspective. In reality, human beings are anything but rational. From guitarists playing around a campfire to opening acts in arenas, more examples of musicians playing without compensation exist than musicians who earn money from their performances.

Despite the lack of money earned through copyright for most musicians, musicians continue fiercely defending copyrights as something that belongs to them as their property right. In their discussions with musicians, Street and Phillips noticed that musicians had very little idea about the letter of the law. "The judgments they made were not bound by the formal requirements of the law, but what they thought was 'right.'"[51] More than anything, musicians care about the morality of copyright if not the law. "Morality could trump the law. Whatever the law required, the issue was what was or was not disrespectful."[52] In other words, musicians do not care about the letter of the law when it comes to their copyrights, but rather they believe fundamental notions of right and wrong exist with copyright. Furthermore, musicians do not necessarily care if they earn money from their music, but they want to ensure that people respect their rights.

I find it important to note that the copyright system did not make people establish a wage relationship with the recording industry. Rather, musicians remained in the position of the romantic ideal of the artist that emerged from the Romantic Period in the nineteenth century. Aram Sinnreich claims that "the modern notion of the 'artist' became necessary only at the moment that culture entered into mass production."[53] Convincing artists to labor for labels (and publishers) required them to think that they own their rights, and the only way to make it was to sign away those rights. As Taylor describes the transition to capitalism for musicians, "they continued to work as artisans, even if they could increasingly rely on concert and publishing infrastructures, as well as new laws such as copyright … to protect the products of their labor in a capitalist market."[54] In order for musicians to continue to believe they retain autonomy in the creation of music, their labor continues to resemble previous phases of capitalism. Specifically, we see artisanal production in which the worker labors over their own creation, and ostensibly, own the products of their labor. This is exemplified among a loose group of musicians who identify themselves as "artist rights" proponents. The popular imaginary constructs the solitary musician writing and performing music as an artist. However, this relation obscures both the role of musicians in the labor process and the ownership of copyrights.

> Because our culture generally holds authors in high regard, it is easy to presume that copyright is in some way designed to reward authors because they deserve reward. This seems so obvious to some that it is a difficult proposition to even investigate… Even as we labor within a corporate industrial system where workers have no rights over the things they help produce, we continue to believe in the principle that we own what we make and we deserve to be paid for what we create. It is important to remember that this is not the case. Rewarding authors has never been the purpose of copyright—it is merely its preferred strategy.[55]

While musician-composers could (hypothetically) work in solitude composing music, they are deeply embedded in social and cultural networks. A composer or songwriter hears other musicians perform, receives training for their skill, and interacts with people throughout their lives. These rich experiences influence the music they create.

Furthermore, the technical apparatus and means of musical production in which musicians create music contribute to the aesthetics of music.

Copyright aids musicians in the commodification of their music, but copyrights actualize their value only when musicians sign away those rights to record labels. "In the industry's own jargon, each piece of music represents 'a basket of rights'; the company task is to exploit as many of these rights as possible, not just those realized when it is sold in recorded form to the public, but also those realized when it is broadcast on radio or television, used on a film, commercial or video soundtrack, and so on."[56] When musicians copyright their music, they make their music commodifiable goods. They can deploy these commodities through recording, performance, and publishing. However, their deployment is only possible because they begin to resemble property. If a musician retains their copyrights in entirety, they can earn money from each usage of their musical work. "It is important to note what actually is traded on copyright markets. When people purchase a vase or a CD, they do not purchase the design of the vase or the copyrights to the sound recording. The only thing purchased is an example of the vase design or a right to listen to the sound recording within certain carefully defined restrictions."[57] As long as they retain the copyright, every time a musician sells a CD, they earn money from the sale. However, musicians can sell their copyrights wholesale by assigning their rights to others.

With copyright enclosure, musicians obtained legal protections for their music, but these government-issued licenses also permitted them to exchange their rights. Copyright enclosure creates a set of intellectual property rights, expropriates labor by forcing musicians into a capitalist economy, and develops a surplus army of labor that suppresses musicians' wages. All three of these parallels to land enclosure create the fertile land for musicians to be exploited, but the exploitation only comes to fruition when musicians trade their copyrights in record contracts.

Contracts and Copyrights

While musicians can commodify music in a number of ways, there is no way for third parties to create profit from the sale of music without copyrights. "The history of world music, and the history of music more generally with the establishment of copyright in the late eighteenth century, has been a history of someone attempting to profit legally from someone else's music."[58] However, copyright alone does not give third parties the ability to profit from musicians' labor; rather, copyright gives musicians the mechanism to trade (i.e., assign) their intellectual property using contract law. Record contracts permit record labels to profit legally from the work of musicians.

Copyright becomes a means of musical production that far exceeds the value of an instrument. But just like land enclosure, the construction of intellectual property rights requires an act of the state and the labor of workers. When musicians create music, there is no inherent value in it, but when musicians copyright their music, the law limits access to their music due to monopoly licenses. Through the deployment of copyrights as a means to make musical creation productive, copyright holders generate surplus value. However, copyrights don't have value for musicians on their own because they need the support of record labels to distribute and promote the recorded music commodity. Holding a copyright of a song is useless in capitalism if the copyright holder does not deploy their rights for sale. Using record contracts, musicians can make their labor productive. "Contracts are the principal means by which companies secure control of the labor and recorded output of their stars and potential stars, preventing artists from taking advantage of attractive offers from competitors and preventing other enterprises from unauthorized access to their artists."[59] When musicians sign record contracts (i.e., become "recording artists"), they take a Faustian bargain to gain the operational heft of record labels and a cash advance in exchange for control of their copyrights. In this exchange, musicians go from workers to owners, while record labels gain the musicians' productive labor in perpetuity.

Much of the music business literature and rhetoric hinges on the idea that music has high production costs and low reproduction costs. "The dominant portion of the costs in copyright industries is attributed to the production of 'the first copy' and the marketing of the title in question."[60] Therefore, record labels argue they take significant risk developing, producing, distributing, and marketing the product that ultimately may not be purchased by an audience. Since their risk is so high, record labels want to recoup their costs before they provide any revenue to the artists. In a standard record contract, recording artists pay back their advance to their record labels through their portion of the royalties, at the same time that record labels earn their own royalties from the sale. Even if it is true that the label takes risks, it does not negate the fact that the musicians are in the same boat with regard to risk. Except, musicians invest money for much longer and participate in music making when they could be earning a wage elsewhere; musicians spend a lot of time practicing their instruments, taking lessons, rehearsing, performing, and promoting their music. Furthermore, when musicians sign a record contract, they labor for a company similar to any other worker, but without a wage. Clearly, musicians take risk developing this skill and pursuing music careers.

By signing record contracts, recording artists submit to the ideology that record labels are the risk takers, while at the same time relinquishing their rights as workers. "The record contract conveys to the company rights over the labor and the recorded output of the artist (and, increasingly, over a range of other activities by the artist). The contract, in other words, plays a role in commodifying and alienating the artist's labor, her recorded output, and the rights to them."[61] Record contracts become the means through which musicians can earn a wage from their labor. However, my description problematizes the idea that record contracts provide a means of subsistence. In fact, the opposite is true. While people must labor to earn a wage, record contracts do not provide signees with a wage, they provide them with a recoupable advance. In some instances, an advance may be a mechanism that allows signees to pay bills using their stipends, but they must repay that money with future sales of their music. This is like buying things to meet your basic needs on a credit card; except in this case, the credit card company is the record label that stands to profit on their labor. With the record label acting as creditor, contracts position recording artists as workers shopping at the company store; the more recording artists spend their advance, the more albums they have to sell to recoup their advance. This is why Courtney Love said a record contract is like a sharecropper's contract. Often times, recording artists are unaware when they are spending money from their advance. Jacob Slichter, drummer from the rock band Semisonic, explains how his band did not know that they paid for expensive catering spreads at promotion events.[62] In one interview, Corey, a bassist signed to a major record label, described a similar situation where his band never once saw an accounting form, but rather the label informed them after they spent all of the advances.

Recording artists cede all of their power to record labels when they sign the record contract. Corey described his experience in Fastbreak, a 1990s alternative rock band, to me in an interview. After recording an album with a reputable boutique indie label, Fastbreak attracted the attention of several major record labels, one of which was their dream label. After some negotiation, Fastbreak signed with their dream label. Furthermore, as a condition to sign with the label, they had to fire the drummer—they lost the ability to make personnel decisions within the band. The label thought the drummer couldn't keep time and was unwilling to sign him. After signing, Fastbreak toured the college circuit, but without a record to promote, they had a difficult time sustaining a fan following. While they toured, they spent some time recording their album and going to promotional events. Meanwhile, the label spent the band's advance (even increasing the size of the advance from $500,000 to $1 million) without informing them. By the time the album was ready for distribution, the label decided not to release it—i.e., it got shelved.

Fastbreak's experience is important because it demonstrates that musicians forfeit their copyrights for opportunity, but in the process, they lose power.[63] Furthermore, this example demonstrates that discussions of risk on the part of the music industry are hyperbole. If Fastbreak's label cared about recouping their advance, they would have used the full force of the label to promote the album. Instead, because of the whims of a new A&R manager, the label decided to cut their losses of over one million dollars without even trying to recoup the money. This is a standard situation in the recording industry. The label either cuts the recording artists or sits on their album. Fastbreak took substantial risk, lost their autonomy, and ultimately has nothing to show for it. Rhetoric about risk ignores the lived reality of the treatment of bands.

Copyright enclosure is dialectic. On the one hand, enclosure of copyrights creates the opportunity for musicians to generate income from their music. On the other hand, the main way that musicians generate income from copyrights is through the wholesale assignment of their rights to record labels. It makes rational sense for musicians to want to earn a living from their musical works. American institutions teach us that we want to find our calling[64] in a job, often obscured in the idea that people want "a career instead of a job." People want to feel fulfilled in their work, so musicians believe their route to labor self-actualization is through employment as a musician. Record contracts give these musicians the means to what they believe will provide them this fulfillment.

Conclusion

Musicians face few barriers to produce music because of the low cost of the means of musical production. Since most musicians own their own musical instruments, they can make music at virtually no cost. Many people thought that the decreasing costs associated with recording and promoting music in the digital environment would make it even easier for musicians to produce their own music; the popular way of thinking is that fewer musicians would sign record contracts as a result. However, the power of the major record labels has not wavered.

Record labels retain their power because the copyright system provides incentive for musicians to sign record contracts. The power stems from the enclosure of copyrights. Similar to the enclosure of land in fifteenth-century England, the enclosure of copyrights creates a set of intellectual property rights, expropriates labor by forcing musicians into a capitalist economy, and develops a surplus army of labor that suppresses musicians' wages. Musicians need a means to turn their unproductive labor into productive labor; copyright provides the means. However, the only way for musicians to actualize their productivity is through the sale of their copyrights to record labels. Largely, signing record contracts does not position the recording artists as labor, but rather the contracts conceal their labor as independent subcontractors.

Nevertheless, the ideology of getting signed obscures the exploitation inherent in copyright enclosure. Musicians believe that signing a record contract will allow them to use their copyrights to leverage obscene amounts of money. They happily participate in their exploitation by signing record contracts.

Notes

1. Frith, "Copyright and the Music Business," 57.
2. Bandcamp is a website that allows musicians to post their music to be downloaded for a donation that the musicians set.
3. Patry, *Moral Panics and the Copyright Wars*, 15.
4. Peterson, "Five Constraints on the Production of Culture," 144.
5. Taylor, *Music and Capitalism*, 2.
6. Adorno, "On The Social Situation of Music."
7. Attali, "Foreword," xi.
8. Marx, "The German Ideology," 154.
9. Wilson and Block, *The NAMM Global Report 2011*, 167.
10. Ibid., 169.
11. Arditi, "Disturbing Production"; Arditi, "Informal Labor in the Sharing Economy"; and Théberge, "The End of the World as We Know It: The Changing Role of the Studio in the Age of the Internet."
12. Verna, "Room with a View's Closing Illustrates Harsh Realities."
13. Arditi, "Disturbing Production."
14. Arditi, "Digital Downsizing."
15. Marx, *Capital*, chap. 23.
16. Ibid.
17. Marx, *Grundrisse*, 305.
18. Harvey, *A Companion to Marx's Capital*, 293.
19. Marx, *Capital*, chap. 27.
20. Ibid., chap. 24.
21. Marx, "The German Ideology," 181.
22. Andrejevic, *ISpy*, 105.
23. Andrews, *The Cultural Production of Intellectual Property Rights*, 81.
24. Vaidhyanathan, *Copyrights and Copywrongs*, 40.
25. Attali, *Noise: The Political Economy of Music*, 52.
26. Boyle, *The Public Domain*, 29.
27. Wikstrom, *The Music Industry*, 18.
28. Boyle, *The Public Domain*, 8; Lessig, *Free Culture: The Nature and Future of Creativity*.

29. Taylor, *Music and Capitalism*, 22.
30. Ibid., 27.
31. Ibid., 28.
32. Ibid., 30.
33. Taylor, *Music and Capitalism.*
34. Patry, *Moral Panics and the Copyright Wars*, 107.
35. Wikstrom, *The Music Industry*, 17.
36. Ibid.
37. Andrejevic, *ISpy.*
38. Klein, Moss, and Edwards, *Understanding Copyright*, 14.
39. Andrews, *The Cultural Production of Intellectual Property Rights.*
40. Boyle, *The Public Domain*, xv.
41. Coombe, *The Cultural Life of Intellectual Properties: Authorship, Appropriation, and the Law*, 6.
42. Marshall, *Bootlegging*, 77.
43. Attali, *Noise: The Political Economy of Music*, 52.
44. Marx, *Capital*, chap. 25.
45. Durkheim, *The Division of Labor in Society.*
46. Taylor, *Music and Capitalism*, 9.
47. Patry, *Moral Panics and the Copyright Wars*, 62.
48. Flanagan, "Grammys 2015."
49. Street and Phillips, "What Do Musicians Talk About When They Talk About Copyright?"; Phillips and Street, "Copyright and Musicians at the Digital Margins."
50. Street and Phillips, "What Do Musicians Talk About When They Talk About Copyright?," 427.
51. Ibid., 429.
52. Ibid., 430.
53. Sinnreich, *The Essential Guide to Intellectual Property*, 30.
54. Taylor, *Music and Capitalism*, 31.
55. Gillespie, *Wired Shut: Copyright and the Shape of Digital Culture*, 23–24.
56. Frith, "Copyright and the Music Business," 57.
57. Wikstrom, *The Music Industry*, 21.
58. Taylor, *Music and Capitalism*, 114.
59. Stahl, *Unfree Masters*, 107.
60. Wikstrom, *The Music Industry*, 24.
61. Stahl, *Unfree Masters*, 111.
62. Slichter, *So You Wanna Be a Rock & Roll Star: How I Machine-Gunned a Roomful of Record Executives and Other True Tales from a Drummer's Life.*

63. Vito, *The Values of Independent Hip-Hop in the Post-Golden Era*, 73.
64. Weber, *The Protestant Ethic and the Spirit of Capitalism.*

Bibliography

Adorno, Theodor W. "On The Social Situation of Music." In *Essays on Music/Theodor W. Adorno*, edited by Theodor W. Adorno, Richard D. Leppert, and Susan H. Gillespie, 391–433. Berkeley, CA: University of California Press, 2002.

Andrejevic, Mark. *ISpy: Surveillance and Power in the Interactive Era*. CultureAmerica. Lawrence, KS: University Press of Kansas, 2007.

Andrews, Sean Johnson. *The Cultural Production of Intellectual Property Rights: Law, Labor, and the Persistence of Primitive Accumulation*. Philadelphia, PA: Temple University Press, 2019.

Arditi, David. "Digital Downsizing: The Effects of Digital Music Production on Labor." *Journal of Popular Music Studies* 26, no. 4 (December 2014): 503–20.

———. "Disturbing Production: The Effects of Digital Music Production on Music Studios." In *The Production and Consumption of Music in the Digital Age*, edited by Brian J. Hracs, Michael Seman, and Tarek E. Virani, 25–40. New York, NY: Routledge, 2016.

———. "Informal Labor in the Sharing Economy: Everyone Can Be a Record Producer." *Fast Capitalism* 13, no. 1 (2016). http://www.uta.edu/huma/agger/fastcapitalism/13_1/Arditi-Informal-Labor-Sharing.htm.

Attali, Jacques. "Foreword." In *Music and Marx: Ideas, Practice, Politics*, edited by Regula Burckhardt Qureshi, translated by Elizabeth Marshman, ix–xii. Critical and Cultural Musicology. New York, NY: Routledge, 2002.

———. *Noise: The Political Economy of Music*. Theory and History of Literature. Minneapolis: University of Minnesota Press, 1985.

Boyle, James. *The Public Domain: Enclosing the Commons of the Mind*. New Haven, CT: Yale University Press, 2008.

Coombe, Rosemary J. *The Cultural Life of Intellectual Properties: Authorship, Appropriation, and the Law*. Post-Contemporary Interventions. Durham: Duke University Press, 1998.

Durkheim, Emile. *The Division of Labor in Society*. Edited by Steven Lukes. New York: Free Press, 2014.

Flanagan, Andrew. "Grammys 2015: Recording Academy's Neil Portnow Uses Speech to Lobby on Streaming Payouts." *Billboard*, February 8, 2015. http://www.billboard.com/articles/events/grammys-2015/6465670/grammys-2015-neil-portnow-streaming-payouts.

Frith, Simon. "Copyright and the Music Business." *Popular Music* 7, no. 1 (January 1, 1988): 57–75. https://doi.org/10.2307/853076.

Gillespie, Tarleton. *Wired Shut: Copyright and the Shape of Digital Culture*. Cambridge, MA: MIT Press, 2007.

Harvey, David. *A Companion to Marx's Capital*. London: Verso, 2010.

Klein, Bethany, Giles Moss, and Lee Edwards. *Understanding Copyright: Intellectual Property in the Digital Age*. Los Angeles, CA: Sage, 2015.

Lessig, Lawrence. *Free Culture: The Nature and Future of Creativity*. New York: Penguin Press, 2004.

Marshall, Lee. *Bootlegging: Romanticism and Copyright in the Music Industry*. 1st ed. Thousand Oaks, CA: Sage, 2005.

Marx, Karl. *Capital: Volume 1: A Critique of Political Economy*. New York, NY: Penguin Classics, 1992.

———. *Grundrisse: Foundations of the Critique of Political Economy*. New York: Vintage Books, 1973.

———. "The German Ideology." In *The Marx-Engels Reader*, edited by Robert C. Tucker, 2nd ed., 146–200. New York: Norton, 1978.

Patry, William. *Moral Panics and the Copyright Wars*. New York, NY: Oxford University Press, 2009.

Peterson, Richard A. "Five Constraints on the Production of Culture: Law, Technology, Market, Organizational Structure and Occupational Careers." *Journal of Popular Culture; Bowling Green, Ohio* 16, no. 2 (Fall 1982): 143–153.

Phillips, Tom, and John Street. "Copyright and Musicians at the Digital Margins." *Media, Culture & Society* 37, no. 3 (April 1, 2015): 342–58. https://doi.org/10.1177/0163443714567018.

Sinnreich, Aram. *The Essential Guide to Intellectual Property*. New Haven, CT: Yale University Press, 2019. https://www.worldcat.org/title/essential-guide-to-intellectual-property/oclc/1055252885.

Slichter, Jacob. *So You Wanna Be a Rock & Roll Star: How I Machine-Gunned a Roomful of Record Executives and Other True Tales from a Drummer's Life*. New York: Broadway Books, 2004.

Stahl, Matt. *Unfree Masters: Popular Music and the Politics of Work*. Durham, NC: Duke University Press Books, 2012.

Street, John, and Tom Phillips. "What Do Musicians Talk About When They Talk About Copyright?" *Popular Music and Society* 40, no. 4 (August 8, 2017): 422–33. https://doi.org/10.1080/03007766.2015.1126099.

Taylor, Timothy D. *Music and Capitalism: A History of the Present*. Chicago, IL: University of Chicago Press, 2015.

Théberge, Paul. "The End of the World as We Know It: The Changing Role of the Studio in the Age of the Internet." In *The Art of Record Production: An Introductory Reader for a New Academic Field*, edited by Simon Frith and Simon Zagorski-Thomas, 77–90. London: Ashgate, 2012.

Vaidhyanathan, Siva. *Copyrights and Copywrongs: The Rise of Intellectual Property and How It Threatens Creativity*. New York: New York University Press, 2003.

Verna, Paul. "Room with a View's Closing Illustrates Harsh Realities." *Billboard*, October 24, 1998.

Vito, Christopher. *The Values of Independent Hip-Hop in the Post-Golden Era: Hip-Hop's Rebels*. Palgrave Pivot, 2019. https://doi.org/10.1007/978-3-030-02481-9.

Weber, Max. *The Protestant Ethic and the Spirit of Capitalism: And Other Writings*. Edited by Peter Baehr and Gordon C. Wells. New York, NY: Penguin Classics, 2002.

Wikstrom, Patrik. *The Music Industry: Music in the Cloud*. 1st ed. Cambridge and Malden, MA: Polity, 2010.

Wilson, Ken, and Erin Block, eds. *The NAMM Global Report 2011*. 2011th ed. Carlsbad, CA: National Association of Music Merchants, 2011.

4

The Digital Turn: Music Business as Usual

In an interview with a label employee, John, I asked him if he played an instrument. This is usually part of my friendly banter with informants as I try to find common ground. As a drummer, I have an easier time relating to people in the industry through our shared experiences playing music. However, in this particular discussion, after stating that he does not play a musical instrument, John explained why a person's musical background is unimportant to working in the music industry: "Signing musical talent doesn't take musical talent, it takes being able to spot musical talent." Of course, spotting musical talent here is not about the musician's talent, but rather their business acumen. Record labels take an interest in artists who have a large following because it both demonstrates that others appreciate their music, and more importantly, demonstrates that they have the right business sense to gain a following. While the mode of production for music is embedded in capitalism where music is always-already a commodity, the notion that music is a commodity is ideological and business-sense pervades any discussion of music.

Alongside the ideology of getting signed, the business ideology shapes much of the activity in the music industry. This separate, but related ideology develops on the part of people who work in the music

D. Arditi, *Getting Signed*,
https://doi.org/10.1007/978-3-030-44587-4_4

industry (managers, A&R, booking agents, venue owners and operators, publishers, etc.). On the one hand, the ideology differs little from any other business perspective: maximize profits. On the other hand, it is quite specialized because of the nuances of copyright law (emerging from the copyright enclosure), and the sense that cultural commodities do not work the same way as other commodities. Musicians learn through their careers that no one cares what they sound like because a million people can do their jobs. As one songwriter-turned-publishing house owner described to me, "If you want to make it in the music business, you have to follow opportunities wherever they go. Piano players are a dime a dozen, so I realized I had to write music. Then I figured-out you need to spend money to make a hit." When you speak with enough people who work in the music industry, their logic begins to seem sensible, but they found the basis of their thinking on the notion that music is a commodity.

For the past 20 years, people both inside and outside the music industry have discussed how much the music industry has changed. Much of the optimistic rhetoric surrounds the idea that anyone can upload music online and be heard. While rhetoric abounds that the Internet enables artists to find success through digital self-release, "it's virtually impossible for most creative people to thrive without the benefits that these enterprises provide."[1] The frequent utopian refrain is that digital technology changed the music industry, then utopians go on about how anyone can use the Internet to distribute and promote their music, which in conjunction with the ubiquity of cheap recording technology, allows musicians to overcome the major label oligopoly. Interestingly, musicians have been far more reluctant than others to share this zeal. While the music industry has transformed with digital technology, I contend that the labels have an outsized role today. Furthermore, when I spoke with aspiring musicians, they continued to exhibit the ideology of getting signed. What changed was the way record labels court prospective recording artists while they continue to exploit the dream.

In this chapter, I identify some of the areas where the logic of business dominates music. First, I explore the divide between musicians and music industry workers and executives. The way the industry positions people changes the way they view the creation of music as an art (musicians) or a commodity (music industry perspective). Second, this chapter expounds on the massive change that accompanied both digital distribution and streaming. The primary shift happened to the way labels "discover" musicians from searching for talent on the touring circuit to examining big data and an act's social media reach. Third, I explore alternatives that have arisen from the datafication of the recording industry. In these alternatives, I see instances where artists continue to hold on to the conventional approaches to the industry, but they must find new ways to make ends meet since labels concern themselves with finding talent through data. While things change dramatically in the recording industry, it is striking how little the change benefits musicians.

Positioning Musicians in the Music Industry

Throughout my study, there was a clear demarcation between music industry professionals (whether they were executives or bar bookers) and musicians around the meaning of making it in music. Most musicians understood the business perspective to the extent that it meant being paid for their work whereas industry professionals view music solely as a commodity that they need to maximize for profits. While the difference between workers and the capitalist class in perspectives can always be seen within any industry (especially craft industries and the arts), the chasm is especially wide and apparent in the music industry where musicians possess a romantic notion about their work and music industry businesspersons care solely about music as a commodity.

In one conversation I had with a high-level booker (and former touring rock bass player) in New York, he said everything changed in the 1990s when "bean counters" took over the executive spots in the recording industry. This trend happened across industries from health care to automotive industries as companies placed people with business or military pedigree in high-powered positions with little to no experience in that specific industry. It corresponds with scandals in the pharmaceutical industry where prices of necessary drugs sky-rocket at the same time that executives pursue research on erectile dysfunction pills. Recently, Gibson guitars hired a new CEO who formerly ran Levi Strauss & Co. (jeans) with the goal of turning the guitar company into a "lifestyle" company.[2] The popular CBS show *Undercover Boss* exemplifies this disconnect as bosses who know nothing about the frontline of their businesses go "undercover" to work alongside their employees only to be ridiculed for their incompetence to do the most basic tasks. If these record executives were placed in a recording studio, most would be completely without skill to do any of the tasks on the frontline.

By positioning musicians as members of "service occupations" who clients pay for a service, Howard Becker highlights the tensions between industry professionals and musicians. "Consequently, the client is able to direct or attempt to direct the worker at his task and to apply sanctions of various kinds," Becker explains, "ranging from informal pressure to the withdrawal of his patronage and the conferring of it on some others of the many people who perform the service."[3] Musicians would like to perform music of their choosing, but if they do so, they risk losing the audience that they depend on to pay for their services. They recognize, as musicians, their job is to serve their client, so they must compromise their expertise about what is best or what is desirable on the part of the client. Becker argues that musicians ultimately decide whether they will sell-out to make money or emphasize art for art's sake:

> The most distressing problem in the career of the average musician… is the necessity of choosing between conventional success and his artistic standards. In order to achieve success he finds it necessary to 'go commercial,' that is, to play in accord with the wishes of the nonmusicians for whom he works; in doing so he sacrifices the respect of other musicians and thus, in most cases, his self-respect.[4]

The decision that musicians make about whether or not they "go commercial" involves a decision about why they perform music: playing for the music or playing for money. Serving a client begins with a willingness to make trade-offs for self-preservation. Note that Becker published *Outsiders* in 1963, so the idea that the non-musician "bean counters" run the industry is far older than the 1990s. Musicians have served a client going back to the monarchy's patronage system[5] and this speaks to the broader political economy of music.

However, the divide between art and commerce is not as stark as we often construct it. "To this day, the idea that the artist and her work somehow stand apart from society remains strong in the realm of classical music, and it is present in rock and jazz," Timothy Taylor asserts, "even though this is an ideology that was produced as a result of music's entry into the marketplace as artists both tried to make a living and at the same time show the world that the fruits of their labors were somehow divorced from the messy business of making a living."[6] In fact, Taylor points out that the contradiction is an outgrowth of the transition of music to capitalism. When capitalism became the dominant mode of production, musicians had to find a way to feed, clothe, and house themselves and their families. To do this, many began working for the aristocracy. Dating back to medieval courts in Europe, the royalty exercised their power by teaching songs to jongleurs and street musicians to go out on the street to play for the people.[7] But as the monarchy grew in power, the royal court began to pay musicians on retainer to work inside the court.[8] This system ensured that musicians had the resources to pay for their means of existence while they worked exclusively at the demand of the sovereign. When the bourgeoisie established itself, working for a patron took on the form of working in a large orchestra for the bourgeoisie to represent their wealth through attendance at concerts.[9] In each case, musicians further diminished their autonomy in exchange for access to a wage. At the same time, the romantic ideal of autonomy grew stronger in which people perceive that the artist operates outside the demands of any other person. Since popular forms of music are supposed to emerge from the people, there must be a certain truth that the author, writer, or performer had some degree of control over its production. "The folk ideology holds that for music to truly be 'popular' it must have emerged from the people."[10] The idea that musicians (and other artists) are autonomous stems from individualism rooted in capitalism.

When musicians decide to go commercial, they do so under the logic of music business. A whole series of "boundary spanners" exist in the music industry whose jobs mandate that they find talent.[11] These boundary spanners internalize the ideology that music is a commodity;

then they seek musicians who adhere to their vision of a potentially successful artist. David Grazian contends that the primary consumer of popular culture is a type of boundary spanner called "surrogate consumers," a network of gatekeepers from film critics to radio DJs who make the decisions about what is commercially viable.[12] These tastemakers also adhere to the logic that a good musician is one who sells a lot of music, tickets, and merchandise. Therefore, John the label employee's position that he can spot musical talent without possessing musical talent begins to make perfect sense. John sells music commodities as his job, and his job is to understand commodities, consumers, and markets. While he has no musical talent, he has business talent. As a boundary spanner, he is only willing to accept the musicians who have the same talent that he has: business savvy.

While self-respect is an important factor determining what type of music a musician will perform, any analysis about whether a musician will go commercial is incomplete without addressing the issues of class and capital. Pierre Bourdieu addresses the issue of class in *The Field of Cultural Production*,[13] where he posits that only artists from a privileged background have the autonomy to pursue art for art's sake. Becker makes a similar claim by noting that families place a strain on a musician's pursuit of music as a career. Whereas "lower-class families" sometimes see a musical career "as a possible mobility route," "middle-class" families oppose a music career.[14] Since working-class musicians often go into music as a means to obtain class mobility, their embrace of the American Dream ideology (to pull oneself from ones bootstraps) makes them willing to go commercial. Because of the surplus of musicians willing to do what the industry wants and the lack of economic stability among working-class musicians, "there are very few symbol creators who are able to disregard economic realities completely."[15] Working-class musicians pursue record contracts and commercialization as a means to overcome the materiality of need. On the other hand, musicians from wealthy backgrounds meet their needs through inheritance and can perform music of their choosing without any commercial interest. Again the notion that people can be delivered from poverty[16] through a record contract drives the ideology of getting signed. Ironically, the people from class backgrounds where business ideology typically incubates, among the bourgeoisie, are the least likely to pursue commercial music and sell-out.

However, musicians in the bourgeoisie class are among the only members of the bourgeoisie who do not consume themselves with business interests. Richard, a very wealthy business person and investor I spoke with from Richmond, VA, has no experience in the music industry outside of his investment in a small music venue. This lack of experience does not stop him from articulating how music is a business like any other, and capitalists should be rewarded for their benevolence:

[Following a long conversation with me and a third person in a bar.]

Me: Record labels exploit musicians by profiting from their creativity without compensating them.

Richard: While I don't have any experience with record contracts, this isn't exploitation. It is no different from any other business. Record labels create value for musicians by strengthening a band's brand. Labels should be rewarded for creating this value. Same as in real estate. If I am going to put the money into constructing a new building, then I expect to receive a profit for taking the initiative to do so. The building wouldn't exist without me. The workers just build the building, and I can pay anyone to do that. I made the investment, I created the value, and I should make money from it. This is the same with music.

His emphasis is on the well-worn narrative of risk—he makes the investment, so he should reap the rewards if there are any. Richard made this statement with an air of expertise even though he self-admittedly lacked any background in performance, songwriting, recording, record contracts, copyright, publishing, advances, touring, publicity, marketing, or promotions. However, he felt the need to explain (maybe that should be capital-splaing) to me (a musician and industry researcher) how labels create value for musicians. There are indeed similarities between how record labels operate and other industries sell commodities, but this misses the point. Richard felt a degree of self-assuredness speaking about business because he has money. If he can sell widgets or prospect real estate, he can sell music. When members of the bourgeoisie decide to pursue a project or business, they do so with the power and wisdom of capitalism—a logic that knows no bounds as long as the purveyors of capital pursue profit.

Musicians create a product (or are a product) for record labels. The businesspeople working for a record label understand how to make money by selling a product. They view musicians as replaceable labor who lack any of the business skills needed to earn a profit on their own because they are ineffective at earning a living without the involvement of a record label. While this sounds condescending, it is the feeling that the industry representatives who I spoke with, observed, and emitted about the industry read throughout my study. To many of the businesspeople, musicians play music because they are too inept at business to make real money (even when the businesspeople admit playing music is difficult).

This business logic does not cease with labels, but permeates every dimension of the music industry. In one conversation I had with Immanuel, a booking agent in Nashville, TN, he insisted he does not care about the talent of a musician, but rather considers a musician's potential to fill his bars. The bars that Immanuel books for largely book cover bands because he says "people want to hear what they know." Immanuel's logic is circular: book bands that play covers because people want to hear covers, but people want to hear covers because they have been socialized to expect covers. More important was the way Immanuel characterized selecting bands to book. After expounding at length about how many bands he books a week, he gave me a sense of the defining characteristics of a band worth booking. While he claims to listen to every tape/CD sent to him for booking, he deemphasized the importance of a band's sound:

Me: With so many acts trying to get gigs, how do you make decisions on who to book?

Immanuel: The tapes don't matter much. They tell me that the band members have a heart beat—at the end of the day, that's all I care about. To book a venue, I think about day of the week, time of the day, and the expected demographics of the show. This tells me what kind of music we need. You may have heard that Nashville is the bachelorette capital of America.

Me: Yeah, I witnessed it last night.

Immanuel: Right, Broadway is teeming with 20-or 30-something women Thursday through Saturday nights. They want to hear the covers that are from Country Radio's Top 40 and hits from their high school and college days. I need bands that will play that music at night Thursday, Friday, and Saturday. It helps if the band has good looking guys, too. These women come here for an experience and we have to meet their needs. The other thing that I'm looking at is their socials [sic], they need a reach on social media. I will take someone not as good if they have a fan base. I gotta see engaged followers—I wanna see likes, retweets, comments—this is not about number of followers. If they can put people in my bar, the bar is happy, the owners are happy, and I'm happy.

In Immanuel's account, the important point is to get people through the door for shows; the bottom line is business, unsurprisingly. Everything he said makes complete sense if all that matters is profit: demographics have to meet the music, bachelorette parties want to sing along, bands with a following will fill the bars. However, there is an unhidden contempt for talent in Immanuel's account of booking for shows. In fact he insisted to me that the musicians do not have to be any "good" to book a show—they need a heartbeat. As we talked, a nationally well-known fiddler played with her band on stage. The phenomenal talent played a 1 pm gig on a Friday to a fairly empty bar because they were not the kind of group that would hold a crowd, in Immanuel's opinion, at night.

According to Immanuel, there was a relationship between a group's seriousness and their ability to draw a crowd, and this term "seriousness" continually emerged in my conversations with people throughout the music industry. A venue manager in Nashville told me that open mic nights are part of an audition process that eliminate unserious musicians. She said, "only serious musicians will advance from open mic night through our multilevel audition process. It takes a lot to put your songwriting on-the-line in front of a crowd of people." In a study of how musicians think about copyright, they identified differences in opinions about copyright depending on the musicians' seriousness about music.

Such contrasts emerged more starkly in the alternatives represented by being an 'amateur' or 'professional' musician. It was the latter categorization, unsurprisingly, that was associated with an explicit, self-conscious awareness of, and concern about, copyright. There was a more subtle variant, or euphemism, for the distinction. This emerged in the idea

> of being a 'serious' musician. Being 'serious' could mean being more business-minded.[17]

Being serious is synonymous in these terms with being business-minded. Part of the emphasis on seriousness deemphasizes musical performance. Some musicians want nothing other than to practice their instruments, write songs, and perform all day; they may be introverted and lack the ability to reach out to people to book gigs or hustle to sell music and fill their shows. Or musicians might be oppositional to dominant norms of capitalism. In some parlance, the ability to be serious may be equivalent to selling-out by placing business interests over musical aesthetics. However, precisely the idea of being serious is a mechanism of exploitation.

Connor, a bass player who also manages other bands, said the following to me:

> It doesn't cost much to get music online. Anyone serious should pay the $30 to CD Baby to get their music on online services. I play in a group and I earn around $800 a month through CD Baby from various streaming services. I mean $30 a year is inconsequential and low risk. Who doesn't have 30 bucks? Give me a break. If bands aren't paying this fee, then they aren't serious about playing music professionally.

The contempt that Connor displayed for musicians who did not want to pay the $30 fee was rather insulting to musicians.[18] In our discussion about CD Baby, I was suspicious about whether he made $800 a month through CD Baby, so I ran a search on Spotify for the number of streams his band received. The total streams for his band two years after our conversation was a meager 400,000 at the Spotify royalty rate, this would have given the entire band about $900 total. The idea that serious musicians pay to play being advanced by a music businessperson is a harbinger for the industry's business zeal. Musicians and music are of little consequence to the music industry except for their potential to redistribute wealth from the poor to the wealthy.

From Bar Gigs to Social Media

Even though digital technology has disrupted the music industry, it has done so only in terms of the way labels conduct business, not as a way to subvert the business itself. The utopian vision of the Internet misses the point. While Chris Anderson's *Long Tail* made waves among the utopian circuit that the Internet makes cultural content available to all,[19] Anderson fails to see that gatekeepers play an important role in filtering infinite content to audiences. As I demonstrate elsewhere, the major labels play an increased role providing power to connect musicians to listeners.[20] When people introduce new technologies, there is often a utopian impulse that the world will change as a result and bring change in the form of democracy and liberation.[21] In this case, digital technology would liberate fans and musicians from the oppressive record label regime. However, all new technologies are embedded in society and contain all of the societal baggage that always-already exists. For the present moment, anything that exists on the Internet exists in society, and we should expect that the uses to which people deploy the Internet will conform to society. Since the Internet exists in a capitalist society, capitalists will find ways to increase profit using new technologies. Here, I consider the way that finding and profiting from talent has changed in the recent past.

There is a long held truism in the recording industry that musicians have to "do your time" performing before a record label will sign them. The basic idea is that musicians have to spend time playing gigs at the local level to build-up a following. Over time, musicians will begin to book gigs at larger venues as their fan base grows. Eventually, buzz builds around the act and label Artist & Repertoire (A&R) representatives will begin to take notice. At that point, musicians begin discussions with A&R reps about potential contracts. Typically, those A&R reps want to see that the musicians have the potential to sell albums; A&R reps want to see the numbers, they want hard data. Historically, the data could be any of the following: attendance at shows, regional and national touring, press coverage, mailing/email lists, album sales, or merchandise sales. Regional and national touring demonstrate to the label a level of commitment in playing professionally; this is not different from the sharks on *Shark Tank* ridiculing a contestant for not quitting their jobs. The shark investors want to know the people running a business do not timidly approach their business; likewise, labels want to see commitment from the musicians, and if the musicians have day jobs, labels cannot tell if they are 100% committed. Many musicians sell their music at shows and in hip-hop a popular expression was to sell music "out the trunk" of a car. Or in the case of a band like Dave Matthews Band, musicians set up their own label and tour the college circuit selling albums and creating an email list. In each case, A&R reps want to see that musicians hustle, and they figure that a hustler will continue to work hard for them. In the "do your time" approach to record contracts, there are echoes of the protestant work ethic described by Max Weber in which "the idea of the duty of the individual to work toward the increase of his wealth, which is assumed to be an end in itself."[22] Musicians have to exhibit an "attitude which, *in the pursuit of a calling*, strives systematically for profit for its own sake…"[23] In context of the ideology of getting signed, musicians must show a restless desire to maximize economic output, resist "idleness," and that they subsumed capitalist ideology. Only then would labels consider signing an act.

The above conventional approach to signing a record contract changed with social media and streaming music, not by reversing the norms, but rather, by hyper-emphasizing data. By using systems of surveillance on the Internet,[24] record labels can extract data not just on consumption and demographics (which become even more data rich in the digital environment), but also by using tracking cookies and following consumers across sites. These data allow record labels to access and assess real-time information about music trends, fan bases, and profitability. Labels can identify that a rock band is popular among 22-year-old women in Denton, TX. They may also find that those women like to drink mojitos from local bar data, they are social activists who read *Ms. Magazine,* and they spend a lot of time tweeting about politics. The drink information can be pulled by mining credit card information, they can figure out the *Ms. Magazine* connection by using tracking cookies, and the Twitter information by paying for Twitter marketing data. A label could use this information to send this band to Denton, recruit Bacardi as a sponsor of the tour, and encourage the band to participate in a protest or attend a rally while they are in town. In order to find a band to sign, the label can use the same data to work in the opposite direction by examining geotag information about popular independent artists who are streamed in a specific location. Recruiting becomes a factor of access to data instead of a gut feeling by A&R reps. On the one hand, this disturbs the power of specific gatekeepers. On the other hand, it rationalizes the creative process by emphasizing hard data over aesthetic judgments.

Earlier, I mentioned a conversation with Immanuel who kept discussing "social media reach" with regard to his willingness to book an act, but this is also an important factor for record labels interested in signing an act. When labels explore signing an artist, they consider not only how many friends, followers, subscribers, etc. the artist has, but also the level of engagement of their followers. In other words, having 15,000 Twitter followers may demonstrate strength for a musician, but if they post a new song and receive 10 likes and five retweets, it indicates that their followers may not pay attention to them. Furthermore, labels can access the number of link clicks, and media engagements on Twitter, which provides even more data about the connection between the artist and their followers. A label would prefer to see an artist with only 2000 followers, but every time they tweet a song it receives 1000 likes, 500 retweets, and 10,000 media engagements. Here is the key difference between the way record labels used to find talent and the way it works today. Instead of A&R reps combing local gigs to find unsigned artists, now they can turn to the trending stars on YouTube, SoundCloud, TikTok, Instagram, Twitter, or Facebook.

In the streaming economy, people pay with their time because it does not cost anything to click on a link to stream a video or a song. A number of authors define this type of economy as the "attention economy" in which attention and time become generators of revenue.[25] "If an economy is the means and rationale through which a given society commodifies and exchanges scarce resources, then the 'attention economy,'" Patrick Crogan and Samuel Kinsley claim, "defines human attention as a scarce but quantifiable commodity."[26] Whereas analyses of the digital economy began to see the evaporation of scarcity because the amount of information on the Internet was limitless, others began to see the scarcity of human attention.[27] As a result of these changes in thinking about scarcity, executives at entertainment industries began to change the way they think about their commodities. Instead of selling specific music to consumers, recording industry executives now think about gaining and maintaining attention for their artists.

Whereas people will only pay for music they enjoy, there is very little opportunity cost to click on something a friend posts on Instagram—whether they think the link is funny, absurd, banal, or interesting does not matter. While we do pay for streams through subscriptions, advertisements, and/or giving up personal data, this does not work the same way as paying cash or credit. Viral content drives the recording industry (among many other industries) to seek out commodities that receive clicks. Virality is a term defined as "a social information flow process where many people simultaneously forward a specific information item, over a short period of time, within their social networks" that traverses to other social networks and accelerates the number of people reached.[28] If a musician can demonstrate that they have the capacity to garner people's attention, then they have immediate value to record labels. At the same time, record labels are agnostic as to the content that the musician creates or the reason why people tune into the content.

Over the past few years, the increase in streaming revenue has led to bidding wars among record labels for new artists who mastered the art of the attention economy. In an article about Juice WRLD's $3 million record deal, *Rolling Stone* writer Meagan Garvey describes the "Sound-Cloud-rap gold rush of the last two years. (The week Interscope signed Juice WRLD, Warner Bros. Records signed Lil Pump in an $8 million deal.)"[29] Interscope decided to sign Juice WRLD because he had the top streaming song, "Lucid Dreams," on SoundCloud in 2018. While the song was huge on SoundCloud, the song went on to gain over a billion streams (and counting) after it gained support from a major label. Because data demonstrate the potential an artist has to garner streams, labels can be confident that their investment will see huge returns. The Internet "is an electric circuit bridging production and consumptions."[30] When data provide certainty, labels avoid overproduction and underconsumption.

Furthermore, the bidding war for new talent advances the ideology of getting signed. "Consider it the American Dream, SoundCloud rap edition: boy skyrockets from obscurity thanks to a perfect song, becomes rich beyond his wildest dreams and moves from Chicago's South Side to a Beverly Hills mansion where he can ride dirt bikes all day and record all night."[31] Most aspiring singers, rappers, and bands today hear about Lil Pump's $8 million deal, Juice WRLD's $3 million contract, and XXXTentacion's $10 million deal. By circulating these stories about massive record contract advances, news outlets help advance the ideology of getting signed, and Garvey's language calling it the "American Dream" is especially significant. In these stories about these fabled contracts, no one describes the terms of the deals—i.e., that these are advances that need to be paid back on the artist's portion of the royalties. This is how ideology operates by providing what Marx called an upside-down picture of reality. "Television and the Internet… portray the present world as inevitable, and as desirable, inundating us with images and texts that seem to have no outside and that never seem to quit."[32] We consume images and texts of those who reach the pinnacle of the entertainment industry, and we believe that record contracts provide the inevitable exorbitant wealth. The one-sided reporting that a record contract is instant wealth distorts the way aspiring musicians think about the music industry.

With the signing frenzy around SoundCloud, Instagram, and YouTube stars, the recording industry reversed the truism that artists need to "do their time" gigging before labels sign artists. While the rise of pop acts in the 1990s coming out of Disney and Nickelodeon television shows began usurping the touring logic, these childhood stars at least had experience performing in some sense. Increasingly, record labels sign young acts who succeed at garnering attention on social media, but have no experience performing. Now these performance novices can record music in the comfort of their bedroom, create viral videos using their phones, and gain massive social media followings from their viral content. Labels want to cash-in on their social media reach. Labels assume that they can teach these artists to perform. "When he signed, Juice had performed in public a grand total of once, when he overcame serious nerves to play a party for his classmates at Homewood Flossmoor High School and

collected a fee of $100."[33] Steve Knopper claims that since almost all of these new signees "inks a 360 deal, sharing revenue with the label from not only albums, downloads and streaming but also ticket and merchandise sales—a common deal structure across the industry over the past decade," labels are willing to train the artists to perform/tour.[34]

When early record labels first began signing musicians to record contracts, the contracts only covered copyrights related to recording. Parallel to record deals, songwriters would sign publishing deals. A publishing deal covers the copyrights related to the writing of a song. For musicians who write their own music, they sign these deals at the same time, but they remain separate packages of rights. For instance, a recording artist could sign a record deal with Universal Music Group and a publishing deal with Sony/ATV Music Publishing. In conversations that I had with publishing executives, this is a fairly common practice. According to my informants, record labels began to cede artist development to publishers in the 2000s and publishing houses began to deploy more artist development contracts. Historically, record labels helped produce, distribute, and market a recording in order to leverage copyrights for profit. However, all of this changed with the move to 360 degree contracts or 360 deals. In these "multiple rights contracts," record labels take a cut of "any facet" of an artist's career.[35] Under these contracts, record labels earn revenue from 360 degrees of an artist's value. This can include recording, publishing, touring, and an artist's image (appearances in television, advertising, film, video games, etc.). These larger record deals become even harder to recoup because labels require signees to pay back their advance through all of these revenue streams. Whereas traditional record contracts were limited in scope, 360 deals can cover most conceivable means through which a musician can earn revenue.

These 360 deals are placing labels back at the center of artist development.[36] This happens as a result of viral sensations who perform in limited situations before their contract. For instance, Atlantic Records sent one group of new R&B and Hip-Hop signees on a packaged tour to Historically Black Colleges and Universities (HBCUs). Before the tour, they had a "five-days-a-week boot camp in New York, with movement, performance and vocal coaches; fitness and media trainers; and musical directors."[37] Similarly, Def Jam Records started "rap camp" "a new program designed to develop and promote the label's fledgling artists... rap camp is more like spring training: an intensive retreat for the label's young guns to write, collaborate and grow creatively under the guidance of seasoned producers and sound engineers."[38] Def Jam developed the idea when they found that taking Fetty Luciano to Hollywood, and removing him from his element, helped cure his writer's block and allowed him to "take instruction" better. So then the executives decided to do that with a roster of new artists. In addition to never performing in front of an audience before, many of the rap camp artists never set foot inside a professional studio.[39]

Furthermore, signing a record contract means something to these young artists by providing them a means to actualize their dreams:

> TJ Porter, an 18-year-old rapper from Harlem with a brash charm, says he ultimately signed for that very reason: Def Jam, he felt, would give him the 'extra push' he needed, rather than 'floating in SoundCloud' forever. 'I was always recording in the projects, in my environment,' he says. 'Now I'm in Los Angeles, I'm in Atlanta, I'm working with new people. It's me on a different level.'[40]

SoundCloud was the jump to help Porter make it by signing with Def Jam; digital distribution is a means to achieve the end—signing a record contract. While he may never make much money, signing the contract signifies living the dream and provides a material movement away from New York to see the world. However, there is a certain conventionality to TJ Porter's dream because ultimately he made music on SoundCloud with the goal of being signed.

At the other end of the spectrum of social media reach are people who sign record contracts because they are viral stars, but may lack any other talent. For instance, viral phenomenon BhadBhabie signed a record contract with Atlantic Records. BhadBhabie, born Danielle Bregoli, appeared with her mom on a Dr. Phil segment titled "I Want To Give Up My Car-Stealing, Knife-Wielding, Twerking 13-Year-Old Daughter Who Tried To Frame Me For A Crime" and accidently started a meme as she yelled "Cash me outside, how bout dat" at the audience.[41] Following her appearance, BhadBhabie recorded a song "These Heaux," and released it on SoundCloud with a video on YouTube. The song received 2 million streams on SoundCloud in two weeks[42] and 21 million YouTube streams.[43] Her first record went gold and she is the one of the youngest to make the Billboard Hot 100. When you read the comments on YouTube, the majority of people commenting on (and likely streaming) the video do so because they find the "cash me outside" girl turned rapper ridiculous. However, Atlantic Records saw the value in her viral social media reach by signing her to a multi-million dollar record contract following two weeks of data that demonstrated the viral attractiveness of the song.[44] Atlantic saw the value and acted as a "network gatekeeper" to "drive information flows in networks"[45] because they recognized BhadBhabie's capacity to generate viral media despite a lack of talent. This is the point: Atlantic does not care why people stream BhadBhabie because they make money based on streams, not intent. Now BhadBhabie has a make-up line and her own Snapchat reality TV series called *Bringing Up Bhabie*. In episode one of *Bringing Up Bhabie*, she repeats the ideology of getting signed when she declares, "I went from sleeping on the floor in a trailer to having a gold record in 6 months and then another one went gold." We can all live the dream of signing a multi-million dollar record deal with no previous experience if we coin a catchphrase on a talk show, acquire 15 million Instagram followers,[46] and deal with universal mockery.

BhadBhabie did not pioneer this cross-platform synergy and this is a fairly standard business model in the recording industry. For instance, Def Jam's rap camp attempted to create a multi-platform marketing scheme to introduce fans to their new roster. Def Jam released a compilation, *Undisputed* (2019), of these recordings. While mix-tapes are standard in hip-hop, this shows the fertile ground of collaboration in the music industry. Record labels recognize that if they put two artists on one song, it opens the song to streaming from each artists' fan base. This "cross-over" strategy is highly visible in the Billboard Hot 100 with songs like "Havana" by Camila Cabello featuring Young Thug (even with a remix by Daddy Yankee) or "I Like It" with Cardi B, Bad Bunny, and

J Balvin. However, Def Jam's approach hopes to build new artists using social media shrewdness.

> The final element of Def Jam's savvy rebranding efforts... a documentary series following the kids and coaches through rap camp as they make music, eat In-N-Out burgers, get tattoos, play basketball, even sit in reality-TV-style confessionals to let off steam (or, more often, to self-aggrandize). It's one part Survivor, one part Real World, one part Making the Band, and when the eight episode show airs on Def Jam's YouTube Channel..., executives hope it reframes the label—and majors in general—as vital.[47]

The logic is circular in generating streams. They signed these artists because of their social media reach. The documentary provides fans with something to watch, which generates revenue for the label. They see an artist they like interacting with other artists, and then the fans can click, watch, and listen to the other artists. All of which can be accessed through social media as the artists share links on Instagram, Facebook, and Twitter. Def Jam earns revenue for every stream even when the streams for each artist may be rather low. "In the end, rap camp and its attendant marketing efforts cost the 'equivalent of an A-list artist rollout,' according to an executive inside Def Jam."[48] By spending the same amount for 10 new artists that they spend on one big artist, Def Jam aims to amplify each artist to new audiences that already exist for the other artists.

When I watched the *Undisputed* documentary, the ideology of getting signed was strong throughout the series. In the first episode, TJ Porter says "I ain't never work no job before cause I want to do music. Like you know people be having plan As and plan Bs, I never had no plan B." The 18 year old, who has been rapping for only 3 years, demonstrates the do or die attitude that many musicians hold with regard to record contracts. Signing a record contract actualizes their American Dream. "Each artist signed with Def Jam for different reasons. While a handful were excited just to be picked, others were leery of giving away too much too soon."[49] These artists wanted to use their record contracts to launch their careers into mega-stardom. Nonetheless, some of the artists recognized that being big on social media was not enough to be big, rather, they needed the inflow of cash from a record label to properly promote their music.

While many recording artists use social media as a springboard to something bigger, the cash flows from the record labels in the opposite direction as well. A new phenomenon of the digital era is the social media influencer. People on social media become "influencers" when they reach a certain number of followers/friends. When they cross that threshold, companies become willing to pay the influencers for influence. This means that the influencer has a certain number of viewers that equates to an audience commodity that would exist on television.[50] Corporations have specific targets for the number of followers that a person must have on different platforms. In the music industry, this could mean that a label pays a YouTuber to have one of its artists to appear on a YouTube video. Increasingly, the labels target TikTok, the popular video sharing app. TikTok, which merged with the lip-synching app Musical.ly in 2017, allows people to create short videos from 3 to 60s that loop after completion. Many of the videos feature the video creator lip-synching to music. Labels developed a number of ways to use this to promote their music. One scheme they use is to pay top TikTok stars to make a video for a song. By paying top users to make a video to their songs, labels drive streams for their music and advertise the music to a broad audience. On the one hand, a top TikTok video creator may be an attractive signee to a record label because of their social media reach. On the other hand, top TikTok users also possess value in their ability to promote a label's artists.

Labels are not the only music industry entities emerging to exploit the new datafication of recorded music. From Apple Music signing a deal with Chance the Rapper[51] to Spotify's forays into bypassing record labels,[52] the new digital music services are developing their own content similar to video streaming services like Netflix, Hulu, and Amazon. However, these music streaming services also look like the original development of record labels. It is important to remember that the term "record label" derives from the label adhered to vinyl records. The companies initially associated with this practice were RCA, Edison

Records, etc.—companies that started selling records to have something to play on the hardware they manufactured—so it is not surprising that "hardware" companies would begin to make content. At the same time, managers are taking steps to provide the same types of services that labels have offered traditionally. "When James Vickery, a 24-year-old R&B singer from London, went viral on YouTube, he quickly landed record-deal offers from two major labels. But instead he decided to sign his first deal with a relative newcomer to the record-label business: artist manager Jake Udell, who isn't going to manage Vickery at all."[53] This is a story of industry insiders wanting more of a piece of the pie. Since labels now sign artists to 360 deals that often take on business areas that managers used to control, it makes sense that managers would begin to involve themselves into recording and distribution. Using their own labels "to secure long-term streaming revenue even after label signees move on, [is] something management deals don't necessarily guarantee."[54] Practically, this means that managers can keep making revenue after artists wash-up or sign elsewhere; the same way labels exploit artist creativity long-after an artist ends their contract. While social media reach can create new avenues for musicians to launch careers, it does not shield them from exploitative practices, but rather creates new ways for the music business to generate profit from their labor.

In this push for new viral artists, there is a cynicism that did not exist in previous music industry business models. While A&R staff conditioned the rest of the industry to believe that they had foresight into what sells based on abstract aesthetic judgments or "instincts,"[55] the industry's current model does not worry about such a pretense. Instead, record labels deploy data analysis to calculate the likelihood that an act will remain viral. They can estimate that if a musician has 1 million followers on Instagram, a certain number of those followers will click on a video or music link. Whereas A&R reps used qualitative judgments to determine who has "it," the new system relies on quantitative data. With easy access to data about a musician, record labels no longer concern themselves about the longevity of an act. In *Before the Music Dies*, the artists interviewed propagate the notion that in 2005 record labels no longer cared about an artist's career, but rather think in terms of quarterly revenue. They argue that if Bob Dylan started his career in 2005, he would have never made it because his music takes an acquired taste. In Questlove's memoir *Mo' Meta Blues*, he further touches on this topic with his experience in The Roots.[56] With hindsight, these sad warnings appear quaint because the situation they mark became amplified a little over a decade later. Now, the music is inconsequential. Whereas artist development used to be a crucial part of a long-term strategy on the part of record labels, the streaming era allows labels to quantify large short-term profits before signing an artist and utilize artist development to extract even more profit.

Alternatives

All of the discussion in the previous section refers to the change from the focus in the recording industry on musicians working the bar circuit to musicians who promote themselves using social media. What about those musicians who continue to play local gigs through regional and national tours? There continues to be a large number of musicians who pursue the conventional route by "doing their time" by playing shows in the hopes of being discovered. These musicians use social media and digital networks to grow their audiences, and use data to make themselves attractive to record labels, too. However, they continue to place an emphasis on performance, and they hope that through their performance they can be noticed. After all, unless someone creates a viral video, song, or meme, they are not likely to generate the types of numbers that interest industry insiders. In the void left by the music industry, there are new opportunities for musicians with conventional performance sensibilities, but these do not offer musicians the kind of utopia promised by technologists. Rather, these alternatives represent a coping mechanism that creative communities establish to deal with the absence of the old system.

In *Beyond the Beat*,[57] Daniel Cornfield discusses some of the innovative strategies that musicians established in Nashville. While the major labels have a strong grip on the music industry in Nashville, a growing number of musicians who migrate to Nashville to try to "make it" realize that their music falls outside the dominant industry business model. For these musicians creating music along the conventional path, music increasingly relies on "entrepreneurial music production" and self-promotion as the recording industry individualizes risk, according to Cornfield. As a result of the informal economy, Cornfield theorizes that artists come together to support each other. Musicians come together under Cornfield's "sociological theory of artist activism" to minimize joblessness for self and peers.[58]

While precarity has always been a part of pursuing music as a career,[59] the change in the industry has left even more musicians without prospects of a steady gig. Taking a long view of the music industry, sound films provided the first major disturbance to musician employment after the development of recording technology because musicians were no longer needed to perform in movie theater pit orchestras.[60] At the time, musicians went on strike using the American Federation of Musicians (AFM) collective strength and barred studio musicians from joining the union.[61] Ultimately, studio musicians won, but their exclusion further weakened the AFM, and made musicians more independent from the corporations for which they worked. Because musicians tend to be independently employed, they do not have much recourse of law or ability to strike, so they must rely on the community. "In the absence of formalized education, bureaucratic norms, or traditional employment relationships, it is the informal community that seizes responsibility for ensuring that rejection does not keep potential group members from joining the community."[62] With the change in the recording industry, there is an increase in the need for musicians to come together to provide the kind of benefits, institutional support, and stability usually provided by more formal employment. For instance, the Future of Music Coalition (a nonprofit that helps musicians) does research about artist revenue streams and provides musicians with information about obtaining health insurance. In a typical employment situation, health insurance would not be a tough subject because employers generally pay for health insurance for their employees in the United States—this is rarely the case for musicians because they are usually self-employed. Cornfield ran into the issue of health care several times in his study of musicians in Nashville.[63] Musicians build community with each other in this situation because the creative labor sector is so exploitative and they need support.

Interestingly, there is a growth of music organizations in cities to establish music cultures. These efforts are remote from major label business models and focus on performance at smaller venues. The role of organizations that I observed fall into two major categories: Chamber of Commerce-led and musician-led. First, I observed several organizations developed by a local Chamber of Commerce or visitor's bureau. These organizations concern themselves with growing the music community with the hope of creating development within the locality. They organized workshops to teach musicians business skills. While I found the information useful at these events for people who want to acquire the logics of the music business, they do not really put musicians' needs first, preferring business acumen instead. Second, I observed organizations created by musicians or people who just want to hear music. These organizations were designed to create community, meet musicians' needs, and advocate musicians' interests, similar to what Cornfield calls "artist advocates." "Artist advocates are creating an arts trade unionism that is attuned to the interests and aspirations of the contemporary generation of enterprising artists in Nashville."[64] The difference in approach between these two organizational types was surprising to me as a supporter of music and musicians. At the former meetings, the focus was on advancing industry logic, while people in the latter groups cared more about creating community. However, in both cases, the musicians who attend the events were ensconced in the traditional bar circuit—these were not the musicians who launch their careers through viral social media. The alternatives they developed aimed to provide support for a residual cultural system of performance in local music venues.

In each case of artist community, what is apparent is that the industry left these musicians behind. While musicians continue to dream of signing record contracts, they seek alternatives to make ends meet.

Conclusion

As the recording industry furthers digital recording, distribution, and promotion, they do so to advance their interests. Every change wrought on music is wrought by large corporate labels' drive to increase profits.

The Culture Industry has not changed much since C. Wright Mills wrote in the 1950s:

> This world is at once the pinnacle of the prestige system and a big-scale business. As a business, the networks of mass communication, publicity, and entertainment are not only the means whereby celebrities are celebrated; they also select and create celebrities for a profit. One type of celebrity, accordingly, is a professional at it, earning sizeable income not only from working, but virtually living on, the mass media of communication and distraction.[65]

Artists like BhadBhabie or reality TV celebrities like the Kardashians provide the quintessential examples of Wright's prestige system. Take Kylie Jenner, one of the stars of *Keeping Up with the Kardashians*, who became the youngest "self-made" billionaire according to Forbes (I'll leave the "self-made" moniker up to the reader's interpretation).[66] Jenner used her fame from *Kardashians* to build her Instagram account and make her the most in-demand influencer. She used her money to buy cheap lip kits and mark up their price. She sold them out instantly and created Kylie Cosmetics. Jenner's talent is not business acumen, but rather Instagram acumen where celebrity produces viral content, and viral content can achieve huge dividends. The music industry is acutely aware of the strength of social media celebrity on its own business model.

Record labels no longer scour bars to "find" talent, but rather look for artists who have a large social media reach. In both cases, labels look for what "sells," and place the commodification of music at the front of their interests. However, there is a noticeable shift to the way labels measure good talent. While many techno-utopians heralded the impact of the Internet, the reality is more of the same where celebrity counts more than ever. "All in all, although advances in digital technologies may at first blush seem to have a 'democratizing' influence, in reality they tend to have the opposite effect: they foster concentration and a winner-take-all dynamic."[67] Record labels are less concerned about making dozens of well-off (dare I say "middle class") musicians with steady income and more concerned with making mega-celebrities like Beyoncé, Ed Sheeran, Taylor Swift, or Blake Shelton—musicians who have the ability to cut through multiple media platforms. Digital music is the music business as usual.

Notes

1. Elberse, *Blockbusters*, 12.
2. Bienstock, "Gibson's Comeback Plan."
3. Becker, *Outsiders*, 82.
4. Becker, 83.
5. Attali, *Noise: The Political Economy of Music.*
6. Taylor, *Music and Capitalism*, 32.
7. Attali, *Noise: The Political Economy of Music*, 15.
8. Attali, 16.
9. Attali, 50.
10. Marshall, *Bootlegging*, 60.
11. Grazian, *Mix it Up.*
12. Grazian, 123.
13. Bourdieu, *The Field of Cultural Production: Essays on Art and Literature.*
14. Becker, *Outsiders*, 115.
15. Wikstrom, *The Music Industry*, 25.
16. Buerger, "The New Style," 49.
17. Street and Phillips, "What Do Musicians Talk About When They Talk About Copyright?," 428.
18. Note that Connor was part of the conversation I had with Richard, the self-assured businessperson, above.
19. Anderson, *The Long Tail.*
20. Arditi, "ITunes"; Arditi, "The New Distribution Oligopoly: Beats, ITunes, and Digital Music Distribution"; Arditi, "Digital Subscriptions."
21. Mattelart, *Networking the World, 1794–2000*; Fuchs, "Social Media, Riots, and Revolutions."
22. Weber, *The Protestant Ethic and the Spirit of Capitalism*, 11.
23. Weber, 19.
24. Arditi, "Disciplining the Consumer: File-Sharers under the Watchful Eye of the Music Industry."
25. Bucher, "A Technicity of Attention: How Software 'Makes Sense'"; Davenport and Beck, *The Attention Economy*; Fuchs, *Digital Labour and Karl*

Marx; Harper, "BEYONCÉ"; Terranova, "Attention, Economy and the Brain."
26. Crogan and Kinsley, "Paying Attention: Towards a Critique of the Attention Economy," 1.
27. Terranova, "Attention, Economy and the Brain."
28. Nahon and Hemsley, *Going Viral*, 16.
29. Garvey, "The Three Million Dollar Man," 40.
30. Agger, *Speeding Up Fast Capitalism*, 17.
31. Garvey, "The Three Million Dollar Man," 40.
32. Agger, *Speeding Up Fast Capitalism*, 40.
33. Garvey, "The Three Million Dollar Man," 40.
34. Knopper, "Teaching Streaming Stars to Tour," 23.
35. Vito, *The Values of Independent Hip-Hop in the Post-Golden Era*, 76.
36. Several executives in the music publishing side of the business told me that since 2000, record labels quit spending money on artist development. They began to see publishing deals as a site of artist development, and when a songwriter began to prove her or himself, they would begin considering signing the songwriter to a publishing deal. The new approach labels have taken with recent signees indicates that they are taking a leading role in artist development once again.
37. Knopper, "Teaching Streaming Stars to Tour," 23.
38. Buerger, "The New Style," 46–47.
39. Buerger, 47.
40. Buerger, 48.
41. *I Want to Give Up My Car-Stealing, Knife-Wielding, Twerking 13-Year-Old Daughter Who Tried to Frame Me for a Crime!*
42. Berry, "BhadBhabie Signs Deal with Atlantic Records."
43. As of May 30, 2019 there are close to a 90 million streams of the video. Staff, "'Cash Me Outside' Girl Signs with Atlantic Records"; Penrose, "'Cash Me Outside' Girl Inks Record Deal with Atlantic Records."
44. Penrose, "'Cash Me Outside' Girl Inks Record Deal with Atlantic Records."
45. Nahon and Hemsley, *Going Viral*, 42.
46. Hyman, "21 Under 21."
47. Buerger, "The New Style," 48.
48. Buerger, 48.
49. Buerger, 48.

50. Smythe, "On the Audience Commodity and Its Work"; Jhally, *The Codes of Advertising: Fetishism and the Political Economy of Meaning in the Consumer Society*.
51. Phillips, "Chance the Rapper Explains How He's Still Independent, Despite Apple Music Deal."
52. Wang, "Spotify Now Lets Artists Bypass Labels and Upload Their Own Music."
53. Wicker, "Managers Jump Into Label Game," 27.
54. Wicker, 27.
55. Negus, *Music Genres and Corporate Cultures*, 93.
56. Thompson and Greenman, *Mo' Meta Blues*.
57. Cornfield, *Beyond the Beat*.
58. Cornfield, 32.
59. Arditi, "Informal Labor in the Sharing Economy."
60. Zinn, Kelley, and Frank, *Three Strikes*.
61. Zinn, Kelley, and Frank.
62. Skaggs, "Socializing Rejection and Failure in Artistic Occupational Communities," 172.
63. Cornfield, *Beyond the Beat*.
64. Cornfield, 121.
65. Mills, *The Power Elite*, 74.
66. Robehmed, "At 21, Kylie Jenner Becomes The Youngest Self-Made Billionaire Ever."
67. Elberse, *Blockbusters*, 186.

Bibliography

Agger, Ben. *Speeding Up Fast Capitalism: Cultures, Jobs, Families, Schools, Bodies*. Boulder, CO: Routledge, 2004.

Anderson, Chris. *The Long Tail: Why the Future of Business is Selling Less of More*. 1st ed. New York: Hyperion, 2006.

Arditi, David. "Disciplining the Consumer: File-Sharers under the Watchful Eye of the Music Industry." In *Internet and Surveillance: The Challenges of Web 2.0 and Social Media*, edited by Christian Fuchs, Kees Boersma, Anders

Albrechtslund, and Marisol Sandoval, 170–186. New York, NY: Routledge, 2011.
———. "ITunes: Breaking Barriers and Building Walls." *Popular Music and Society* 37, no. 4 (2014): 408–24.
———. "The New Distribution Oligopoly: Beats, ITunes, and Digital Music Distribution." *Media Fields Journal*, no. 10 (November 14, 2015): Online.
———. "Informal Labor in the Sharing Economy: Everyone Can Be a Record Producer." *Fast Capitalism* 13, no. 1 (2016). http://www.uta.edu/huma/agger/fastcapitalism/13_1/Arditi-Informal-Labor-Sharing.htm.
———. "Digital Subscriptions: The Unending Consumption of Music in the Digital Era." *Popular Music and Society* 41, no. 3 (2018): 302–18. https://doi.org/10.1080/03007766.2016.1264101.
Attali, Jacques. *Noise: The Political Economy of Music*. Theory and History of Literature. Minneapolis: University of Minnesota Press, 1985.
Becker, Howard S. *Outsiders*. Paperback. New York, NY: Simon and Schuster, 1963.
Berry, Peter A. "Bhad Bhabie Signs Deal With Atlantic Records." *XXL Mag*, September 15, 2017. https://www.xxlmag.com/news/2017/09/bhad-bhabie-signs-deal-atlantic-records/.
Bienstock, Richard. "Gibson's Comeback Plan: Les Paul Maker Emerges From Bankruptcy Like a '125-Year-Old Startup.'" *Billboard*, February 13, 2019.
Bourdieu, Pierre. *The Field of Cultural Production: Essays on Art and Literature*. Edited by Randal Johnson. New York: Columbia University Press, 1993.
Bucher, Taina. "A Technicity of Attention: How Software 'Makes Sense.'" *Culture Machine* 13 (July 22, 2012).
Buerger, Megan. "The New Style." *Billboard*, March 2, 2019.
Cornfield, Daniel B. *Beyond the Beat: Musicians Building Community in Nashville*. Princeton, NJ: Princeton University Press, 2015.
Crogan, Patrick, and Samuel Kinsley. "Paying Attention: Towards a Critique of the Attention Economy." *Culture Machine* 13 (2012): 29.
Davenport, Thomas H., and John C. Beck. *The Attention Economy: Understanding the New Currency of Business*. Revised edition. Boston, MA: Harvard Business Review Press, 2002.
Elberse, Anita. *Blockbusters: Hit-Making, Risk-Taking, and the Big Business of Entertainment*. New York: Henry Holt and Co., 2013.
Fuchs, Christian. "Social Media, Riots, and Revolutions." *Capital & Class* 36, no. 3 (October 1, 2012): 383–91. https://doi.org/10.1177/0309816812453613.
———. *Digital Labour and Karl Marx*. New York, NY: Routledge, 2014.

Garvey, Meaghan. "The Three Million Dollar Man." *Billboard*, March 9, 2019.
Grazian, David. *Mix It Up: Popular Culture, Mass Media, and Society*. 2nd ed. W. W. Norton, Incorporated, 2017.
Harper, Paula. "BEYONCÉ: Viral Techniques and the Visual Album." *Popular Music and Society* 42, no. 1 (January 1, 2019): 61–81. https://doi.org/10.1080/03007766.2019.1555895.
Hyman, Dan. "21 Under 21: Bhad Bhabie on What You Don't Understand About Her." *Billboard*, October 12, 2018. https://www.billboard.com/articles/news/21-under-21/8479251/21-under-21-bhad-bhabie-interview.
I Want to Give Up My Car-Stealing, Knife-Wielding, Twerking 13-Year-Old Daughter Who Tried to Frame Me for a Crime! Talk-Show, 2016. http://www.imdb.com/title/tt5758066/.
Jhally, Sut. *The Codes of Advertising: Fetishism and the Political Economy of Meaning in the Consumer Society*. New York, NY: St. Martin's Press, 1987.
Knopper, Steve. "Teaching Streaming Stars to Tour." *Billboard*, November 10, 2018.
Marshall, Lee. *Bootlegging: Romanticism and Copyright in the Music Industry*. 1st ed. California: Sage Publications Ltd, 2005.
Mattelart, Armand. *Networking the World, 1794–2000*. Minneapolis, MN: University of Minnesota Press, 2000.
Mills, C. Wright. *The Power Elite*. New York: Oxford University Press, 1956.
Nahon, Karine, and Jeff Hemsley. *Going Viral*. Polity, 2013.
Negus, Keith. *Music Genres and Corporate Cultures*. New York: Routledge, 1999.
Penrose, Nerisha. "'Cash Me Outside' Girl Inks Record Deal with Atlantic Records." *Billboard*, September 15, 2017. https://www.billboard.com/articles/columns/hip-hop/7965832/bhad-bhabie-cash-me-outside-record-deal.
Phillips, Amy. "Chance the Rapper Explains How He's Still Independent, Despite Apple Music Deal." *Pitchfork*, March 17, 2017. https://pitchfork.com/news/71701-chance-the-rapper-explains-how-hes-still-independent-despite-apple-music-deal/.
Robehmed, Natalie. "At 21, Kylie Jenner Becomes The Youngest Self-Made Billionaire Ever." *Forbes*, March 15, 2019, Online edition. https://www.forbes.com/sites/natalierobehmed/2019/03/05/at-21-kylie-jenner-becomes-the-youngest-self-made-billionaire-ever/.
Skaggs, Rachel. "Socializing Rejection and Failure in Artistic Occupational Communities." *Work and Occupations* 46, no. 2 (May 1, 2019): 149–75. https://doi.org/10.1177/0730888418796546.

Smythe, Dallas Walker. “On the Audience Commodity and Its Work.” In *Dependency Road: Communications, Capitalism, Consciousness, and Canada*, edited by Dallas Walker Smythe, 230–56. Norwood, NJ: Ablex, 1981.

Staff. “‘Cash Me Outside’ Girl Signs With Atlantic Records: ‘A Real Star With Undeniable Talent,’ Says Label Executive.” *Variety*, September 16, 2017. https://variety.com/2017/music/news/cash-me-outside-girl-signs-atlantic-records-contract-1202561216/.

Street, John, and Tom Phillips. “What Do Musicians Talk About When They Talk About Copyright?” *Popular Music and Society* 40, no. 4 (August 8, 2017): 422–33. https://doi.org/10.1080/03007766.2015.1126099.

Taylor, Timothy D. *Music and Capitalism: A History of the Present*. Chicago, IL: University of Chicago Press, 2015.

Terranova, Tiziana. “Attention, Economy and the Brain.” *Culture Machine* 13 (July 22, 2012): 19.

Thompson, Ahmir “Questlove,” and Ben Greenman. *Mo’ Meta Blues: The World According to Questlove*. Reprint edition. New York: Grand Central Publishing, 2015.

Vito, Christopher. *The Values of Independent Hip-Hop in the Post-Golden Era: Hip-Hop’s Rebels*. Palgrave Pivot, 2019. https://doi.org/10.1007/978-3-030-02481-9.

Wang, Amy X. “Spotify Now Lets Artists Bypass Labels and Upload Their Own Music.” *Rolling Stone*, September 20, 2018. https://www.rollingstone.com/music/music-news/spotify-artists-direct-music-upload-726352/.

Weber, Max. *The Protestant Ethic and the Spirit of Capitalism: And Other Writings*. Edited by Peter Baehr and Gordon C. Wells. New York, NY: Penguin Classics, 2002.

Wicker, Jewel. “Managers Jump into Label Game.” *Billboard*, December 8, 2018.

Wikstrom, Patrik. *The Music Industry: Music in the Cloud*. 1st edition. Cambridge and Malden, MA: Polity, 2010.

Zinn, Howard, Robin D. G. Kelley, and Dana Frank. *Three Strikes: Miners, Musicians, Salesgirls, and the Fighting Spirit of Labor’s Last Century*. Boston: Beacon Press, 2002.

5
On Competition in Music

I began the Introduction to this book exploring an interaction I had with a co-headlining band at a gig I played in Blacksburg, VA. The members of the other band insisted on playing second because they were on the verge of signing a contract. In doing this they were performing their superiority and reproducing a hierarchy that expresses the competitive nature of gigging. As Sarah Cohen notes of musicians in Liverpool, England: "The order in which bands performed was... important at most gigs besides those of the more famous bands and bands often argued over it, firstly because it supposedly reflected the popularity of each band..."[1] Inherent in conflicts about the order of performance is a sense of competition. Bands show up to gigs ready to demonstrate that they are "better" than other bands. Musicians at shows exhibit this sense of competition in a number of ways; they may refuse to talk to the other band, size up the other band, refuse to share equipment, speak with audience members about how a musician has better chops than the one performing (even if it is clearly not the case), discuss sponsorships, boast about big gigs, or of course, brag about any attention they received from music industry insiders or good press. From the guitarist exercising their best rifts warming up to the tensions before the show. These interactions

D. Arditi, *Getting Signed*,
https://doi.org/10.1007/978-3-030-44587-4_5

demonstrate a desire by musicians to prove superiority over other musicians through their performance, discussing their greatness, or a crowd's reaction.

Gigs are drenched in an atmosphere of competition as musicians from one band stand-back and observe the others. From the moment they arrive, they judge each other. Most musicians at a show are easy to spot in the crowd—standing in the back with their arms crossed, locked-in on one musician on stage—whether or not they are performing at that show. They eye-up the competition to try to determine whether they can play the riffs of the current performer. Many musicians that I observed in my study demonstrated this attitude through their actions at gigs. In fact, I could usually find a musician in the crowd to talk to by their demeanor. Very few embraced an atmosphere of sincere and appreciative listening as would be demonstrated by musicians complimenting each other, applauding, asking each other questions about technique, or exchanging information (i.e., networking).

In a *Rolling Stone* interview Paul McCartney confirms that being "the best" was a clear motivator behind how The Beatles viewed playing in a band.

> *Interviewer (Kory Grow)*: Are you competitive with other touring acts?
> *Paul McCartney*: It's just an instinct: In the Beatles, we always wanted to be the best band in Liverpool. Then we tried to be the best band in England, then we tried to be the best in the world.[2]

Paul McCartney identifies one of the critical components of the ideology of getting signed: competition—it reflects and reproduces a capitalist logic that is obscured under the rhetoric of artistry. Every musician wants to be "the best." How do they demonstrate they are the best? On the road from being the best in Liverpool to the best in England, The Beatles would need financial support to publicize their music. In the 1960s, no other way existed to publicize music than to sign a record contract. Since record contracts have been so important for success in the recording industry, record contracts became a mechanism to demonstrate to others one's success. Yet record contracts do as much to demonstrate success to other musicians as they do to demonstrate success to the self.

In American society, competition is a dominant ethos. From a young age, we learn that winning at a competition is a form of success.[3] Borrowing from Adam Smith's belief that competition among firms optimizes the market,[4] we live in an ideological era dominated by a belief in competition. Today, that dominant ideology is that of neoliberalism, "a theory of political economic practices that proposes that human well-being can best be advanced by liberating individual entrepreneurial freedoms and skills within an institutional framework characterized by strong private property rights, free markets, and free trade."[5] Whereas free markets dominate the economy, "Neoliberalism sees competition as the defining characteristic of human relations."[6] People acquiescing to neoliberal ideology believe that competition improves the world the same way sunshine grows plants. Even though competition is the defining characteristic of social relations under neoliberalism, capitalists never want to compete with each other and actually seek every chance to avoid competition: from government support to monopoly. However, the competitive ethos requires that workers compete with each other; in Marx's terms competition results specifically from the propertyless masses because capitalism forces them to compete for work.[7] Competition is not for capitalists, but rather the workers. To convince the masses of the necessity of competition, capitalism articulates competition's importance at every turn. Within the music industry, musicians learn that they must compete with others for chairs in orchestras, spots in a band, and with other band for gigs and record contracts. From the perspective of musicians and fans, the competition is logical and natural, but it is really ideological—an upside-down vision of reality—because it aids the material relations of corporate firms.

Why do musicians participate in competitions? How do they demonstrate their talent to others? In this chapter, I argue that competition is an underlying drive that incubates musicians' beliefs in the ideology of getting signed. First, I explore the role of competition in American society. Second, I demonstrate the unique qualities and role of competition in the entertainment industry with a specific focus on the music industry. From early experiences in music education to Battles of the Bands, competition is ubiquitous in entertainment fields. Finally, I contend that competition happens among musicians as opposed to among record labels. The illusion that musicians need to compete for record contracts reifies the role of record contracts in a musician's career, while giving record labels surplus labor to sign.

Competition in American Society

Right next to the American Dream, competition figures as a key ideological term that drives the engine of capitalism in America. As Paul Smith asserts, "Probably the single most important ideological keyword for millennial capitalism is competition."[8] Specifically, capitalists and ideologues on the local, national, and international level advocate for "free enterprise" to create competition between firms to make products better and drive profit. "Attempts to limit competition are treated as inimical to liberty."[9] Competition becomes the arbiter of freedom, equality, and progress. Some will argue that in order to have great products like the iPhone, we need competition. Smith contends that "Competition appears in these exhortations as a mysterious but natural force…"[10] They do not need concrete examples of why competition creates better commodities nor should we expect them to defend their position—keep in mind that the Soviet Union dominated the space race for nearly two decades. Competition is natural and does great things, neoliberal ideologues tell us, but please ignore all of the inequity, suffering, and waste that it produces.

The wealthy deploy an ideology of competition to obscure "what they preserve materially from the past for the furthering of their new enterprise," which Horkheimer and Adorno posit "is evidence for the contention that the entrepreneur has always gone about his competitive business with more initial capital than his mere physical capacity."[11] Inheritance—money preserved from the past and given to future generations—is the not-so-hidden reason why the vast majority of wealthy people possess capital. In other words, the wealth owned by most people derives not from competition among equals, but through claims to property enforced by the state. Furthermore, accumulation by dispossession[12] allows capitalists to enjoy tax breaks to build large projects. For example, Amazon received a total of more than $2 billion in tax incentives to build headquarters in New York and Virginia including a helipad in Virginia paid for by the state.[13] Amazon has monopoly control over online shopping and increasingly broader areas, becoming one of the largest companies in the world, and making Jeff Bezos the wealthiest person in the world in 2018 and 2019.[14] However, Amazon and Bezos create profit by underpaying their employees for their work. By giving Amazon tax breaks and incentives, the state reduces competition as it favors Amazon even more. While capitalists benefit from that which they did not earn, they pretend that all else is equal. Since American ideology claims that everyone is equal, competition separates the good from the bad.

In many ways, the ideology of getting signed develops from the American capitalist ethos of competition: eat or be eaten. Free enterprise in the liberal economic tradition espouses a type of economic Darwinism that contends that businesses succeed through survival of the fittest.[15] "Competition—between individuals, between firms, between territorial entities (cities, regions, nations, regional groupings)—is held to be a primary virtue" under neoliberalism.[16] However, capitalist ideologues and corporations view "competition as a sacred principle" at the same time that they broaden "the actual practice of decreasing competition."[17] They sell the idea of competition while they resist actually competing with others. Both Paul Smith and David Harvey surmise that competition occurs among contractors at lower-levels in an organization to help reduce the costs of the means of production. Nowhere is this competition more acute than among workers. When workers sell their labor-power on the market, they compete with other workers who sell their labor-power, too. Workers need to improve their skills to make them more competitive for a specific job, but at the same time that they attempt to improve their skill, other workers attempt the same. According to Marx, capitalism benefits from a surplus army of workers who have the proper skill to work a particular job thereby making more people eligible for a position of employment and forcing them to compete with each other by lowering their wage.

The promotion in American political discourse of Science, Technology, Engineering, and Math (STEM) fields as the most desirable degrees to obtain gainful employment illustrates the logic of competition at work. In the early 2000s, people graduating with bachelor's degrees in computer science regularly earned $70,000 ($101,000 in today's dollars) as a starting salary straight out of college. Then came this myth that the United States needed to educate its workers in STEM fields or else the inability to produce Americans with these degrees would result in the export of those jobs overseas. Federal and state governments followed by investing heavily in STEM fields at colleges and universities. Since this push for STEM workers, more people earn STEM degrees because they believe it is the best route to a well-paid job. However, the increase in STEM degrees did not bring a parallel increase in STEM jobs. This created a surplus army of workers that had the effect of depressing wages. Now, in order to receive a good-paying computer job, computer scientists and computer engineers need to seek graduate degrees. If they do not, they often end up working in information technology (IT) jobs that previously did not require a college degree. Now students with an MS in computer science can expect about $80,000 in their first jobs, considerably less than someone with a BS less than 20 years ago when adjusted for inflation. People with STEM degrees compete so that firms do not have to compete for them, and this lowers wages.

While workers compete for jobs, this reduces competition among capitalists because there are plenty of available (properly skilled) workers to work a job. The industry is irrelevant under this logic. Record labels and IT companies work to reduce competition among each other as they increase competition among workers. At the same time, schools, parents, and the press teach workers that in order to "compete" they must pick up skills to make themselves more competitive. Capitalists force workers to compete in the "hunger games" while they observe from afar and stoke the need to compete.

At the same time, America is supposed to be a land of meritocracy. Part of the ideology of the American Dream hinges on merit. In a meritocracy, people earn their position in life based on possessing specific qualities that mark them as more qualified for a job than other people. Those who are most qualified always earn their due in a meritocracy. This meritocratic rhetoric begins in grade school and continues through college where people receive grades as a basis of evaluation. Every year, I have the discussion with at least one student that I did not "give" them a grade, but rather, they "earned" their grade. By making this distinction, teachers eliminate their subjectivity because they point to objective qualities and the student's agency to decide whether they want to do the work. If a student "earns" a grade, they receive it based on the work they put into the assignment or course. While meritocracy in employment relations is an ideology that pacifies workers into thinking that one person "deserves" more than another, the lack of emphasis in creative employment is notable because winning emphasizes competition between people over the one individual's meeting the required qualifications.

Since the American ethos of competition requires a platform to be disseminated, it becomes visible to the populace through entertainment. Sports competition is the most obvious and least metaphorical site of competition. When athletes play a game, match, or race, they explicitly compete—this is the high neoliberal ideal of competition. The first person to cross the finish line in a race wins; the highest score in a basketball game wins; the longest or highest jump wins. I do not dispute the idea of a winner. However, translating that idea to the rest of society often unfairly pits one desperate (potential) worker against another, and in entertainment fields this means that one entertainer must be victorious over another. Next I map the American ethos of competition onto the entertainment fields, specifically within musical performance.

Competition as Unique to Music and Other Entertainment Fields

Competition has a special place in the entertainment industry. Performance culture valorizes public competition through performance as a fair way of picking the most deserving performers for a job. "The competition is an attractive method for identifying those 'worthy of support' because it is believed to be fair and democratic."[18] This goes for both competitions and auditions, which provide two approaches to obtaining musical status in a public and competitive means. Accountants do not compete to see who adds using spreadsheets the best. Job interviews happen behind closed doors. Even in academia we do not "compete," even though there is always underlying competition to be published, present at conferences and for jobs. Entertainers must compete in sports-like competitions to succeed in their craft. For musicians, an important sign of success in competition involves signing record contracts.

Winning/Losing

When musicians and other artists in the Culture Industry think about getting a gig, they think about it as "winning" a position. Yet, there is a chasm between the verb "to win" and the verb "to earn." To win means to overcome in a contest, competition, or battle. Only one person or group can win in most uses of the term. Sometimes, people win because of chance, not because of skill (i.e., lottery winners). However, to win a gig means to vanquish one's enemies or defeat one's competitors. When one person wins a gig, it means that someone else loses. On the other hand, to earn has greater connotations within a capitalist system. When we work, we "earn" a wage in exchange for our labor. The verb to earn implies receiving something in return for one's efforts. To earn also resembles the verb "to obtain" more closely. If one obtains a gig, it means that they possess that position, or as the title of this book uses "to get." None of these other verbs position competition as part of the process. On the one hand, if someone obtains, earns, or gets a job, this remains rather opaque as to the other people who did not receive the job. Earning regards the solitary individual's efforts. On the other hand, if one wins at something, others lose; this puts people in direct conflict with one another. Of course, in both cases, the results are zero-sum because whether one wins or earns a job, no one else can have the job.

Competition pits one person against another instead of both being at the mercy of an employer. For instance, in a race, the winner is clear because they cross the line first. However, when someone interviews for a job, the employer chooses one person or the other. This is the curious contradiction between winning and earning. Winning in competition signifies outright objectivity while earning connotes a certain degree of deserving, but it also includes subjectivity. Again, crossing a line first is objective, but choosing the best performer is immensely subjective.

Whereas qualification for a position could *potentially* be objectivized, creative performance cannot translate into any objectivity. Furthermore, selecting a musician or an actor involves criteria beyond talent: Do they have the right look? Can the guitarist dance? These are random questions, but the judges for a creative job wrestle with them. Take auditioning a guitarist for a pop band as an example, the judges may have to wrestle with whether she can play pop music, sing, dance, and look right with the rest of the band. While the tour manager may have an idea about the right "fit" for the position, it also means that the person with the most talent at guitar could be overlooked. As such, auditions become important sites of musical aesthetic development and present "useful settings in which to observe musical judgments at work because they are here made explicit: musicians are being judged, discussed, against each other."[19] As a site of musical judgment, auditions also help to reinforce the social constructedness of musical value. Ability to pull off a successful audition can be a product of one's received "musical capital."[20] Class becomes an important marker as to whether a performer recognizes the skills they need to demonstrate their value at an audition.[21]

These ideologies about winning at auditions present themselves throughout the popular culture press. For example, an article in *Rolling Stone* magazine about the popular BBC America television show *Killing Eve* contained the following caption about one of the actors: "Comer won the part of Villanelle in a field of about 70 actors."[22] The caption did not claim that Jodie Comer earned, gained, or received the position. It highlights simply that she beat about 70 other actors to win the competition for the part. If you apply for a job as an accountant, you rarely know how many other people applied for the position and you earn the position based on qualifications. The academic job market, especially in the liberal arts, is very competitive, but even though hundreds of applicants apply for a job, we do not think of the successful applicant as "winning" the job; they earn/obtain/receive/get the job. Only in creative jobs do we think of obtaining a job as winning.

In music performance culture, competition begins from an early age through school music competitions.[23] From the time that students begin to learn to play music in public schools, they audition for positions in their school bands. School orchestras/bands assign "chairs" to students signifying who plays better. This competition scheme has its own irony because schools cannot post students' grades publicly without violating the Family Educational Rights and Privacy Act (FERPA). In other words, music students learn from an early age that musical performance follows a different set of rules where competition is valued. Beyond the school, students compete in district, regional, and statewide competitions. Bands compete in a variety of music competitions[24]: from parades and district competitions to spring high school band trips. These school competitions solidify the competitive ideology of musical performance. "Competitions have become standard pedagogical practice… In both popular and high art musical genres, competition prizes are staples of promotional media, resumes, and biographies of aspiring and professional musicians alike."[25] We expect musicians not only to perform well, but they have to demonstrate that they have won competitions to show that they vanquished their competitors.

While Lisa McCormick studies the Van Cliburn International Piano Competition, a classical piano competition, her insights are valuable for thinking about the ideology of getting signed. She describes that on the "narrative level, the ultimate purpose of the event is 'the discovery of the world's finest young pianists' and their introduction to the musical public which includes not only an adoring audience, but respected critics and concert presenters."[26] Competitions help situate performers to establish their credibility and résumé, which leads to more gigs. These public competitions establish not only the best performers, but also McCormick claims they favor particular modes of playing (i.e., "higher, faster, louder") over other ways of performing the piano—she identifies the Cliburn as reinforcing masculine ways of playing over feminine characteristics of performance. Competition leads to reinforce social constructions about performance and music.

In Fort Worth, the same city that holds the Van Cliburn International Piano Competition, I had the opportunity to attend the *Fort Worth Weekly* (*FW Weekly*) Music Awards in two consecutive years. While a local popular music competition as opposed to an international classical competition, the *FW Weekly* competition provides performers with many of the same benefits McCormick describes about the Cliburn. Each year dozens of bands enter the competition to say they are the greatest in

Fort Worth. *FW Weekly* gives awards for Best Band, Best Venue, Best Artist, Best Talent Buyer, many genres (Rock, Country & Western, Texas Music, Rap, etc.), and Best Instrumental (Guitarist, Drummer, Bassist, and Vocalist) Performance of the Year, among others. Attendees vote for their favorite musicians using a ballot that is available online and at the event. By issuing ballots for viewers/listeners/fans to vote, the competition reinforces the concept of democracy. However, voting creates an illusion that allows the ideology of competition to continue to function. Max Horkheimer and Theodor Adorno posit that "The industry submits to the vote which it has itself inspired."[27] The acts with the most votes will be the ones with the largest fan base of people willing to go to a show for the competition and submit a ballot. As such, voting places the logic of the market over aesthetics. By allowing the public to vote, the competition negates expertise in favor of perceived democracy. I frequently see large crowds at local shows where the act is popular for reasons other than performance—I return to this in the discussion about battle of the bands shows below.

I never thought much about the reasons for performing in these music competitions because in the music world, they are ubiquitous. My attendance at the competition was solely as a site where I could find a lot of musicians who would be easy to speak with, and I surmised they would exhibit a high degree of the ideology of getting signed. After all, the initial idea for the project came in part from conversations I had with a colleague who performed at South by Southwest (SXSW) in Austin—they informed me that most bands performing at SXSW walked around with a chip on their shoulder that they were the "next big thing" and about to be signed. In this regard, the competition did not disappoint me because a number of musicians displayed this affect, but I found the desire to win the *FW Weekly* Music Awards as its own phenomenon embedded in competition.

When I went to see an R&B band play at the same *FW Weekly* Music Awards, the singer repeatedly intoned the audience to vote for her band. Her repeated calls to vote spoke for itself to me. In my mind, she wanted to win to say that she won. This band displayed the best musicianship and performance of any act I saw over the course of the two-day competition (note: they did not win any of the competition categories). People packed the venue, but they seemed more there for the food and patio on a beautiful day than for the music—it was a rare Texas summer day with highs in the 80s in late June. A nearby couple observed me taking notes and struck a conversation about what I was doing there. They stumbled upon the event by chance because they went there for drinks to enjoy the nice weather. As the singer reminded the audience to vote between songs, the couple asked:

Couple: what do they get for winning?
Me: There is an awards ceremony in a couple of weeks. The winners get an award and *FW Weekly* lists the winners. Some of the winners are invited to play at the awards ceremony.
Couple: That's it?
Me: Well, they get to say they are the best band or musician in Fort Worth.
Couple: Oh, doesn't seem like much.

The simplicity of this interaction with a couple who happened to stumble upon the competition provided me with more to think about than the rest of the competition. Why do musicians compete in a local competition? The answer is a degree of symbolic and social capital, even if it provides no immediate monetary capital. After a performer wins one of the categories, they use the win to further their career. For some of the winners, this means advertising the win on their website or press release information, which provides information to prospective bookers, venues, and even audiences—people who see a flyer that says "winner of the *FW Weekly* Music Awards" might be more likely to go to a show. Local venues are more likely to book winning bands because they know that the performers have a degree of local support—i.e., enough people must like them to vote for them and votes could mean bodies at a show—which means an audience and people buying drinks from the bar.

Winning also holds cultural significance to the local music scene. It announces to other musicians and people in the music scene that the winning musician is the "best." Every music scene is a small community. "A musical scene… is that cultural space in which a range of musical practices coexist, interacting with each other within a variety of processes of differentiation, and according to widely varying trajectories of change and cross-fertilization."[28] The local music competition is a site where cross-fertilization occurs and musicians interact. Because musicians in the scene believe the competition is culturally significant, they reinforce and enhance the legitimacy of the results giving those results symbolic capital. "*Symbolic capital* refers to a degree of accumulated prestige, celebrity, consecration or honour and is founded on a dialectic of knowledge (*connaissance*) and recognition (*reconnaissance*)."[29] Local music competitions act as a type of consecration for performers that enhances their prestige and celebrity in the local music scene.

Because local music scenes are tight-knit communities (even across genres), a musician's career history also determines their ability to obtain future gigs. "Previous group experience is used as a sample of personnel qualifications in much the same way as a visual artist's qualifications are shown by a portfolio."[30] Therefore, winning a local music competition has a lasting impact on a musician's career because it remains an important part of their resume with other local musicians. The impact this has on a musician's résumé is a result of social capital. For Pierre Bourdieu, "Social capital is the aggregate of the actual or potential resources which are linked to possession of a durable network of more or less institutionalized relationships of mutual acquaintance and recognition – or in other words, to membership in a group– which provides each of its members with the backing of the collectivity-owned capital, a 'credential' which entitles them to credit, in the various senses of the word."[31] Social capital provides musicians with further networking abilities beyond their immediate position. If person A played guitar with band X, and band X won best rock band in Fort Worth, then, when band Y in Fort Worth needs a new guitarist, they will be aware of person A's reputation. Whereas winning a local music competition provides symbolic capital that builds a band's credentials helping them to obtain gigs, the contest's social capital exists within the potential for musicians to continue their music careers with other groups.

These local music competitions are standard in cities across the United States. In Dallas, I attended the *Dallas Observer* Music Awards. Unlike its Fort Worth counterpart, the Dallas awards contest was determined by a panel of judges, but the *Dallas Observer* incorporated fans to interact in the contest at the initial stages with a voting mechanism to help determine who could perform in the contest. In 2018, I attended the *Dallas Observer* Music Awards, dozens of bands played at a handful of venues. The Dallas event charged admission, whereas the Fort Worth competition was free. In both cases, many bands demonstrated the ideology of getting signed. The most outright display came from a grunge rock band singer who said at the end of the performance, "Please vote for us, we've been talking to two labels, maybe this will push them over the top." Rock bands and hip-hop emcees displayed the aesthetic more so than performers in other genres of music. People clearly perform in these competitions with the hope that they will be noticed, book gigs, and sign contracts.

Battle of the Bands

Beginning in the 1930s among jazz big bands, "a battle of bands is an event in which several groups compete by attempting to outplay one another for a specific prize."[32] While battle of the bands competitions used to be more popular than they are today, they still strike the popular imaginary as a rite of passage for aspiring musicians. At a University of Utah battle of the bands, one performer described his participation in the competition this way:

> "I would come to Velour all the time and see shows," said Austin Oestreich, Indigo Waves guitarist. "I was like a big fan of Imagine Dragons and stuff like that growing up, and so it was really cool to see people make it you know. Not that we're trying to make it, but make a difference in music, and to see that someone in Utah could do that."[33]

The battle marks a clear opportunity for bands to "make it" as this student demonstrates. While SXSW may be "Rock 'n' roll's version of the lottery… [where] hordes of obscure musicians hoping a mythical record-label Mr. Big will turn them into stars with a wave of the magic fountain pen,"[34] every battle of the bands represents this opportunity for aspiring musicians.

When I spoke with musicians at battle of the bands competitions, they always came back to the hope/feeling that someone from a record label may be in the audience. At the second battle that I attended for this project in 2017, I went backstage to interview some of the musicians. Junior, the bass player of funk band Inner Space Explosions told me about his dreams of signing a record label:

Me: How long have you been playing with Inner Space?
Junior: We've been playing for about 2 years, and we're on the cusp.
Me: What do you mean "on the cusp?"
Junior: On the cusp of making it, you know what I mean, signing with a label.
Me: Oh yeah? Have you been talking to any labels?
Junior: No, we still gotta find the A&R folks. That's why we're playing here. We heard label dudes are coming. We're really starting to connect with crowds, and we're starting to tour. Last week, we played in Tulsa [OK] and we had 100 people at the show. 100 people, and this was our first show in Oklahoma! How did people know about us? Things are poppin'!

Junior's optimism met with the reality that no label representatives attended the show. Inner Space Explosions came in second that night. After the show, I caught up with Junior:

Me: How did you think things went tonight?
Junior: I'm feeling down since there weren't any label types here, less so than the L [i.e. loss]. But it's cool, man. This spring, we're going to Austin for the first time. I'm sure good things will happen to us there since that place is teeming with labels.

While Junior is an extreme case of optimism with regard to signing a record contract from playing a battle of the bands, most people I spoke with desired more of an outcome than was guaranteed by the prizes like the intangible outcome of being noticed by audiences.

Part of this desire stems from the mythical history of battle of the bands. Myths present "illusory visions of reality [that] are plainly political in their thorough inversion of social realities."[35] These myths of massive successes create momentum that perpetuates the belief that they will receive something from the competition. For instance, the 1981 International Battle of the Bands took place in Nashville, Tennessee where 3000 country acts competed for the title of "International Band of the Year," which included a prize of $1,000 and a record contract.[36] Aside from the top prize, semi-finalists won the chance to record a 45-RPM record and received 100 copies of the recording.[37] Today, *The Voice* and *American Idol* fulfill the larger role of competitions like the International Battle of the Bands in the American ideology of success. However, battle of the bands remains a constant on the local music scene.

A battle of the bands that I attended at a medium sized college in 2017 illustrates the tensions inherent in these competitions. The school's student union arranged the battle of the bands, and the audience voted for the winner on paper ballots handed out to the audience. The winner would be invited to perform at a yearly springtime music festival on the college's campus. One of the bands was 3rd Earth, a hip-hop band that consisted of a contingent of musicians who were sought after in the local music scene as some of the best players in town. Their competition consisted of some other bands who regularly gigged around town with decent followings, and a rock band, Bean Counters performing in front of people for the first time. 3rd Earth played a great set and had good crowd response. However, Bean Counters, a band associated with a fraternity, brought all of their fraternity brothers and a sorority to the show, providing a majority of the crowd; their band won. The student union was disappointed by the results, and they decided to invite 3rd Earth to open for a major touring hip-hop act who would perform at the school in the spring. I spoke with Lisa, the president of the student union about the event:

Me: What did you think of the result?

Lisa: The winners are not who I would have picked, but the people spoke. I'm a fan of Ecstatic Condition and 3rd Earth. I've seen both bands play around town a few times. Ecstatic Condition brings energy to every show and 3rd Earth has such good music… they jam.

Me: How do you think Bean Counters will fit with the festival?

Lisa: Stylistically, I think Bean Counters are on brand with the national acts coming to campus. But I wonder if these guys are going to put on a good show.

Me: "On brand," you sound ready for the music industry, is that your goal?
Lisa: Yes! I joined [the student union] to gain experience booking shows. I also work at [local bar] now as the booker.

By turning the voting over to the crowd, this group of students turned the forces of the show to a pseudo-democratic result. In a way, the voting resembled the voting of the American Music Awards—anyone can vote, but only a specific population votes; this holds true for television talent shows as well. The organizers of the battle of the bands placed their trust in the crowd, but they did not plan for a group that brought their own crowd. Bean Counters could use winning the competition to pad their résumé for better shows, and the festival helps even more in that regard. While the bands played the show to win, their hope was to play the festival for the chance to be noticed by the other acts at the festival. In an interesting twist, Lisa was the best contact at the show for aspiring musicians even though she is aspiring a place in the industry herself.

Not all battles involve bands, a frequent form of similar competition is the rap battle. Rap "battles are lyrical duels and dissing contests. Opponents take turns dissing each other or hyping themselves up."[38] Jooyoung Lee describes the way that audiences choose the winners and losers in these informal battles. They are informal because they happen without organization. For the community Lee studied, battles had less to do with "blowin' up" than demonstrating one's lyrical prowess, but rather, these battles helped young emcees develop the skills to move to the next level. In fact, Lee claims that for rappers to "blow up," they had to develop battle rapping and freestyling skills before they move on. However, the rap battle scene confirms the presence of competition across genres.

While battle of the bands competitions by no means represents the interests of all musicians, they do provide fertile ground to see the way competition explicitly encompasses the lives of musicians. Battle of the bands competitions act as a rite of passage for many musicians, but I didn't come across anyone who regularly plays them—once is usually enough. However, the competitive ethos is dominant in these shows. By instilling competition among musicians (i.e., labor), labels do not have to compete as much with each other.

Competition Between Musicians, Not Labels

In the recording industry, there is competition between labels, but the labels compete with each other over the acquisition of talent. When a record label begins looking at an artist, other record labels begin to notice the artist as well. Once one label begins the process to sign an artist, more record labels make moves to acquire the artist. This often results in a bidding war. Artist & Repertoire (A&R) staff attend gigs, wine, and dine the artists, and promise the world. If one label shows genuine interest in an act, the other labels see value in them. They want to make sure that they do not miss profiting from the latest talent. If they cannot sign a specific artist, they try to replicate it as part of an overall strategy to minimize risk.[39] At the turn of the twentieth century, the quest for blonde bubblegum pop stars illustrated this drive for talent. Since Jive Records (at the time a member of BMG Entertainment) signed Brittany Spears, the other labels were desperate to corner that same blonde teenage girl market. Columbia Records (at the time a member of Sony Music Entertainment) followed by signing Jessica Simpson, who looked the same, but added a wholesome Christian aesthetic. Meanwhile, RCA signed Christina Aguilera who looked and sounded very similar to Spears and Simpson, but with a Latin musical flare.[40] Ultimately, the acquisition of talent in this manner resembles a risk management strategy on the part of record labels. Industry insiders believe that "all hits are flukes" and as a result attempt to imitate successful cultural commodities.[41] As Keith Negus contends, "strategic calculation provides a means (or so it is assumed) of applying order, increasing predictability and enforcing accountability."[42] By creating music that resembles that which is already popular, record labels reduce musical diversity while increasing competition between firms. While this produces bland music, it produces large profits for record labels. Furthermore, competing for a contract and getting it does not necessarily translate to success.

Bidding wars are pervasive in the recording industry because A&R staff do not want to miss a profitable act. However, the latecomer labels to a bidding war do not necessarily demonstrate interest in the artist for the same reasons as the original label, but rather, see a value in keeping the first label from profiting from the artist. The problem stems from competition. If the second (or third, etc.) label does not sign the artist, their already-signed artists may lose sales to the new act—i.e., in the above scenario, Jive Records may want to sign Jessica Simpson to limit competition. In a lengthy chat I had with Joann, a manager for several bands in DFW and a 20-year veteran in the business, she mentioned some of the hurdles acts she worked with faced with record contracts.

Me: What has been your experience with acts signed to record contracts?

Joann: It runs the gamut. From bands that struggle to receive attention from labels to a band that has made a successful career touring and released four albums with a label. At this point, I encourage bands and artists who I manage to avoid labels unless they can demonstrate a strength in the market. They need to sell albums on their own, pack venues regionally, and receive radio airplay before I'm ready to deal with labels. I've seen too many acts suffer from record contracts.

Me: What types of problems have you run into with record contracts?

Joann: Too many to list right now [laughs]. Several bands I worked with signed with labels, but their label failed to put the album out. It's frustrating and sad, but it happens consistently with different labels. The label thinks the album isn't good enough or the artist wasn't going to work hard enough to sell the album—or any other reason. This is why I now emphasize that they need to do the work ahead of time to show their strength.

Me: What do you mean they won't put the album out?

Joann: Basically, labels refuse to put any more money into an album after it is recorded. Labels can sit on the album, artists can't do anything with it because the labels own the rights. In some cases, the artists can't even tour. But the artists are stuck… trapped.

Me: I've always had this theory that labels sign acts to limit competition…

Joann: Yes, absolutely. That isn't a theory, that is what they do. I've seen it happen.

Joann's insistence that labels sit on albums to stop competition emphasizes where the power lies in the recording industry.

Part of a label's power stems from its ability to sign artists, whether they plan to promote albums or not. After a label signs an artist, the label possesses all of the decision-making power about the band's music.

> The label may decide not to record the artist once they are signed. The label may want to do this because they have found some other artist who really gets them excited, or because they are running out of money to invest in new recordings, or because the artist in question has committed some major public relations problem... The label may not accept the finished master or refuse to release it... The label may release the record but only put a minimum amount of marketing money into it...[43]

However, the label's intentions and interests are never transparent with the recording artists. I consistently heard about record labels refusing to put out an album (i.e., sitting on it or shelving it[44]) when I spoke with musicians. A singer (Clarke) in a rap-metal band I spoke with immediately responded to my questions about record deals the following way:

> *Clarke*: I don't want anything to do with record labels unless I have clear assurances that they will release our album. Too many of my friends signed deals only to have the labels sit on their albums.
> *Me*: Why did labels sit on their albums?
> *Clarke*: In two cases, it was clear they didn't want them [the bands] competing with acts on their rosters. In another case it was "artistic differences."

The idea that labels will sit on an album is pervasive and veteran musicians in my research understand labels sign acts to reduce competition. "An artist can also get held up because of competition between labels. If a certain kind of sound is suddenly in demand, labels might rush to sign similar artists — either to profit off them themselves [sic], or to simply sit on them and claim them" according to former Future of Music Coalition deputy director Casey Rae.[45] Importantly, the label's intention is never clear to the artists they attempt to sign. Labels seduce artists with dreams of making it big even when they have no intention to release their music.

In Sara Bareilles' "Love Song," she walks the listener through the process where the label seduces her by making her feel like she is the greatest, but then they demand her to be someone she does not want to be. While the song sounds like a love song (about not writing a love song), the textual meaning of the song demonstrates that Bareilles' label wanted to dictate the music that she writes, performs, and sells to her audience. When the label first approached her, she alludes to multiple labels' interest in signing her and "they all say things you wanna hear."[46] After she signed with Epic Records, they made Bareilles feel like they "made room" for her as if they did her a favor—keep in mind that she had several labels interested in signing her. Since her label positions itself as doing her a favor, it uses the favor to leverage her compliance with its demands. Ultimately, the label threatens to sit on her music if she does not want to play by its rules. She gave Epic Records the poppy love song they wanted in order to release the album, but the song turned out to be a critique of the record label's A&R management.

For these reasons, it is important to be suspicious about entertainment industry rhetoric that only a small percentage of artists (or films) become hits on which they have to offset the costs of the risk they take on all of their investments. In the above scenarios, labels do not take risk by signing artists, they actually minimize risk by signing a number of unsuccessful acts—they are unsuccessful because the label does not promote them. Copyright "is one of many instruments used by organizations and individuals within a complex web of industrial relations in order to make money, reduce risk, and manage competition."[47] Notice how reducing risk and managing competition are two sides of the same coin here. If a label signs an act that could be competition, they reduce the risk that they will have to compete with them. When record labels point to data about how many acts they sign versus how many acts are successful, they obfuscate the active role that they play in the industry as tastemakers. They do not provide information about successful recording artists against data about all albums that they released and promoted. Record labels work on an active strategy to propel certain acts to blockbuster status "rather than spreading resources evenly across product lines… and vigorously trying to save costs in an effort to increase profits, betting heavily on likely blockbusters and spending considerably less on the 'also rans' is the surest way to lasting success in show business."[48] Their self-serving strategies muddle their motivations by turning their desire to limit competition into an asset because they can

argue that they sign a number of artists who do not succeed. Successful artists become mythical and not easily replicated because labels argue that they do not know what makes them so popular. However, the reason one act becomes successful directly correlates to the money spent on the act. Meanwhile, the majority of artists receive very little support from their labels.

Musician and journalist Helienne Lindvall writes that there "are many reasons why a label goes cold on an act: the person who signed them might have been sacked, leaving them without a champion; they might not have delivered a record that's good enough; or the label might have been bought by a bigger company (which is what happened to me)."[49] In one conversation I had with a 1990s rock guitarist, Jonathan, he described his band's move from potential stardom to obscurity partly because the A&R person who signed them left the label. After recording an album in New York City with a fairly well-known independent label, a major-subsidiary label approached Jonathan's band. They signed with the label, and everything looked great—they were touring and beginning to record another album. Behind the band's back, the label purchased the original album from the independent label for $1 million. The label felt like this was the quickest way for the band to release their first album on the label. However, by the time they received the master recording, the A&R executive who signed them left the label. At that point, the new A&R staff decided not to release the album (i.e., shelve), and the band's career sputtered to obscurity. Jonathan's band is an example of a band that pursued the ideology of getting signed only to realize the harsh reality about record contracts after it was too late.

The pinnacle of competition results in the achievement of celebrity within the star system.[50] When musicians become celebrities, they demonstrate to everyone else that through competition people can become successful—here, successful means rich and famous. "The professional celebrity, male and female, is the crowning result of the star system of a society that makes a fetish of competition."[51] With the advent of reality television, celebrity and competition become the same game, and the lines between celebrity, capital, and competition become blurred. When CBS launched *Survivor* in 2000 it brought together exhibitionists looking for their 10 minutes of fame in a television game show. Donald Trump honed the competition as path to celebrity and money on *The Apprentice* in 2004. Ultimately, *Shark Tank* created the quintessential model to combine competition with capital and celebrity in 2009 as "entrepreneurs" compete for investors in a mock venture capitalist meeting room. *Shark Tank* sells the quintessential American Dream ideology that if you work hard enough you too can be Mark Cuban (or at least have your invention sold at Bed Bath & Beyond). Sports create their own realm, as C. Wright Mills illustrates, "In America, this system is carried to the point where a man who can knock a small white ball into a series of holes in the ground with more efficiency and skill than anyone else thereby gains social access to the President of the United States."[52] While Mills belittles the skill it takes to knock a ball into a hole, his point is that golf can gain social access, which highlights the importance of competition in the American ethos.

Competition becomes the marker of success in America and a cause for celebration. "It is carried to the point where a chattering radio and television entertainer becomes the hunting chum of leading industrial executives, cabinet members, and the higher military. It does not seem to matter what the man is the very best at; so long as he has won out in competition over all others, he is celebrated."[53] Musicians signify success by signing record contracts. By coveting a record contract, musicians gain access to more opportunities that again signify more success. For instance, musicians can only play certain gigs if they have a contract: Live Nation, the largest event promoter in the United States, tends to book only signed acts; large music festivals (e.g., Coachella) reserve most slots for signed performers. Every blockbuster or celebrity recording artist signed some type of record deal to establish their careers; even famed unsigned artist Chance the Rapper has a deal with Apple Music.[54]

At the point when a musician becomes a star, competition reverses itself and labels compete for them. The "competition for the few stars at the top is so severe that the pressure on entertainment businesses is getting pretty intense: the truth is that often they can barely afford to compete for the most sought-after performers, but at the same time they cannot afford not to do so."[55] When a blockbuster becomes available, creative industries have to compete or risk suffering the losses of not signing talent. For example, in 2009 the Walt Disney Company purchased Marvel Entertainment for $4 billion, which at the time seemed like a risky move.[56] However, after ten years of hits, Disney has made exponentially more in revenue and now has bought 20th Century Fox, a move that will reunite the rest of the Marvel characters.[57] In 2016, Sony signed singer-songwriter Adele to a three album record deal for $130 million.[58] Adele's album *25* was the largest grossing album of 2015[59] and was the third in a string of chart-topping albums. Sony not only wanted to profit from signing Adele, but also, they did not want another label to profit from Adele's hits.

However, Adele is the exception to the rule. Most signed artists sign record contracts for advances that they will never recoup. Musicians feel intense competition among themselves, while labels enjoy watching them compete. By creating a surplus of creative talent angling for record contracts, labels ensure a decreased cost to sign acts; therefore, competition lowers costs and raises profits for labels.

Conclusion

While competition supposedly drives success in the music industry, it creates tensions and paradoxes in the process of instilling the competitive ethos in musicians. As a society, we learn that cooperation is the key to success (there is no I in team). However, competition contradicts cooperation. In many ways competition among bands conflicts with the greater ethos of cooperation within bands. Teams, groups, and bands need to work together to compete with external competitors, but the drive to compete can result in competition within a group of people otherwise tasked to cooperate (I look further at these internal tensions in Chapter 6). This is where ideological tensions in capitalism collapse.

Capitalist ideology in all its forms stresses that competition is a fundamental characteristic of capitalism. "When banks compete, you win" (LendingTree motto) or the idea that competition reduces costs. Capitalists would have us believe that competition makes things better, but they do everything they can to avoid competition. In the music industry, this means that musicians compete with each other because labels retain monopoly rights issued by the state in the form of copyright. Competition becomes ingrained in musicians from an early age as they aim to be the best. However, "the best" remains marred in someone else's opinion of the performer. While musical performance is always judged in someone else's opinion, a fundamental disconnect exists between what musicians want and what other people want from musicians. It results in musicians seeking their own system of rewards that comes from their status markers. For musicians, the ultimate status marker is signing a record contract—the ideology of getting sign is a musician's main form of motivation.

Notes

1. Cohen, *Rock Culture in Liverpool*, 84.
2. Grow, "McCartney Shares His Touring Secrets."
3. Nicholls, *The Competitive Ethos and Democratic Education.*
4. Smith, *The Wealth of Nations.*
5. Harvey, *A Brief History of Neoliberalism*, 2.
6. Monbiot, "Neoliberalism—The Ideology at the Root of All Our Problems."
7. Marx, "The German Ideology," 162.
8. Smith, *Millennial Dreams*, 26.
9. Monbiot, "Neoliberalism—The Ideology at the Root of All Our Problems."
10. Smith, *Millennial Dreams*, 27.
11. Horkheimer and Adorno, *Dialectic of Enlightenment*, 61.
12. Harvey, "Neoliberalism as Creative Destruction."
13. Casselman, "A $2 Billion Question."
14. "Billionaires 2019."
15. The "survival of the fittest" economic narrative does not match the reality of government support. Most large corporations succeed specifically because of government programs and policies from copyrights and money for research and development to tax breaks and public resources such as roads. Free market capitalists quickly argue that they support a limited government, but in actuality, they support a very large government that supports their interests. In fact the neoliberal state "trumpets the virtues of

competition while actually opening the market to centralized capital and monopoly power." Harvey, *Spaces of Global Capitalism*, 25.
16. Harvey, *A Brief History of Neoliberalism*, 65.
17. Smith, *Millennial Dreams*, 30.
18. McCormick, "Higher, Faster, Louder," 11.
19. Frith, *Performing Rites: On the Value of Popular Music*, 56.
20. Nylander and Melldahl, "Playing with Capital."
21. Bourdieu wrestles extensively with the idea about how class impacts the access to cultural capital in *The Field of Cultural Production: Essays on Art and Literature*.
22. Morris, "The Twisted Thrills of 'Killing Eve,'" 36.
23. McDow and Stiffler, "Statewide Public School Music Competitions/Festivals in Kansas and Oklahoma."
24. McDow and Stiffler.
25. McCormick, "Higher, Faster, Louder," 6.
26. McCormick, 10.
27. Horkheimer and Adorno, "The Culture Industry: Enlightenment as Mass Deception," 134.
28. Straw, "Systems of Articulation, Logics of Change," 37.
29. Johnson, "Editor's Introduction: Pierre Bourdieu on Art, Literature and Culture," 7.
30. Bennett, *On Becoming a Rock Musician*, 35.
31. Bourdieu, "The Forms of Capital," 248–49.
32. Davis, "Battle of Bands," 38.
33. Carroll, "Battle of the Bands."
34. Christensen, "The Ultimate Battle of the Bands Comes to Austin."
35. Luke, *Screens of Power: Ideology, Domination, and Resistance in Informational Society*, 24.
36. "Battle of the Bands."
37. "Battle of the Bands."
38. Lee, *Blowin' Up*, 110.
39. See: Negus, *Music Genres and Corporate Cultures*, chapter 2; Grazian, *Mix it Up*, chapter 6.
40. Coincidentally, all three pop stars signed with labels that ultimately became part of Sony Music Entertainment following the merger between Sony and BMG in 2004.
41. Bielby and Bielby, "All Hits are Flukes."
42. Negus, *Music Genres and Corporate Cultures*, 31.

43. Hull, Hutchison, and Strasser, *The Music Business and Recording Industry: Delivering Music in the 21st Century*, 199.
44. Vito, *The Values of Independent Hip-Hop in the Post-Golden Era*, 52–54.
45. Zafar, "What It's Like When a Label Won't Release Your Album."
46. Bareilles, *Love Song*.
47. Sinnreich, *The Essential Guide to Intellectual Property*, 78.
48. Elberse, *Blockbusters*, 4.
49. Lindvall, "Behind the Music."
50. Horkheimer and Adorno, "The Culture Industry: Enlightenment as Mass Deception"; Mills, *The Power Elite*.
51. Mills, *The Power Elite*, 74.
52. Mills, 74.
53. Mills, 74.
54. Phillips, "Chance the Rapper Explains How He's Still Independent, Despite Apple Music Deal."
55. Elberse, *Blockbusters*, 8.
56. Barnes and Cieply, "Disney to Buy Marvel and Its 5000 Characters for $4 Billion."
57. Schwartz, "Disney Officially Owns 21st Century Fox."
58. Ellis-Petersen, "Adele Signs £90m Contract with Sony."
59. Caulfield, "Adele's '25' Official First Week U.S. Sales."

Bibliography

Bareilles, Sara. *Love Song*. Little Voice. Epic, 2007. https://genius.com/Sara-bareilles-love-song-lyrics.

Barnes, Brooks, and Michael Cieply. "Disney to Buy Marvel and Its 5000 Characters for $4 Billion." *The New York Times*, August 31, 2009, sec. Media. https://www.nytimes.com/2009/09/01/business/media/01disney.html.

"Battle of the Bands." *The Skanner (1975–1988); Portland, Or.* July 1, 1981.

Bennett, H. Stith. *On Becoming a Rock Musician.* University of Massachusetts Press, 1980.

Bielby, William T., and Denise D. Bielby. "'All Hits Are Flukes': Institutionalized Decision Making and the Rhetoric of Network Prime-Time Program Development." *American Journal of Sociology* 99, no. 5 (1994): 1287–1313.

"Billionaires 2019." *Forbes*, Online edition. Accessed May 1, 2019. https://www.forbes.com/billionaires/.

Bourdieu, Pierre. "The Forms of Capital." In *Handbook of Theory and Research for the Sociology of Education*, edited by J. G. Richardson, 241–58. New York, NY: Greenwood Press, 1986. https://www.marxists.org/reference/subject/philosophy/works/fr/bourdieu-forms-capital.htm.

———. *The Field of Cultural Production: Essays on Art and Literature*. Edited by Randal Johnson. New York: Columbia University Press, 1993.

Carroll, Jeffrey. "Battle of the Bands." *University Wire; Carlsbad*. October 26, 2018, sec. Newsline. https://search.proquest.com/docview/2125437023/citation/542C8F2E31B84257PQ/1.

Casselman, Ben. "A $2 Billion Question: Did New York and Virginia Overpay for Amazon?" *The New York Times*, November 14, 2018, sec. Business. https://www.nytimes.com/2018/11/13/business/economy/amazon-hq2-va-long-island-city-incentives.html.

Caulfield, Keith. "Adele's '25' Official First Week U.S. Sales: 3.38 Million." *Billboard*, November 25, 2015. http://www.billboard.com/articles/columns/chart-beat/6777905/adele-25-sales-first-week-us.

Christensen, Thor. "The Ultimate Battle of the Bands Comes to Austin." *The San Diego Union-Tribune*, March 17, 2000, sec. Lifestyle. https://advance.lexis.com/document/?pdmfid=1516831&crid=532d5bdf-2b22-4d58-bc3b-fb0dd71acad9&pddocfullpath=%2Fshared%2Fdocument%2Fnews%2Furn%3AcontentItem%3A3YTS-1290-00RR-W43P-00000-00&pddocid=urn%3AcontentItem%3A3YTS-1290-00RR-W43P-00000-00&pdcontentcomponentid=11811&pdteaserkey=sr0&pditab=allpods&ecomp=bfyk&earg=sr0&prid=72dddf9b-c37c-41bd-b3ef-8e337cb09257.

Cohen, Sara. *Rock Culture in Liverpool: Popular Music in the Making*. New York: Oxford University Press, 1991.

Davis, John S., ed. "Battle of Bands." In *Historical Dictionary of Jazz*, 38. Lanham, MD: Scarecrow Press, 2012. http%3A%2F%2Flink.galegroup.com%2Fapps%2Fdoc%2FCX2781000110%2FGVRL%3Fu%3Dtxshracd2597%26sid%3DGVRL%26xid%3Dda2570df.

Elberse, Anita. *Blockbusters: Hit-Making, Risk-Taking, and the Big Business of Entertainment*. New York: Henry Holt and Co., 2013.

Ellis-Petersen, Hannah. "Adele Signs £90m Contract with Sony." *The Guardian*, May 23, 2016, sec. Music. https://www.theguardian.com/music/2016/may/23/adele-set-to-sign-90m-sony-deal.

Frith, Simon. *Performing Rites: On the Value of Popular Music*. Cambridge, MA: Harvard University Press, 1996.

Grazian, David. *Mix it Up: Popular Culture, Mass Media, and Society*, 2nd ed. W. W. Norton, Incorporated, 2017.
Grow, Kory. "McCartney Shares His Touring Secrets." *Rolling Stone*, July 13, 2017.
Harvey, David. *A Brief History of Neoliberalism.* Oxford and New York: Oxford University Press, 2005.
———. *Spaces of Global Capitalism.* London and New York, NY: Verso, 2006. http://www.loc.gov/catdir/toc/ecip067/2006002202.html.
———. "Neoliberalism as Creative Destruction." *The Annals of the American Academy of Political and Social Science* 610, no. 1 (2007): 21–44.
Horkheimer, Max, and Theodor W. Adorno. *Dialectic of Enlightenment*. New York: Herder and Herder, 1972.
———. "The Culture Industry: Enlightenment as Mass Deception." In *Dialectic of Enlightenment*, xvii, 258. New York: Herder and Herder, 1972.
Hull, Geoffrey P., Thomas W. Hutchison, and Richard Strasser. *The Music Business and Recording Industry: Delivering Music in the 21st Century*, 3rd ed. New York, NY: Routledge, 2011.
Johnson, Randal, ed. "Editor's Introduction: Pierre Bourdieu on Art, Literature and Culture." In *The Field of Cultural Production: Essays on Art and Literature*, 1–25. New York, NY: Columbia University Press, 1993.
Lee, Jooyoung. *Blowin' Up: Rap Dreams in South Central*. Chicago: University of Chicago Press, 2016.
Lindvall, Helienne. "Behind the Music: When Artists are Held Hostage by Labels." *The Guardian*, April 15, 2010, sec. Music. https://www.theguardian.com/music/musicblog/2010/apr/15/artists-held-hostage-labels.
Luke, Timothy W. *Screens of Power: Ideology, Domination, and Resistance in Informational Society*. Urbana: University of Illinois Press, 1989.
Marx, Karl. "The German Ideology." In *The Marx-Engels Reader*, edited by Robert C. Tucker and Robert C. Tucker, 2nd ed., 146–200. New York: Norton, 1978.
McCormick, Lisa. "Higher, Faster, Louder: Representations of the International Music Competition." *Cultural Sociology* 3, no. 1 (March 1, 2009): 5–30. https://doi.org/10.1177/1749975508100669.
McDow, George H., and Daniel L. Stiffler. "Statewide Public School Music Competitions/Festivals in Kansas and Oklahoma: The Beginnings of the School Music Contest Movement in the United States." *Journal of Historical Research in Music Education*, November 19, 2018, 1536600618810783. https://doi.org/10.1177/1536600618810783.
Mills, C. Wright. *The Power Elite*. New York: Oxford University Press, 1956.

Monbiot, George. "Neoliberalism—The Ideology at the Root of All Our Problems." *The Guardian*, April 15, 2016, sec. Books. https://www.theguardian.com/books/2016/apr/15/neoliberalism-ideology-problem-george-monbiot.

Morris, Alex. "The Twisted Thrills of 'Killing Eve.'" *Rolling Stone*, no. 1326 (April 2019): 36–36.

Negus, Keith. *Music Genres and Corporate Cultures*. New York: Routledge, 1999.

Nicholls, John G. *The Competitive Ethos and Democratic Education*. Harvard University Press, 1989.

Nylander, Erik, and Andreas Melldahl. "Playing with Capital: Inherited and Acquired Assets in a Jazz Audition." *Poetics* 48 (February 1, 2015): 83–106. https://doi.org/10.1016/j.poetic.2014.12.002.

Phillips, Amy. "Chance the Rapper Explains How He's Still Independent, Despite Apple Music Deal." *Pitchfork*, March 17, 2017. https://pitchfork.com/news/71701-chance-the-rapper-explains-how-hes-still-independent-despite-apple-music-deal/.

Schwartz, Matthew. "Disney Officially Owns 21st Century Fox." *NPR.Org*, March 20, 2019, Online edition, sec. Business. https://www.npr.org/2019/03/20/705009029/disney-officially-owns-21st-century-fox.

Sinnreich, Aram. *The Essential Guide to Intellectual Property*. New Haven, CT: Yale University Press, 2019. https://www.worldcat.org/title/essential-guide-to-intellectual-property/oclc/1055252885.

Smith, Adam. *The Wealth of Nations*. Edited by Edwin Cannan. Vol. Bantam classic. New York, NY: Bantam Classic, 2003.

Smith, Paul. *Millennial Dreams: Contemporary Culture and Capital in the North*. The Haymarket Series. London and New York: Verso, 1997.

Straw, Will. "Systems of Articulation, Logics of Change: Communities and Scenes in Popular Music." *Cultural Studies* 5, no. 3 (October 1, 1991): 368–88. https://doi.org/10.1080/09502389100490311.

Vito, Christopher. *The Values of Independent Hip-Hop in the Post-Golden Era: Hip-Hop's Rebels*. Palgrave Pivot, 2019. https://doi.org/10.1007/978-3-030-02481-9.

Zafar, Aylin. "What It's Like When a Label Won't Release Your Album." *BuzzFeed*, May 12, 2013, sec. Music.

Part II

6

We're Getting the Band Back Together: Social Cohesion and Solidarity in Bands

The title of this chapter reflects a phenomenon with which any casual music listener is familiar. A band breaks up, for a myriad of reasons, only to re-form for a reunion tour, usually for financial exigencies. The phrase "we're getting the band back together" is so ubiquitous that it is a trope used whenever people are getting a group of friends together after a long absence. The *Blues Brothers* popularized the phrase and it is even the title of a musical. However, it points to a real problem for musicians, that is, finding a way to make a group of people working closely with each other continue to work with each other. Therefore, my interest here is less about the re-formation of a group than the social cohesion in the first place. What factors help to determine whether a band stays together? Record contracts are a primary means for keeping a band together. Bands form within a specific system (i.e., the major record label system) at a specific time that places particular constraints on musicians at the same time that it shapes their motivations to ultimately sign record contracts. Signing a record contract is a primary mechanism to keep bands together, which adds to the ideology of getting signed.

When a band forms, a number of factors determine its success. The commitment that individual members have to playing in their band is

D. Arditi, *Getting Signed*,
https://doi.org/10.1007/978-3-030-44587-4_6

a decisive factor of a band's success. Their commitment usually parallels the degree to which they want to earn a living from it. Does an individual band member see himself or herself as a musician or as a band member? How does this affect the desire for a record contract? How does it have an effect on cohesion? These questions address the motivations of band members, but they also situate the bands and band members in broader social, economic, and historical forces. In this chapter, I argue that while capitalism creates the circumstances that threaten a band's cohesion as individual members seek economic activity to fulfill their needs, record contracts enable solidarity in bands by allowing for productive activity under capitalism. Musicians in bands believe in the ideology of getting signed because they see a record contract as a mechanism to solidify their bands.

This chapter addresses these questions by discussing how the division of labor under capitalism relates specifically to the division of labor in the production of music. I address how both Émile Durkheim and Karl Marx conceive of the division of labor. Then I develop a model I call "strained solidarity" that addresses the dialectic tension within a band. While Durkheim and Marx both look at the broader relations in society, I think their concepts provide important insights into the interworking of the micro-level within bands. Finally, I discuss a case study of a band that helps elucidate my theory of strained solidarity. I chose this band as a case study because the timing of my interview elaborates the foregoing theory—my discussion with them occurred after the band moved to Nashville, but before they broke-up.

Division of Labor

The very idea of a band implies a division of labor. According to Merriam-Webster's dictionary, a band is "a group of persons, animals, or things; *especially*: a group of musicians organized for ensemble playing." The fact that musicians organize within an ensemble points to the division of labor. A band doesn't organize for playing in an ensemble outside of the economic and social forces of society, but rather musicians form a band because of social norms, cultural expectations, and economic need.

Alternatively, a rock band is a "group banding together of individuals for the purpose of achieving something that none of them can get on their own: money, fame, the right sound, something less easy to put into words."[1] At each moment in history, the mode of production plays a determinant role in organizing the social relations of production. Since many bands form to earn money, bands are sites of economic organization. While the division of labor itself reflects the mode of production, cultural and social norms drive the specific circumstances and alignments of that division. Any given band organizes within the artistic conventions of society.[2] For instance, a rock band requires at the very least drums, an electric guitar, and an electric bass. Outside of a one-man-band, it is very difficult to produce music without a division. But even the one-man-band exists because of particular structural forces. For instance, Ed Sheeran made a name for himself by using looping pedals extensively to layer percussive, vocal, and guitar sounds while performing alone; however, Sheeran connects to the singer-songwriter tradition where only a singer playing guitar or keyboard is necessary for the music. Furthermore, the singer-songwriter is part of a longer tradition of troubadours, minstrels, and jongleurs.[3] In a typical rock band, the drummer plays the drum kit and the bass player plays the electric bass; the drummer may be capable of playing the electric bass, but it is impossible for them to do so at the same time as playing drums under current conventions of a rock band. The division of labor is necessary in order for the band to perform. While the division of labor within a band reflects conventions about the organization of sound, this division of labor creates the circumstances under which bands decide to sign record contracts.

In *Noise: The Political Economy of Music*,[4] Jacques Attali demonstrates that music possesses the potential to predict the broader organization of society. Music's "styles and economic organization are ahead of the rest of society because it explores, much faster than material reality can, the entire range of possibilities in a given code."[5] The social and economic organization of music predicts the social and economic organization of society. For Attali, music is the organization of noise, and this organization speaks to the operation of power. As such, the organization of the social relations of production (i.e., the division of labor) in which people create music predicts a future time's division of labor. While Attali does not focus on the division of labor, this division is the underlying basis of his political-economic description. Broadly speaking, during the phase Attali names "sacrificing," music's division of labor focuses on the individual; in his second phase, "representing," labor organizes in the large orchestra; and during the third phase, "repeating," small groups of people working in a recording studio (and by extension touring together) characterize the division of labor.

While the division of labor changes over time, older formations continue beside newer divisions. Older divisions of labor never fully go away. Orchestral music continues alongside rock bands, hip-hop groups, and electronic dance music (EDM) DJs; however, the latter did not exist during the early nineteenth century at the high point of orchestral music. Even older forms of musical organizations continue to exist today such as minstrels. Whereas troubadours, jongleurs, and minstrels were expected to play different instruments and styles of music, orchestral music decentered the musician as a jack-of-all-trades because orchestras required musicians to be virtuosos on a singular instrument. "The capitalist mode of production systematically destroys all-around skills where they exist," Harry Braverman contends, "and brings into being skills and occupations that correspond to its needs."[6] As capitalism erodes the position of the solo-musician, it replaces their singular craft production with a division that better reflects the needs of capital in a given moment. The virtuoso violinist is no more or less talented than the jongleur, but the skill set is remarkably different in character. Skill itself evolves with each change in the mode of production.

The changes to the division of labor often cause great social upheaval as musicians contend with labor circumstances following the development of new divisions. This is exemplified in the early-to-mid-twentieth century as studio musicians supplanted orchestral musicians[7]; as "talky" moving pictures became popular, musicians were displaced from their jobs playing music along with silent movies in theaters to a smaller number recording music in Hollywood studios. Movie theaters across the United States required a large labor force of musicians to perform along with silent films; this labor force was unionized and they recognized the vulnerability that their craft faced due to the use of recording technologies.[8] Capital deployed these technologies to change the social relations of production in order to lower the cost of labor-power. A similar process occurs once again in late twentieth-century recording studios as recording tasks producers with more elements of music production at the expense of work for studio musicians.[9] As musicians react to the changes in the political economy of music for the aptly named gigging economy, marked by greater precarity for musicians, evidence demonstrates that musicians prepare by re-organizing unions and support groups once again.[10] Of course, the driving forces behind these changes include the "perfection of the machine and the replacement of human forces of labor through mechanical forces."[11] The social organization of society and available technology intricately binds the division of labor for the creation and performance of music.

While the general organization of the relations of production for the creation of music is important, equally important is the division of labor that characterizes their interaction with other sectors of the music industry. Within the music industry, two divisions of labor exist that interest me here. First, there is the division within a band. This is what I view as a horizontal division of labor. Each band member plays their instrument while each instrument's part is necessary for the production of the band's music. No one band member can perform as the band without other musicians dividing the labor to perform music. Very close proximity of the musicians working together characterizes the division of labor. There is little degree of alienation in the horizontal division because the band members know each other, have personal relationships, and see each other perform. Because of the low degree of alienation between members of the band, this division points to a pre-capitalist organization of the means of production. The horizontal division of labor exists within a hierarchy both within and outside of a record label, which constitutes the second division of labor on a vertical axis. Record contracts construct bands, and recording artists more generally, as independent contractors for the record labels because of the way labels write these contracts. The record labels have a division of labor between and among departments. Looking at organizational charts at major record labels, the major departments at a record label include Artist & Repertoire (A&R), Marketing, Publicity, Legal, Business Affairs, Promotion, Artist Development, Distribution, and New Media. Record labels divide labor between and within each department. Even these neat organizational charts obscure the division that takes place within a record label. Furthermore, the broader major label "group" includes both labels and publishers, an additional division of labor within the industry. Record labels operate not just within departments, but across departments. However, the most glaring omission in any major record label organizational chart is the recording artists because technically and legally recording artists do not work for record labels. In the broader vertical division of labor within record labels, there is a greater degree of alienation—i.e., workers in one division do not see what workers in another division of the label do every day. Furthermore, the specialization and skill required in positions outside of the band lend themselves to greater interchangeability; with lower skill and less specialization, more workers can replace any given worker within a record label.

As an often overlooked aspect of corporate music production and mass distribution, I think it is important to interrogate the division of labor within the recording industry. The division of labor is the site where conflict, cohesion, and solidarity originate within a band. A band holds the power of collective cooperation, but it operates within the constraints of the larger capitalist system. Furthermore, the division of labor helps explain why so many musicians desire to sign record contracts.

Solidarity

Different mechanisms exist that encourage social cohesion within a band, which in turn depend on the band's structure. Depending on how a band is structured changes the long-term prospects of the band's ability to maintain cohesion. At one end of the spectrum is a band with a singular leader; if a band is defined with a particular leader in the group, the goals of the band align with the leader's goals. In this case, the leader can make decisions and individual band members can decide if they want to continue with the group—these musicians are merely workers and can decide their commitment level, at the same time the leader has the power to fire band members. At the other end of the spectrum is a band of equals; if everyone in the band is equal, and members disagree about the direction of the band, there is little cohesion, and the band risks breaking up at any time. In both cases, band members may differ with regard to the reasons why they play in the band, but in the former, each band member is replaceable whereas in the latter, a difference in opinion contributes to tension that can disintegrate the band. Here I am less concerned with bands working in a group with a leader and more concerned with the situation where a band is a group of equals. Within a band, there are contradictory forces that work to hold a band together or rip a band apart, and the division of labor helps to explain the tensions that affect a group's solidarity.

Émile Durkheim develops social solidarity based on the degree of the division of labor within a society. The greater the division of labor, the stronger the social bonds across society. While Durkheim focuses on the macro-level division of labor by exploring the impact that the division of labor has society-wide, I think his concepts of mechanical and organic solidarity are useful to explore with regard to the relationships in a band. Durkheim posits that a low degree of division of labor creates what he calls "mechanical solidarity." Mechanical solidarity is a form of social cohesion in which there is a strong "collective conscience" within the group. There is little division of labor within such a society, and the people have similar religion, education, and day-to-day existences. As the division of labor grows within society, each person develops a unique task within the division of labor. While people become further removed from each other (what Marx calls alienation), Durkheim contends that the dependence on one another grows and the bonds between people actually intensify. The greater division of labor creates what Durkheim calls "organic solidarity"—a society where "each one of us depends more intimately upon society the more labor is divided up."[12] Organic solidarity operates like the parts of a machine or the parts of a living body—the organs of a human body all do entirely different tasks, but each task is vital to the life of the body.

On the one hand, a band represents a quintessential case of organic solidarity because each member of the band performs an essential task in the division of labor. Ultimately, the band ceases to perform without the labor of each individual instrumentalist just like an organism. The necessary parts that allow a band to function are social constructions of the artistic conventions in the style of music. Howard Becker describes the conventions that organize the division of labor in art worlds, in this case popular music, as determined by genre. "Each kind of person who participates in the making of art works, then, has a specific bundle of tasks to do. Though the allocation of tasks to people is, in an important sense, arbitrary—it could have been done differently and is supported only by the agreement of all or most of the other participants—it is not therefore easy to change."[13] While these conventions are arbitrary, they are necessary nonetheless. If the conventions of a rock band call for a singer, a bass player, lead guitarist, rhythm guitarist, and a drummer, all four positions are necessary for the performance of music. Of course, there are substitutions where any member of the band could be the singer or it may be possible to have a keyboardist instead of the rhythm guitarist, but there is an aesthetic requirement that overdetermines the configuration of the band. As a particular band develops by writing, performing, and recording music, the specific demands of particular instruments within the band grows stronger (can "Stairway to Heaven" exist without guitar?). Sara Cohen observes that the more musicians performed together "relationships between their members intensified which often … led to stronger solidarity and egalitarianism."[14] This develops a dependency between the specific musicians within a band beyond the artistic conventions of the genre. Since popular music is often unwritten, each member of the band becomes irreplaceable to an extent because it is difficult for a new band member to learn a band's corpus of music. "Band members may become indispensable, and thus powerful, because of their business acumen, social skills, or longtime familiarity with the band repertoire."[15] The indispensability of specific band members acts to solidify organic solidarity.

On the other hand, bands also resemble aspects of mechanical solidarity. Musicians in a band are not alienated from each other, in fact, their lives are intertwined in very personal ways; they intimately know each other. One former bandmate of mine once described being in a band as similar to being in an intimate relationship. By that he meant that you have personal feelings for each other, you want to make each other happy, but you also can become engaged in bitter fights over the direction of the relationship. This can make firing a band member extremely difficult because it resembles breaking-up with a significant other. Alternatively, some describe bands as "a bit like being in a family."[16] Band relationships blur the line between professional and social relationships. In some ways, bands exhibit forms of ritual punishment found in societies of mechanical solidarity. This can be present in the form of hazing band members, ridicule, signifying, or public shaming; a ritual I witnessed numerous times in my research. Often these mechanisms are used to force a band member to practice or grow humility, but the key is that these practices do not resemble the formal system of justice found in a society with a high degree of the division of labor. While band members can appropriate rhetoric about professionalism, the personal nature of a band's relationship alludes to a more mechanical sense of solidarity.

In an analysis of the evolving division of labor in Nashville, Daniel Cornfield uses Durkheim to demonstrate how musicians come together to support each other.[17] His work extends beyond the bounds of a band to conceptualize the division of labor in a music community. According to Cornfield, music increasingly relies on "entrepreneurial music production" and self-promotion as the recording industry individualizes risk. As a result of the informal economy, Cornfield theorizes that artists come together to support each other. Musicians come together under Cornfield's "sociological theory of artist activism" to minimize joblessness for self and peers, but at the same time they reduce the division of labor. Increasingly, musicians take on the role "artist-as-intermediary," which Kait Kribs defines as a musician who "creates, records, and produces her/his own music" along with promotion and distribution through social media.[18] Cornfield tries to reconcile this streamlining of the division of labor by thinking about Durkheim:

> In Durkheimian terms, reconstituting a post-bureaucratic community of artists entails the development of a new 'social solidarity' or sense of togetherness based in a simplifying occupational division of labor. In a community built around a complex division of labor of occupational specialists, 'organic social solidarity' was achieved from the

> interdependence among specialists. In contrast, 'mechanical social solidarity' was achieved in a community based on an occupational sameness that prevailed in a simple occupational division of labor.[19]

Cornfield addresses the difficulty of understanding musical solidarity through Durkheim's analysis of the division of labor. A unique and evolving division of labor surrounds musicians; while the division of labor is highly complex, musicians have never really left the craft/artisan mode of production.[20] In fact, the rhetoric of musicians as artists demonstrates their connection to artisanal labor, as opposed to industrial labor. Whereas Cornfield discusses the movement of Nashville musicians from a corporate/industrial model of labor to a craft model where precarity dominates the lives of musicians, I argue musicians have always remained in a craft model of labor that is precarious for the vast majority of musicians while being subsumed by the rationalization of the Culture Industry[21] on every other level of cultural production. The ideology of getting signed perpetuates musicians' position as craft labor, as I explored in Chapter 3.

Understanding the division of labor within a band requires the concept of solidarity. Musicians work in close proximity with each other in a band, and they form personal relationships with each other, as a result. The organization of the division of labor in a band develops a unique hybrid between mechanical and organic solidarity. However, a discussion of the division of labor within a band is incomplete by discussing Durkheim alone because the division of labor exists within capitalism.

Marx

Under capitalism, the primary way that people satisfy their needs is through earning a wage. In "A Critique of the German Ideology," Karl Marx exhorts that the "first premise of all human history is, of course, the existence of living human individuals. Thus the first fact to be established is the physical organization of these individuals and their consequent relation to the rest of nature."[22] In other words, the only way to understand what motivates people to live a certain way is to comprehend the organization of the world in which they live. Fulfilling needs motivates people to act; therefore, the organization of society shapes the conditions through which people meet their needs. For instance, under a subsistence economy, people hunt and gather to satiate hunger in societies with little division of labor beyond the division of the sexes. However, under capitalism, and a complex division of labor, most people work for a wage that they use to pay for everything from housing to beer, and electricity to entertainment. Furthermore, Marx adds that the mode of production "is a definite form of activity of these individuals, a definite form of expressing their life, a definite mode of life on their part. As individuals express their life, so they are."[23] Capitalism encompasses the individual's life so much that people constitute who they are based on what they do to satisfy their needs. A musician who wants to "be" a musician must be able to earn a living from making music.

However, obeying the logic of capitalism does not satisfy the requirements of individual members of society; in fact, capitalism runs counter to the livelihood of the vast majority of people. Particular trades do not conform to capitalism when they don't allow capital to profit from labor; the arts are the quintessential trades that don't necessarily create room for profit. Band members need to pay their bills, but performing in a band isn't necessarily productive labor. "Briefly, labor that contributes to the accumulation of capital, which creates surplus-value, is said to be productive," according to Jacques Attali, "and labor is unproductive if it is only of interest to the purchaser for the use-value of its product."[24] Earning a living through the performance, recording and sale of music runs counter to the typical forces within capitalism because performing music is not productive labor when musicians perform music for themselves.[25] Music doesn't produce profit or surplus value for someone if a band remains independent because they work for themselves. Productive labor is exploited labor. Productivity has an inverse relationship to the fair compensation of labor. The more a worker produces, but makes the same wage, the more productive the worker is. The low cost of the means of production contributes to a musician's unproductivity because musicians own their instruments making it more difficult for capital to exploit them. However, music as unproductive labor also results from organization because bands do not exploit themselves to generate surplus value—here is where record labels come in. The primary characteristics of a band are in tension with capitalism because they are not productive, but there is a requirement for people living under capitalism to labor productively.

The contradiction that performance in a band is unproductive while people have to be productive to survive in a capitalist system creates tension between band members because different members may envision their own productivity and the goals of the band differently. "Friction concerning finances often arose" in Cohen's work on bands in Liverpool, England as the primary source of tension.[26] Throughout my interviews, it became clear to me that people often have individual interests based on their perception of the best way to fulfill their needs. When I spoke with a lead guitarist in a popular local R&B band, he described his band's situation this way:

> I've been playing with [name of the R&B band] for 2 years. [Bass player] and I were playing together in some other bands when we met [singer]. I called [drummer] and pretty soon we had a band. [Bass player] is good at getting gigs, so we started playing shows about once a week. But I don't know what will happen with the band. [Singer] works at a local bar, and he seems in it for the girls, I'm not sure he has much business sense. You have to know how the business works. [Drummer] is a real pro, but he's in five bands at any given moment. I want to do this thing, I want to make it, you know? But I'm not sure everyone is in it at the same level. Our keyboardist is a CPA with a wife and kids, is he going to leave that for a tour? I don't know man.

This guitarist provides an assessment that I heard repeatedly from a number of bands. Whereas the drummer may be playing in the group to have fun (and have a "real" job), the guitarist may be dedicated to the band for a living, the keyboardist has a "day job" to supplement band income, and the bassist may be playing in several groups with the hope of sticking with whichever group becomes the most successful. Not only do the band members' visions for the band diverge, but also this divergence happens because of how each band member defines oneself. People who have a "real" job do not perceive themselves as musicians; whereas a band member dedicated to earning a living through performing music views themselves as a musician first. These varied interests have a way of coming into conflict with each other within a band.

After a band forms, the band holds together within a cloud of uncertainty because there is nothing officially holding them together (like a contract). Their varied interests have the potential to rip the band apart because members of the band do not define themselves as members of a band, primarily. In the United States, people define themselves through their labor more than in different parts of the world. Americans making small talk ask people "what do you do?" In this question, what people do to earn a living explicitly links them with who they are. The simplest way to see if a band is a band member's primary job, and as a result is how they earn a living, is to ask them what they do. In Mary Ann Clawson's study of local musicians in the Boston area, she observed that "Although many of these bands were well known locally, none of their members supported themselves through performing. Instead they worked at a variety of day jobs ... Nonetheless, respondents commonly identified music as their principal work activity and as the focus of long-term ambition and artistic aspiration."[27] Being a musician is a strong identity marker that often supersedes the way people earn a living as a measure of how they see themselves, but a musician's response to this question can still be significant. As a result, I would often informally ask people in my research "what do you do?" before I would interview them. There is a strong correlation between how people answer this question and the strength of a person's identity as a musician. For instance, one informant whose show I went to is the leader of his band—it is his band, and the supporting musicians change. However, before I even introduced myself as a professor, he introduced himself as a professor at a university in Washington. If every member of a band does not answer this question in casual settings that they are a musician, there is little likelihood of the band staying together for little more than a fun gig every once in a while. My research shows that these conflicting interests, where one band member wants to play for fun and another wants to play for a living, result in the failure for most bands to move beyond local performance, and ultimately ends the band.

In order for the band to hold together, the typical route is to come together contractually—the contract can be through a management contract or a record contract. While either contract can bind a band together, the record contract is the stronger of the two, and Marx helps to explain the record contract's adhesive strength. Since musical performance is unproductive labor, the record contract develops the commodity that transforms a group to productive labor, as I discussed in Chapter 3. Record contracts stipulate that recording artists sign away their copyrights to the label in exchange for an advance. This is the site of what Marx calls primitive accumulation. Because the ownership of instruments, sound equipment, and today even recording equipment is relatively cheap, musicians tend to own their means of production. They may operate as a small business playing shows, and selling CDs that they recorded in their homes. The entrance cost to perform is relatively low, and most musicians pay for the investment to perform long before there is an opportunity to perform. Within the current music industry, copyright becomes the key to the means of production. Without a record contract, a band solely owns its means of production. However, a record contract allows a band to sign their recording rights away in exchange for an advance. As soon as a band signs a record contract, they no longer own the means of production, and their record label acts to commodify their performances by recording the band and selling those recordings for profit.

On the one hand, capitalism is the force that threatens to rip a band apart as band members seek a way to make a living. Their self-interest driven by the need under capitalism to pay bills forces the individual band members to find productive work. Bourgeois ideologues argue that these people are driven by self-interest, but this self-interest is a result of the economic system. The economic system that structures the music industry assures that the vast majority of aspiring musicians will fail to be able to pay their bills performing music. In a Mertonian analysis of country songwriters' attempts to break-in, Richard Peterson and John Ryan assert the "active competition among many people to achieve high goals with rich rewards, in which some are more likely to fail than others, is a recurrent condition in American society."[28] While the condition is recurrent, it depends on the system and apparatuses that proselytize these goals. Ideology is the mechanism that obscures the real relations of production. Musicians think they need to abandon their dreams of playing music for a living because they face the reality that they need to pay their bills. Self-interest is not something that manifests within the individual, but rather represents something that is forced upon the individual from external forces. Each band member operates within a system where they must find ways to secure their basic and social needs. If the band does not earn enough money for individuals in the band to feel financial security, they will seek financial security by other means. This is not to say that conflict does not otherwise exist within bands, but rather to demonstrate that in the quasi-familial atmosphere of a band, members concern themselves with affirming relationships. Those relationships can be strained, but their strain results from their closeness. Paying bills stands as the primary form of tension that threatens the cohesion of a band.

On the other hand, record contracts appear as a means to cohere the group and turn its members into productive labor. Without the contract, individuals work together to the extent that they receive personal benefit from playing collectively. For Durkheim, the "contract is indeed the supreme legal expression of cooperation."[29] If we think in terms of solidarity, the contract is necessary in a division of labor characterized by organic solidarity because it forces diverse people doing diverse tasks to work together. The record contract does two things to bind a band: (1) obligates them to execute a task; (2) turns the band into productive labor. A contract obligates a band to work through legal force. With this obligation, the idea that some individual will pursue their own interest fades. The drummer quits their "real" job, the keyboardist quits their "day" job, and the bassist quits their other bands, while the guitarist fulfills their dream of the band making it. The band works together, but they do so for the abstracted reason to serve their record contract obligation instead of reaffirming social relationships within the band.

Further, the band becomes productive labor because the contract creates the circumstances through which record labels can create profit through the exploitation of musician labor. Under their record contracts, bands no longer own the rights to their music. They no longer own their means of production, and their labor becomes alienated. First, alienation originates in the band's loss of autonomy because as recording artists, they work for the label, which determines the sound of the final product.

Second, bands are alienated from the final product because producers and engineers, at the direction of label (A&R) staff, change the band's sound. Finally, they are alienated from their fans as the band spends more time in the studio and listening to label staff about what consumers want.

Strained Solidarity: A New Model of the Division of Labor

Of course, when the record contract proves to be insufficient for sustaining the needs of band members, the band usually succumbs to the original tensions and dissolves as members of the band pursue earning a living by other means outside of the band. Most bands never realize the dream of earning a living from music because they never move from unproductive labor to productive labor. Even under the coercive mechanism of the record contract, bands dissolve because record contracts do not enable musicians to meet their needs; musicians rarely recoup their advances or earn salaries from selling and performing music. Friction from finances continues "particularly when a band signed a contract."[30] Record contracts represent a strained solidarity somewhere between organic and mechanical solidarity. Strained solidarity is the condition bands exist in when musicians navigate the tumultuous situation where band members feel a part of something larger, but still ultimately fail to meet their needs. As the internal mechanical solidarity of the band rubs against the organic solidarity found within the label and the broader division of labor, musicians feel new strain from their failure to earn a wage while they do a highly specialized job. While band members have assurance through a contract that their bandmates will not bail on them, they still do not earn enough money to survive. Strained solidarity recognizes that band members seek a contract to alleviate the forces within capitalism that compel people to pursue productive labor while at the same time recognizing that this behavior is a coping mechanism that would be unnecessary outside of the current mode of production. In many cases, the strained solidarity embodied in a record contract fails to meet each individual's financial needs resulting in the dissolution of the band.

Durkheim describes the way that our solidarity operates on a continuum between the collective and the individual. According to Durkheim, "individuality cannot arise until the community fills us less completely."[31] In other words, as we feel that our community does not fulfill our needs, we recognize those needs and pursue them as an individual. "Here there are two opposing forces, the one centripetal, the other centrifugal, which cannot increase at the same time."[32] Durkheim's use of terms from physics is apt for the scenario of bands. On the one hand, the forces of the mode of production act to tear apart the band as individual band members pursue behavior that fulfills their material and social needs—this is a centrifugal force. On the other hand, a centripetal force acts on a moving body by pulling it back to the center; here ideas of the collective aim to hold the band together, but a record contract is the ultimate centripetal force that holds a band together. Record contracts act as the definitive centripetal force within the recording industry for bands because they define the band as a legal unit; to pursue one's interest outside the band is to break the contract. Before the band signs a record contract, everything is informal—for instance, playing a gig or going on tour may interfere with someone in the band's "real" job. However, after a band signs a record contract, the band is the "real" job. The centripetal force of the record contract forces a band to record and promote an album, and tour.

The centrifugal and centripetal forces are not the only forces acting upon a band. As I discussed in Chapters 4 and 5, record labels often sit on albums keeping the bands from ever having a chance to sell music to recoup their advance. This is another state of strained solidarity. But other forces include an unenthusiastic response to a band's music, poor management, a tragedy for one of the musicians, etc. My model of strained solidarity is not universal, but represents something many bands experience. While experiences vary, the tensions bands feel exist in their peculiar division of labor.

Another definition of "band" according to Merriam-Webster's dictionary is "something that confines or constricts while allowing a degree of movement." Here the dictionary refers to an object such as a rubber band or a hairband that acts to bind by grouping without permanently binding, like a staple. These are similar forces to the centrifugal and centripetal forces I discuss above. A rubber band does an adequate job at holding together 5 pencils, but one pencil can easily be removed from the group, the rubber band can be removed, one can twist the pencils until several fly out, or the rubber band can be cut. Record contracts bind stronger than a band. A record contract holds a band together with legal authority, and it does so under the auspices of fulfilling each individual's basic and social needs. However, record contracts bind according to a record label's desire to extract surplus value from productive labor instead of a desire for community or creativity. Under a record contract, a record label acts to establish a complex division of labor. While record labels leave bands on the periphery of their corporate hierarchies, record contracts establish bands as a cog in the record label's machine.

However, the important point here is not the record contract itself, but rather the competing forces that fight a band's solidarity. On the one hand, individual band members want to pursue a source of income; on the other hand, individual band members receive something from performing in the band (e.g., comradery, fame, attention, money, recreation, fun, etc.). Record contracts are one means to an end (i.e., keeping a band together). Through my research, I had the opportunity to speak with one band that exemplified some of these challenges. A case study of that conversation follows.

Solace: A Case Study of Strained Solidarity

As an interesting case study to this chapter, I had the opportunity to interview a fairly popular indie folk band, Solace.[33] This band was unsigned and touring medium-size venues (500–1000 person capacity) in the southern United States when I interviewed them. The band formed in 2009 as a group of college students in a college town. While the town is known as a music town and sits in a larger metropolitan area, Solace felt the need to move to Nashville. One band member, Rick, described the move like this:

> Although [college town] is like a really cool town, and it's cool for artistic inspiration, it is not really good for furthering your business. If you want

> to be one of those guys that hates people for success and says you want to do it the old fashioned way so to speak, then [college town] is the place for you. But I spent 6 years after graduating from college there, playing in different bands, nothing is happening there. There aren't that many important people there that I can buddy up with. There's not any other opportunity for any other type of 'oh you want me to go on your tour and you are going to pay me' – everyone's friends but there aren't opportunities.

Rick, who only began playing with Solace six months earlier, points to two issues. First, his analysis illuminates the pitfalls of performing in a small town. There are very few opportunities for a band to perform in front of new audience members, which in the long-term limits fan base. Second, while Rick is a member of Solace, he clearly thinks about personal career opportunities. This is not surprising coming from a band member who only began playing with the band 6 months earlier. Clearly, Rick wants to perform music to make a living, but he lacks commitment to the band because he actively seeks opportunities to go on tour; this was a description he initiated in the presence of the other band members. Solace presents Rick with the opportunity to make a living playing music, but the fact that he plays with the band to make money is known to the band, and he may not be as committed to the band himself.

For the other members of Solace, having access to Nashville was the motivation for moving to Nashville. First, Solace described to me that Nashville is a one day drive from 70% of the population of the United States. This is common reasoning among many musicians who decide to move to Nashville. Second, John, the bandleader, describes the presence of a community of musicians:

> I think it's the difference between having a lot of musicians with a music scene and having the actual music industry. And it just so happens that Nashville has an office for all the music record labels. There's a lot of industry ... In Nashville, it makes it nice for meeting people, dating people, and making friend because being a musician is something everyone there intrinsically understands. Everyone has a musician friend with a house, a car, and babies. So it doesn't seem weird to people to

> be a musician. You don't get a lot of [speaking with a pejorative country accent] 'What do y'all actually do?' Your family's like 'You just bang on drums. You make money off that? I'm worried about you, I'm worried about y'all' whereas people in Nashville say 'you should meet my friend Kenny he plays upside down jazz piano in between Kenny Chesney stuff.'

For Solace, Nashville represents a place that not only has music industry workers/executives, but also has people who understand them. They don't want to live in a place where they have to describe why being a musician is a normal job. Here John conducts a bit of identity construction because he sees himself as a musician. Since he sees himself as a musician, and ostensibly the other band members as well, then John and Solace define themselves in their labor as musicians. They desire to avoid speaking with strangers and family members who do not see "musician" as a way to pay bills. In other words, they are not living a pipe dream and what they do is real productive labor.

However, the idea to move to Nashville always seemed a bit of a pipe dream to me. Having known quite a few musicians who moved to Nashville, it is a terrible place to move to try to make it. The pull to Nashville is real, but once there, the gigs do not exist. I think about the migration of musicians to Nashville like the migration of actors to Los Angeles and New York, or people wanting to work for a nonprofit or the government moving to Washington, DC. While the move seems like a good idea, it is far easier to get gigs in cities with fewer musicians. I asked Solace about their luck getting gigs in Nashville.

> *Me*: What is it like getting gigs in Nashville?
>
> *John*: Never, no, don't even try. You live in Nashville, to drive from Nashville, not to play in Nashville. Total waste of time.
>
> *Bill*: There's always potential. I had a friend who was playing and Steven Tyler showed up and watched him play … things like that can be good, but because the market is so saturated and because there are probably a bunch of people hoping to be discovered, there is no financial benefit to playing in Nashville. Venues will pay you 20 bucks to play, so there is no money.

Bill and John are painfully familiar with trying to gig in Nashville. However, they perceptibly conceal that gigging in Nashville is about putting you and your band in front of industry folks. While using Nashville as a tour launching point is a good reason for migrating there, Bill alludes to the idea of being discovered by someone; other places are within a one day drive from 70% of the US population, but no other place has the concentration of musicians and the music industry.

The move to Nashville also demonstrates the strain caused within a group when different group members have different visions and goals for the band. For instance, when Solace decided to move to Nashville, they were a six piece band. Two members of the band quit before moving and the remaining four members auditioned and found replacements before the move. Between the time the band moved and our interview, they reduced the size of the band to four and had to hire a replacement for another member. At the time of our interview, the band was a four-piece band with only three of the original band members. Since Solace is a democracy, the consensus decision to move to Nashville forced two members out of the band. In Daniel Cornfield's analysis of musicians in Nashville, the issue of democracy came up frequently: "As a partner in a band, he characterized the constant give-and-take between self and group as a 'nasty democracy.'"[34] In an interview with *Rolling Stone*, Sting alludes to the break-up of his former band the Police as a product of these tensions. He says, "A band is a democracy ... Or the semblance of democracy. You have to pretend more in a band."[35] When people are equal in a band, their different visions for the group can cause internal friction among the musicians. With new members in Solace, the power dynamic changes as newcomers do not feel as if they have as much power as original members, and their goals of playing in the band may run orthogonally with the goals of the band.

We had a lengthy discussion about the problems with record contracts. Even though Solace showed contempt for record contracts, they clearly moved to Nashville for contact with label representatives. Several months before my interview a smaller record label offered Solace a contract. They said, "We were offered one, it was a bad contract. They delivered it on April 1st, we thought it was a joke." They continued:

Bill: We talked to them for a while. These guys approached us. They said 'We like this stuff, and we have some ideas.' They took us to a lot of lunches, they bought us a lot of lunch ... They paid for a little bit of studio time, they paid for a little bit of rehearsal space. They introduced us to people in the business that we would get if we signed with them. They buttered us up and they sent us an April fool's joke, and they haven't said just kidding yet.

John: It ended with a bad phone call. From me to the other guy that we'd been working with. I basically said 'this doesn't make any sense,' in a mean way. This doesn't make any sense because they do this thing that they don't really explain which is the recoup rate and the royalty rate. The recoup rate was 50% which seems great until you realize the record label spends, in this case 100k, and they make 200k before you make $1. No other business would ever agree to that. If you took that kind of business on *Shark Tank*, they would laugh you right off the show. What they would say is I'll give you 200 grand for 50% of your business, which is totally different… The record contract is extremely exploitative. And I don't think it is a good business practice, I think it is a bad business model, it's such a risky model. And I don't think it used to be that way. I think, back in the day, a record label would actually choose an artist that they thought was good and then they would work with them until their career hit. And they don't necessarily do that anymore. Maybe it would have been cool for us, maybe we would have gotten on Jimmy Fallon or whatever.

Rick: And I think that was the other thing. We looked at their roster of bands, and were like 'who are these people?'

John: It was one of those things where the terms seemed really good. Until we got the actual contract. The actual contract was spelled out in such thick legalese that it took some sifting to really get at what the terms were. If we had been presented with those terms we would have said 'no thanks' or we would have milked out as many free lunches as possible. Everyone likes a $30 steak with truffle butter.

Solace pursued a record contract, but ultimately decided against signing it. By the time they were offered the record contract, they were too experienced to fall in the trap of signing away their rights for an advance that would cost them twice the advance before they saw revenue. However, their pursuit of a record contract blunts their post-offer jadedness. This is precisely why an ethnographic researcher must read between the lines when interpreting an informant's views on a subject. When I spoke with Solace, the band appeared to me not to desire a contract, and the contract this record label offered conformed to their original trepidation about record contracts. However, as I transcribed the interview it became clear to me that throughout our conversation, they expressed a desire for attention from record labels. While Solace couch their move to Nashville in the city's central location, their discourse signifies a deep desire to be near the industry's apparatus in order to prove to themselves, their families, friends, and peers that they "made" it playing music. Nashville represents making a commitment by all of the band members who moved there to be dedicated full-time musicians, and signing a record contract represents the definitive remuneration for the move. The contract offered to Solace disappointed them because they expected something from it that was not in the fine print.

In John's comment, you also see a common perception about how things used to be different. Musicians in the 2010s think there was this heyday in the 1990s, i.e., before digital music, when record labels cared about artists. This theory of better times in the past comes-up in Cornfield's research on artist activists in Nashville,[36] and the music documentary *Before the Music Dies*[37] describes this situation in the 2000s. However, a long view of record contracts shows this exploitation going back much further. For instance, the drummer for the 1990s one-hit-wonder Semisonic describes his band's bad experience with record contracts.[38] Courtney Love described record contracts as that of a "sharecropper"[39]; Prince said he was the record label's "slave."[40] In a deeper historical analysis, Richard Peterson describes how Ralph Peer perfected the system of exploiting artists in the 1920s.[41] While John experienced the terms of the "joke" contract as something new and unique, a long history exists in which record labels exploit musicians through similar record contracts.

At the time I interviewed Solace, they were on a small tour through Texas consisting of five shows. Solace played four shows following the night I interviewed them, then after several weeks of silence, they announced their final show together. When I interviewed Solace, there must have been turmoil within the band. They gave me no indication that they were breaking up. Underneath their contempt for record contracts seemed a palpable bitterness toward the bad deal the record label offered them. The band endured years of turmoil after some band members refused to make the move to Nashville, and the band struggled to retain band members after the move. In our interview, band members openly spoke of opportunity in Nashville to better their own careers, they speculated on how much better a record contract would work for a solo artist, and doing so they exhibited the strain of keeping a band intact.

Record contracts have the ability to bind a band, but for Solace, the missed contract accelerated their break-up. It is not clear to me that all of the band members opposed signing the record contract because when we began discussing the offered contract one band member sat in silence. Signing the record contract would have created legal commitments for Solace thereby forcing some configuration of the band to record an album. However, the lack of contractual obligation with each other, either through a record contract or a management contract, encouraged the band members to go separate ways.

Conclusion

Bands sit uncomfortably between Durkheim's two poles of solidarity (mechanical and organic) because of the division of labor in the music industry under contemporary capitalism. While musicians come together to perform for a number of reasons, the drive for financial security threatens the stability of any given band because bands rarely earn enough money to provide for all of their members. A centrifugal force caused by the need for each member of the band to meet their basic and social needs threatens the unity of the band, while weak centripetal forces keep them together for the good of friendship and performance. Often band members regard record contracts as mechanisms that legitimate their identity as musicians. Contracts legitimate their identity as a musician for two reasons. First, the record contract establishes that they can earn a living performing and recording music. The contract allows them to quit their day job and offers proof to questioning relatives and friends that they "made it" playing music. Second, record contracts aid the process of transforming the unproductive labor of performing music into productive labor. In the process of legitimating musicians' identities, this also signifies where the rubber meets the road for the ideology of getting signed. Musicians and their familial networks believe that record contracts represent making it in the industry, so musicians pursue getting signed.

However, the strained solidarity that record contracts strengthen doesn't solve all problems experienced by bands. This is the dialectic relationship embodied in a record contract's strained solidarity. While the record contract resolves the tension between organic and mechanical solidarity, it does not resolve the conflicts underlying the desire to sign the contract. Since very few record contracts result in financial security, one of the main forces driving bands to sign record contracts remains in place. After bands discover that recording, promoting, and touring produces very little, if any, money, they begin to see the fallacious thinking in their desire to sign a record contract. Ultimately, these bands break-up because band members still fail to be able to meet their basic and social needs. In most cases, the centrifugal force is too strong and rips bands apart.

Notes

1. Marcus, *Mystery Train: Images of America in Rock "n" Roll Music*, 4th rev. ed.: 40.
2. Becker, *Art Worlds*.
3. Attali, *Noise: The Political Economy of Music*.
4. Attali.
5. Attali, 11.
6. Braverman, *Labor and Monopoly Capital: The Degradation of Work in the Twentieth Century*, 57.
7. Burlingame, *For the Record*; Zinn, Kelley, and Frank, *Three Strikes*.
8. Burlingame, *For the Record*; Zinn, Kelley, and Frank, *Three Strikes*.
9. Arditi, "Digital Downsizing."
10. Cornfield, *Beyond the Beat*.
11. Adorno, "On The Social Situation of Music," 414.
12. Durkheim, *The Division of Labor in Society*, 102.
13. Becker, *Art Worlds*, 11–13.
14. Cohen, *Rock Culture in Liverpool*, 28.
15. Clawson, "When Women Play the Bass," 207.

16. Cohen, *Rock Culture in Liverpool*, 36.
17. Cornfield, *Beyond the Beat*.
18. Kribs, "The Artist-as-Intermediary," 2.
19. Cornfield, *Beyond the Beat*, 4–5.
20. Arditi, "Digital Downsizing"; Arditi, "Disturbing Production."
21. Horkheimer and Adorno, "The Culture Industry: Enlightenment as Mass Deception."
22. "The German Ideology," 176.
23. Marx, 177.
24. *Noise: The Political Economy of Music*, 38.
25. Marx, *Capital*, chap. 16.
26. Cohen, *Rock Culture in Liverpool*, 55.
27. Clawson, "Masculinity and Skill Acquisition in the Adolescent Rock Band," 100.
28. Peterson and Ryan, "Success, Failure, and Anomie in Arts and Crafts Work: Breaking into Commercial Country Music Songwriting," 307.
29. Durkheim, *The Division of Labor in Society*, 97.
30. Cohen, *Rock Culture in Liverpool*, 55.
31. *The Division of Labor in Society*, 101.
32. Durkheim, 101.
33. Solace is a pseudonym for the band. All names for band members are pseudonyms as well.
34. Cornfield, *Beyond the Beat*, 37.
35. Rodrick, "Sting's Rock & Roll Salvation."
36. *Beyond the Beat*.
37. Shapter, *Before the Music Dies*.
38. Slichter, *So You Wanna Be a Rock & Roll Star: How I Machine-Gunned a Roomful of Record Executives and Other True Tales from a Drummer's Life*.
39. Love, "Courtney Love Does the Math."
40. Orwall, "Purple Drain."
41. Peterson, *Creating Country Music: Fabricating Authenticity*.

Bibliography

Adorno, Theodor W. "On the Social Situation of Music." In *Essays on Music/Theodor W. Adorno*, edited by Theodor W. Adorno, Richard D. Leppert, and Susan H. Gillespie, 391–433. Berkeley, CA: University of California Press, 2002.

Arditi, David. "Digital Downsizing: The Effects of Digital Music Production on Labor." *Journal of Popular Music Studies* 26, no. 4 (December 2014): 503–20.

———. "Disturbing Production: The Effects of Digital Music Production on Music Studios." In *The Production and Consumption of Music in the Digital Age*, edited by Brian J. Hracs, Michael Seman, and Tarek E. Virani, 25–40. New York, NY: Routledge, 2016.

Attali, Jacques. *Noise: The Political Economy of Music*. Theory and History of Literature. Minneapolis: University of Minnesota Press, 1985.

Becker, Howard Saul. *Art Worlds*. 1st ed. Berkeley, CA: University of California Press, 1984.

Braverman, Harry. *Labor and Monopoly Capital: The Degradation of Work in the Twentieth Century*. New York: Monthly Review Press, 1998.

Burlingame, Jon. *For the Record: The Struggle and Ultimate Political Rise of American Recording Musicians Within Their Labor Movement*. RMA Recording Musicians Association, 1997.

Clawson, Mary Ann. "Masculinity and Skill Acquisition in the Adolescent Rock Band." *Popular Music* 18, no. 1 (1999): 99–114.

———. "When Women Play the Bass: Instrument Specialization and Gender Interpretation in Alternative Rock Music." *Gender & Society* 13, no. 2 (April 1, 1999): 193–210. https://doi.org/10.1177/089124399013002003.

Cohen, Sara. *Rock Culture in Liverpool: Popular Music in the Making*. New York: Oxford University Press, 1991.

Cornfield, Daniel B. *Beyond the Beat: Musicians Building Community in Nashville*. Princeton, NJ: Princeton University Press, 2015.

Durkheim, Emile. *The Division of Labor in Society*. Edited by Steven Lukes. New York: Free Press, 2014.

Horkheimer, Max, and Theodor W. Adorno. "The Culture Industry: Enlightenment as Mass Deception." In *Dialectic of Enlightenment*, xvii, 258 pp. New York: Herder and Herder, 1972.

Kribs, Kait. "The Artist-as-Intermediary: Musician Labour in the Digitally Networked Era." In *RE: TURNS*. Toronto: eTopia, 2016. http://etopia.journals.yorku.ca/index.php/etopia/article/view/36768.

Love, Courtney. "Courtney Love Does the Math." *Salon*, June 14, 2000, Online edition, sec. Entertainment News. http://www.salon.com/2000/06/14/love_7/.

Marcus, Greil. *Mystery Train: Images of America in Rock "n" Roll Music*. 4th rev. ed. New York, NY: Plume, 1997.

Marx, Karl. *Capital: Volume 1: A Critique of Political Economy*. New York, NY: Penguin Classics, 1992.

———. "The German Ideology." In *Karl Marx: Selected Writings*, edited by David McLellan, 2nd ed., 175–208. Oxford and New York: Oxford University Press, 2000.

Orwall, Bruce. "Purple Drain." *Saint Paul Pioneer Press (Minnesota)*, January 15, 1995, Sundary Metro Final Edition, sec. Main.

Peterson, Richard A. *Creating Country Music: Fabricating Authenticity*. Chicago: University of Chicago Press, 1997.

Peterson, Richard A., and John Ryan. "Success, Failure, and Anomie in Arts and Crafts Work: Breaking into Commercial Country Music Songwriting." *Research in the Sociology of Work* 2 (January 1983): 301–23.

Rodrick, Stephen. "Sting's Rock & Roll Salvation." *Rolling Stone*, December 15, 2016.

Shapter, Andrew. *Before the Music Dies*, 2006.

Slichter, Jacob. *So You Wanna Be a Rock & Roll Star: How I Machine-Gunned a Roomful of Record Executives and Other True Tales from a Drummer's Life*. New York: Broadway Books, 2004.

Zinn, Howard, Robin D. G. Kelley, and Dana Frank. *Three Strikes: Miners, Musicians, Salesgirls, and the Fighting Spirit of Labor's Last Century*. Boston: Beacon Press, 2002.

7

The Voice: Popular Culture and the Perpetuation of Ideology

When I reach Globe Life Park in Arlington, Texas, to observe *The Voice*'s 2018 auditions, there is an atmosphere of hope. Across the street from the ballpark, friends and family wait in folding chairs and on blankets in the 100-degree Texas heat. They accompanied their aspiring singers with the belief that they will be good enough to land on *The Voice*. Everyone is friendly to me and to each other, even among those auditioning for the show. While the show is pure competition, I observe auditionees exchange phone numbers, bum cigarettes, and engage in friendly banter. However, they are all there to fulfill a dream to be on TV, compete to sing, and win a record contract.

Contestants begin arriving to the ballpark at 4 a.m. for a 7 a.m. audition time. Most travel with friends, family, and/or significant others when they take their spot in line. The line runs the length of one side of the ballpark, separated from the rest of the sidewalk by red queue tape. After they say bye to their supporters, they make new friends in line who share their desire to become the next winner of *The Voice*. Now the waiting begins. They wait for the 7 a.m. audition slot when security ushers them into the ballpark. At this point, show workers split the contestants into groups of 10. The groups of 10 will be in a row until

D. Arditi, *Getting Signed*,
https://doi.org/10.1007/978-3-030-44587-4_7

the point they go into the audition room. All 10 aspiring singers arrive at the audition room as new friends. Several singers described the change that happens as they enter the audition room as going from a very loose friendly atmosphere to one of thick anxiety. Anne Grace, a 25-year-old singer, said, "as soon as we entered the audition room, the anxiety fell on us like a fog." When they audition, each person in the group of 10 sings a song of their choosing in front of 1 judge and the other 9 singers. If they receive a red card with *The Voice* logo on it, they come back for the second round the next day when judges request that they sing a song in the current Billboard Hot 100. Unfortunately, most groups of 10 discover their dream is over with the judge saying "I'm sorry, but there will be no callbacks for this group" according to 30-year-old gospel singer, Kiki.

When I started this project, I had a vague sense that television talent shows would play a role in the contemporary construction of the ideology to sign a record contract. However, as I spoke with musicians, and they confirmed the role of television talent shows as a path to achieving the goal of getting a record contract, these artists exposed some disturbing patterns to me. I spoke with a number of informants from around the country who had varying degrees of connection to the show, including five artists who made it to the final rounds of the show. While these informants provided me with significant information and stories, I decided to incorporate their accounts judiciously because as I searched contracts, available on the Internet, it struck me that *The Voice* could sue my informants—something I will discuss below. While my informants had informed consent and they protected specific information, it seems to me that their accounts could identify and incriminate them. As a result, I chose to suspend some ethnographic accounts and focus on a cultural studies reading of the show. To do this, I found contracts on the Internet and scoured news accounts of the show—most references by name to contestants in this chapter come from accounts in newspapers, magazines, and Internet sources—when I do refer to people who auditioned for the show, I use pseudonyms. I conduct a critical reading of these texts to demonstrate not only the ideology of the show, but the power inequities that exist in the Culture Industry.

While *The Voice* is but one talent show among many, the show's underlying social forces exemplify the ideology of getting signed. How does *The Voice* advance the ideology of getting signed? How are power dynamics within the show emblematic of power in the recording industry? By selling an instantaneous rags-to-riches rise to stardom on television, I argue in this chapter that *The Voice* reinforces the ideology of getting signed while increasing the precarity of most musicians.

Because of the social relations of production, a number of contradictions become evident in the show. *The Voice* offers record contracts, where record contracts no longer exist. The producers require obedience from contestants without compensation. Coaches earn millions per season, while contestants receive room and board during the show's production. Recordings are for sale on iTunes for profit, but producers bar musicians from earning money from their sale. Producers own everything contestants do outside of the show, while still a contestant.

Contracts on *The Voice* are the negation of record contracts. They provide the means of exploitation without the promise of riches. Contestants must record without royalties; they must perform without compensation. Someone will win a contract and $100,000, but no one will be a superstar, or even recoup their advance. If the goal of the show is to find the next superstar with the best voice in America, or what *Billboard* describes as a "career-turning turn of the chair,"[1] then the winner's inconsequential celebrity negates the very premise of the show. No one will "make it" in a given season—one person will receive a record contract, and the winner will go back to oblivion. However, the artifice of the show perpetuates the ideology of getting signed.

Following a critical description of the show, this chapter proceeds by discussing the precarity of labor for the show's contestants. Then, I argue that *The Voice* becomes the quintessential purveyor of the ideology of getting signed.

The Show

NBC's music competition, *The Voice*, first aired on April 26, 2011. What NBC offered was a new spin on the decades-old talent show format. Whereas other shows in the genre focus on celebrity judges, *The Voice* uses "coaches." These coaches begin by selecting their teams from a pre-auditioned cast of singers. *The Voice* holds auditions across the United States to find singers to compete on the show. Each season a limited number of singers are flown to Los Angeles where they audition in front of the coaches and a studio audience, which is aired on television. However, at the beginning of these auditions, the coaches don't see the contestants. Each singer walks onto an empty stage in front of four chairs that hold the coaches. Contestants see the backs of the chairs as the coaches face the audience. The coaches remain in this position until they hit a button. Coaches press the button when they decide they want the auditioning singer on their team. After they press the button, the chair turns around to show the coach the singing contestant. When the performance ends, all remaining coaches swivel around. The moment the chairs pivot marks the moment when coaches receive their first glimpse of the contestant. If no coaches turn their chairs around before the end of the performance, the singer is dismissed from the show, often with kind words from the coaches. If only one coach presses their button, the singer goes to that coach's team; however, in cases where more than one coach hits their button, the coaches begin to lobby the singer to join their team—the singer makes the decision on which team.

The coaches on *The Voice*, who are celebrated performers in their own right, play the role of coaching the performers to be celebrities like themselves. Coaches teach contestants the affective aspects of performance that include everything from the best way to hold a microphone to singing lessons. "Coaches dedicate themselves to developing their team of artists, giving them advice and sharing the secrets of their success."[2] Even though coaches supposedly work closely with contestants, some contestants report having very little contact with their coaches.[3] Through their coaching, they teach the contestants how to perform like them. However, there is far more to acquiring success in the recording industry than performance. Coaches know this detail all too well because they not only have had successful careers as performers, but their business acumen landed them on the highly lucrative cast of *The Voice*—coaches have earned $2–17 million per season. Furthermore, aside from a large salary for their coaching services, their appearance on the show boosts their record sales and song streams. Few artists know the record business as well as these coaches, but they do not provide that information to the contestants.

During early rounds of each season, coaches make decisions about who will be excluded from future rounds of the show. Each season these early rounds differ with regard to the rules about how the selection process works. The key to these early rounds is that the coaches act more like judges or coaches deciding whom to cut from the team—an analogy to sports teams. Ultimately, "America" votes for who they want to continue to the next round and win. *The Voice* introduced a new form of voting that differs from *American Idol*, *America's Got Talent*, *Sing-Off*, *Sunday Best*, etc., because the show allows viewers to download a contestant's performance on Apple's iTunes, which counts as a vote.

While *The Voice*'s contest rules differ from other talent competition shows, the format itself is as old as television. *Original Amateur Hour* was the first television music-talent show that began airing in 1948 after a 15-year run on radio.[4] In my formative years, the popular talent show competition was Ed McMahon's *Star Search* (1983–1995). Each week contestants competed head to head in different categories (female vocalist, male vocalist, teen vocalist, etc.): challenger vs. champion. In order to win $100,000 on *Star Search*, the champion had to fend off challengers for a number of weeks. No one became particularly famous, but then again, the end-goal was not to win a record contract. *American Idol* changed the goals of the talent competition show by introducing the record contract-as-prize. The revamped talent show format made the ultimate goal to sign a record contract a centerpiece of the show.

From the first commercial that I saw for *The Voice*, I thought the show would be complete artifice. While the show sells itself as about the singer's voice, dozens of people see the contestants before they hit the stage. Then, the coaches turn around (for some reason they are always surprised when their stereotype for the voice they hear does not match the singer); from that point forward, the show is about everything *but* the singer's voice. For instance, while battling for a contestant to choose her in the first round of the show, Gwen Stefani often mentions to women contestants how they would have access to her wardrobe; thinking about your coach as a stylist is hardly about a person's voice. Aspiring singers learn what they need to look like, dance like, and *be* like, while watching at home. While aspirant performers absorb the superstar affect, producers avoid any coaching about negotiating the record business. As an ideological formation, *The Voice* inspires singers to pursue their dreams at the same time that the show conceals the power relations in the recording industry. Specifically, producers are adept at concealing the precariousness of the singers' day-to-day lives, especially, while on the show.

Precarity

For the hope of one day receiving a record contract and $100,000, producers of *The Voice* expect contestants to labor without pay for 5–8 months, depending on the season of the show. After *The Voice* selects contestants from the Open Call Auditions held across the United States, the producers fly contestants to Los Angeles to start the show.[5] The first round is a nine-day jaunt to determine the final roster of candidates to appear on the show. According to the eligibility requirements for Season 13, "If you are selected as a participant, you must be willing to travel to and reside at one or more undisclosed locations in the United States for several weeks at any time in September 2017 through May 2018 (or as otherwise scheduled by Producer). Economy travel to be paid for by Producer." In other words, participants have to be willing to live for the show with no other commitments and no pay for the majority of the year. Their life becomes characterized by precariousness. "Precariousness (in relation to work) refers to all forms of insecure, contingent, flexible work – from illegalized, casualized and temporary, to homeworking, piecework and freelancing."[6] Competing on a talent show exemplifies insecurity because contestants do not know if they will continue on the show from week to week without a wage. Contestants commit to the show, but the show makes no commitments to the contestants. While on the show, precariousness defines contestants' lives because they do not know how they will pay bills, whether they will have a job when the show is complete, or to what degree the show will help their careers.

This isn't a unique case for contestants on television singing contests, but rather permeates society, especially among freelance positions across the Culture Industry.[7] In industries where talented freelancers are willing to work without pay to "break" into an industry, this decreases the value of all workers in that industry.[8] While working for no wage other than to build one's reputation makes sense at an early stage, David Chandler[9] posits the presence of unpaid labor brings the value of established workers down. Eventually, this hurts the person willing to do the work without a wage in the end because after they begin earning money from their craft, others remain willing to work for free to break into the industry. By dedicating themselves to "making it" in the music business, *The Voice* contestants perpetuate not only their own exploitation, but also the exploitation of all freelance musicians.[10] Whereas gigs could pay sustainable wages for all, the willingness of a few musicians to break into the industry creates perpetual precariousness as the norm for most musicians.

The current condition of flexible labor is not unique to the music industry, but rather can be viewed through the lens of the problems that musicians have faced for over a century. Musicians play gigs at night and work part-time jobs or teach music lessons during the day to supplement their income. Since musicians perceive being a musician as flexible and casual, they accept other forms of flexible and casual employment to supplement their income. Musicians have perceived their labor as freelance and flexible throughout the recording era.[11] As more jobs become subsumed by the concept of "flexibility," Jacques Attali's declaration that the political economy of music foreshadows the broader political economic system becomes more germane because the global social relations of production now reflect the contingent nature of employment for musicians. Andrew Ross establishes that capital deploys precarious labor at all levels and in all types of labor.

> Capital-owners have won lavish returns from casualization – subcontracting, outsourcing and other modes of flexploitation – and increasingly

> expect the same in higher-skill sectors of the economy. As a result, we have seen the steady march of contingency into the lower and middle levels of the professional and high-wage service industries.[12]

Ross' term "flexploitation" signifies the degree to which flexible employment exploits labor; in the Marxist sense, exploitation is the condition in which capitalists pay workers less than the full value of their labor-power.[13] Companies implement flexploitation through the language of creativity and creative workers by contending that in order for workers to be the most productive and happiest, they must be given the space to have a flexible work environment. While *The Voice* owes nothing to contestants because of the flexibility of their relationship, there is little prospect that any contestants will gain anything from their experience.

Precariousness, or precarity, characterizes contestants on *The Voice*, and freelance or sub-contractors more generally. As labor flexibility increases, it increases the reserve army of labor. For Marx, the reserve army of labor is the large number of unemployed properly skilled workers to do a particular job.[14] With more people seeking work than jobs available, a reserve army of labor has the effect of lowering wages. Flexible workers in the music industry increase the size of the reserve army of labor because they are often underemployed. As David Grazian discusses the broader reality TV business model, by "casting amateur participants willing to work for free, rather than professional actors, producers also avoid paying industry-standard union wages to members of the Screen Actors Guild."[15] Contestants on *The Voice* receive twice the exploitation here as they are neither protected by the Screen Actors Guild nor the American Federation of Musicians. Furthermore, participation in the show weakens the strength of unions because these gigs dilute the overall pool of gigs. With so many musicians performing in the music industry, the competition depresses wages. For example, if *The Voice* viewers download recordings on Apple Music to "vote" for their favorite contestant, they spend that $1 on the contestant who makes no money from the download instead of downloading a different song that pays a recording artist with the same $1 (more on this below). When some musicians are willing to perform without a wage, all musicians compete with this free labor. Or simply watching the television show instead of going to a bar to listen to music provides another example of how the show undercuts musician wages. "Contestants on talent shows thus have become amateur performers and thereby have replaced the professional performers or celebrities."[16] Unpaid labor on *The Voice*, and other talent shows, replaces high wage celebrities that would otherwise take these positions. Flexibility is a ruse that perpetuates mass unemployment because "[w]hat is called the flexibility of the labor market means that no job is secure."[17] Without job security, even flexible workers who earn a wage never know if that wage will continue, and that is why it is important to consider the effect of such precariousness on labor.

When singers sign-up for the show, they put their regular lives on hold for 5–8 months. In my interviews with singers auditioning for *The Voice*, this came up several times. Jamal, a 30-year-old gospel singer, previously made it through the initial rounds of BET's *Sunday Best*, but he decided not to pursue the 8-week taping of the show because he would have to quit his job as an insurance broker; then he would have no means to pay his bills. Another singer, KJ, I met at *The Voice* Auditions made it to the second round of *America's Got Talent*, but he was unsure if he would continue because it conflicted with his job coaching at-risk youth. After singers agree to the show, they do it knowing that they will not earn a wage while appearing on the show, and producers prohibit them from doing so. How is it legal for people to work for a company without pay? Contract law supersedes labor law; since contestants sign a contract stating that they are independent contractors agreeing to do the work without compensation, they can work without pay. Contestants work for the show without being employed by the show—this is the same contractual condition of recording artists who sign record contracts with major labels, as discussed in Chapter 3. Therefore, the producers do not owe contestants anything beyond a bare minimum of living expenses that they agree to up front. This makes it impossible for contestants to meet their basic and social needs while they are contestants. As human beings, Marx explains, we need to meet our basic and social needs, and the way we fulfill those needs is determined by the mode of production.[18] Under capitalism, we meet our needs by earning a wage and paying for our needs with that wage. The relationship in which contestants find themselves is one where the producers pay for their most immediate basic needs as long as they are on the show. How do contestants pay for their mortgage or car payments back home? How do contestants pay their cell phone bills? If contestants become sick, how do they pay for health care? When they are not on stage, how do they afford new clothing? Producers do not concern themselves with these questions, but rather focus on profit. By agreeing to be contestants on *The Voice*, these aspiring singers agree to forgo their ability to meet their necessities of life.

Some people may contend that the contestants seek out this precarity by auditioning at the open call auditions. While I don't think it matters how someone finds their way to a job (everyone deserves a fair wage), I would like to point out that the premise is incorrect. Many people who participate as contestants are solicited by producers through managers to audition, bypassing the first several rounds of auditions.[19] In these cases, the singers have successful independent careers touring and performing around the country. *The Voice* producers learn about these singers the same way that record label Artist & Repertoire (A&R) staff discover new talent. Producers encourage these singers to place their careers on hold to perform on the show. Singers willingly become contestants because they believe this will launch their careers; they relinquish what they have for the possibility of what they may gain. These are professionals who producers make feel as though this is the answer to their problems. Therefore, two types of performers participate in *The Voice*: those who audition in the open calls and those the producers invite to audition at higher levels. In my interviews, there was a noticeable difference in career trajectories between these two types of contents. Those who attended the open calls were more likely not to have much professional experience, they tended to perform at weekly karaoke events, sing at open mics, but some also performed professionally. Singers who skipped the open call by definition have some experience performing professionally. In fact, all five singers I spoke with who made it to the top 10 skipped the open call auditions. However, regardless of their way onto the show, vocalists deserve to be paid as any other laborers. Precarity envelops the lives of both types of aspiring singers, so they think this will be their ticket to security, but the show paves the way for more despair.

While contestants labor without wages, *The Voice* generates large sums of money through their labor. As I mentioned earlier, coaches earn staggering salaries ($2–17 million per season) with regular coaches Adam Levine and Blake Shelton earning $13 million per season each while coaching on two seasons per year. Viewers watch *The Voice* because it is a musical competition show; therefore, the contestants matter at least to the extent that without contestants, there would be no show. The producers use contestants' stories to construct narratives that entice viewers to watch.[20] At the same time, the contestants themselves are largely unknown to the audience. Producers would like viewers and contestants to believe that since contestants are interchangeable, they have very little value. However, there are a myriad of positions that support the show from finance to lighting where workers possess skills that could easily be interchanged, but still receive a wage. In fact, the coaches, aside from Levine and Shelton, consistently change, and they are the largest earners. In other words, whether a worker has an interchangeable skill does not affect whether they are or should be paid. We do not know the camera operators' names for *The Voice*, but the median income for a camera operator in Los Angeles, California, is $44,246.[21] And, again, most viewers do not tune in to *The Voice* because of a camera operator—they do a job, the same as contestants. "From the viewpoint of labor theory, these 'relatively cheaper' or 'even unpaid' amateur singers compose an amazing percentage of the 'industry reserve army' that enables the television station a part of the music industry chain, to cut their costs very efficiently."[22] The unpaid precarious labor of contestants allows for the obscene wages of coaches on *The Voice*.

Fans generate revenue for *The Voice* by watching the show, voting, downloading and streaming music, and watching commercials. For every dollar spent on iTunes to listen to (and vote) for a contestant on *The Voice*, fans spend money that may otherwise be spent on other recording artists who record labels pay for their performance. Or at least this is the logic that the recording industry has peddled since the inception of Napster. There is a twisted irony in the precarity that these contestants face that highlights the overall predicament of musician labor in the music industry. For years, the Recording Industry Association of America (RIAA) and major record labels have belabored what I call the piracy panic narrative.[23] In the piracy panic narrative, the industry claims that downloading music for free through file-sharing networks is the same thing as stealing from artists. Then, at the 2015 Grammy Awards show, Neil Portnow, president of the Recording Academy, claimed "What if we're all watching the Grammys a few years from now and there's no Best New Artist award because there aren't enough talented artists and songwriters who are actually able to make a living from their craft?"[24] Portnow went on to scoff ad-supported streaming services as the new miscreant trying to exploit artists. Coincidentally, *American Idol* winner, Jennifer Hudson, accompanied and took part in Portnow's speech at the 57th Grammy Awards. However, Portnow and the RIAA abstain from articulating anything about the lack of wages for contestants on musical competition shows—much less musicians performing in clubs. When the music industry decides not to compensate musicians, industry representatives are silent because that is business as usual; record labels have no qualms about expropriating wages from these contestants.

Furthermore, *The Voice* has sponsors for which the contestants work directly during the course of the show. In Season 1, for instance, *The Voice* had a special room, called the V-Room where contestants went to interact with fans using social media during live broadcasts. "In the V-Room, the contestants were seen using their Samsung tablets with the suggestion that they were at that moment on social networks, engaging with audience members."[25] By forcing contestants to tweet during the show using Samsung tablets, *The Voice* simultaneously forced contestants to work (unpaid) for both Samsung and the show. In subsequent seasons, producers of *The Voice* rebranded the social media room and changed sponsors to Sprint, but contestants could still be seen typing away at their social media accounts. Samsung or Sprint pay *The Voice* the value contestants' labor produces, but the show's producers do not pay the contestants for this work. This practice is legal because contestants give up all rights to their likeness in the "Participant Agreement, Release and Arbitration Provision" which they sign to participate in the show:

> I further irrevocably grant to Producer and Distribution Entities, the right to use the my Likeness and the Material (including without

> limitation the Recordings and Statements) in and in connection with the Program, including without limitation, any promotion, publicity, marketing, advertising or merchandising in connection with the Program or for Producer and Distribution Entities or otherwise in any manner whatsoever. I hereby grant Producer and Distribution Entities the irrevocable right to reproduce, edit, dub, subtract from, add to, modify or juxtapose any part of the Material (including without limitation the Recordings and Statements), and/or my Likeness in any manner and to combine them with any other material. I grant the rights hereunder whether or not I am selected to participate in the Program in any manner whatsoever.[26]

Since a contestant no longer controls their likeness, *The Voice* can use contestants to promote anything without compensation. A contestant's willingness to forgo their rights for a chance to make it in the music business increases precarity.

However, a contestant's precarity does not stop with performance, producers require contestants to work as social media specialists. Performing as part of the competition is one type of labor, but tweeting to fans on Twitter is another type of labor that is often performed by social media marketers. "By Season 3, the show also displayed contestants' Twitter usernames. In doing so, it fueled 'social chatter' among audience members and between audience and contestants, thus stimulating a sense of interaction without necessarily having to incorporate comments into the show."[27] While Karin van Es discusses the problematic power dynamics between producers and viewers with *The Voice*'s social media strategy, this concern unearths a further power dynamic between the show and its contestants. Participating in *The Voice* allows contestants to increase their number of followers on social media accounts. Musicians notoriously self-promote using social media accounts to alert fans to recordings, concerts, merchandise, etc. But to what degree does cultivating a social media network help contestants with their careers?

Producers, past contestants, and news reports state that the benefit of going on the show is a national platform through which contestants can harness publicity otherwise unattainable without help from a major record label. However, the only self-promotion that contestants can utilize while they are on the show is for their performances on *The Voice* because contracts ban contestants from performing, recording, or otherwise using their likeness while they are on the show. The "Participant Agreement, Release and Arbitration Provision" states that the producers of the show own any recordings made while the singer is a contestant on the show. In order for contestants to benefit from being on the show, they need to be able to connect fans with a product while they are on *The Voice*, but their contracts bar them from doing so. There is no way for contestants to appropriate the platform to advance their careers because:

1. contestants cannot record an album while on the show;
2. they cannot perform concerts while on the show;
3. they cannot arrange a tour to commence when they leave the show;
4. they cannot use their likeness to promote other products.

The ideological position of the show implies that contestants can grow a fan base through the publicity of the show and change this social capital to money capital upon any contestant's release from the show. "But as soon as *The Voice* cranks out one success story, a completely new batch rotates in for their chance in the spotlight. A new season of the NBC show airs every six months, meaning America falls out of love with contestants just as quickly as they fell in."[28] Since a new season of the show begins so quickly, the fleeting celebrity of contestants is continually replaced with a new cast of temporary celebrities. Graeme Turner contends "television's production of celebrity can truly be regarded as a manufacturing process into which the product's planned obsolescence is incorporated."[29] By thinking in terms of planned obsolescence, this helps demonstrate that *The Voice* creates a (re)consumable product without pursuing mechanisms that would create sustained careers for its performers. This becomes clearer through first-hand accounts from contestants. Paige Skinner of the *Dallas Observer* interviewed several past contestants from Dallas–Fort Worth.[30] Through the interviews, it becomes clear that the contestants quickly lost support of their fans. From declines in attendance at shows to albums that they failed to release, their appearances on *The Voice* did little more than build their resume—a frequent reference on a number of my informants' bios includes participation in a reality TV show from *American Ninja Warrior* to *America's Got Talent*. In other words, the only thing they gain is the possibility of a larger number of social media fans/followers. But they do not have a way to leverage their new fan base until it is too late. Viewers quit paying attention to these contestants quickly, especially since they do not have anything to hold on to immediately.

By signing up for *The Voice*, contestants open themselves to precarity. Contestants accept the logic that they will gain a following from television exposure while neglecting to acknowledge the inevitable—their position on the show will not develop their careers or help them to achieve their goals. Whereas contestants work hard to become celebrities, their participation in *The Voice* blocks them from being able to achieve tangible results in their careers. Most musicians live in the condition of precarity, but shows such as *The Voice* utilize precariousness while they propagate the ideology of getting signed.

Ideology

In many respects, *The Voice* represents a strong articulation of the ideology of getting signed at the same time that it points to the inability of record contracts to serve recording artists. Singers compete on the show for the ultimate chance to make it, which includes a $100,000 prize and a record contract. However, to win the show, singers must sign away their rights for the chance to be further exploited by a label through a record contract. Viewers watch the show and internalize the ultimate goal of signing a record contract, but they lack the awareness of the business models at work in the background. Mass media disseminate the dream of signing a record contract to viewers at home. The "idea of a rock band and the possibility of starting one are derived from commercial mass media."[31] So we must look to commercial mass media to understand the goals of musicians. With television singing competitions, commercial mass media define what it means to be a successful pop vocalist. While *The Voice* seems to address the dreams and aspirations of contestants performing on the show, it (re)produces the dream of signing a record contract for viewers at home.

Whether a viewer comes to watch *The Voice* as a listener of popular music, fan of one of the celebrity coaches, aspirant singer, or someone with nothing better to do, they all observe the same ideological construction. They absorb the idea that ordinary people can one day pull themselves from obscurity to become a celebrity through hard work and determination. Furthermore, these performers reach their dream of becoming music stars through a democratic meritocracy where "the people" vote for the best performers. While I focus on *The Voice*, several authors describe the perpetuation of ideology through a number of talent search shows. Miaoju Jian and Chang-de Liu observe the same phenomenon in China on the popular show *Supergirl*. Producers "reduced costs by exploiting the labor of contestants and audiences willing to 'work' for 'invisible' payments based on an ideology."[32] They continue that "These voluntary laborers are symbolically paid in 'dream-fulfillment' within the apparent democracy of a singing contest."[33] Here, contestants and viewers work to produce revenue for the show because they believe in both the ideology of the dream to become recording artists and the show's ideology of democratic support.

Two contradictory ideals become apparent within the dream that contestants can achieve their dreams through singing competitions. On the one hand, viewers develop the impression that achieving celebrity is easy, but rare, similar to winning the lottery—while your chances of winning the lottery are slim, all you have to do to win is buy a ticket. Katherine Meizel spoke with several people who auditioned in early rounds of *American Idol*. Her interviews chronicle the belief that auditioning for *Idol* results in "a seemingly easy path to fame and fortune."[34] While *Idol* winners in early seasons did win substantial sums, these contestants express a narrow view of "ease." I observed this in my interviews where auditionees had a "can't hurt to try" mentality. Catherine, a 20-year-old pop vocalist, postulates, "Most people here are good, all it takes is a bit of luck." On the other hand, the ideology is imbued with concepts of hard work. Junhow Wei terms the ideology that inspires singers to audition for talent shows "meritocratic ideals" because "contestants emphasize that anybody could potentially find success through the show, despite their regular Joe backgrounds. Furthermore, contestants attribute success on the show specifically to individuals' vocal talent."[35] Meritocracy implies that people are deserving of the time that they put into preparations for a position. Singing talent shows are grueling and take significant work to participate. Furthermore, any talented singer spends countless hours learning to sing, dance, and negotiate the music business. The idea that contestants win based on merit structures the entire show.

In order to increase viewership, show producers construct narratives about the contestants. Matthew Stahl observes that the biographical information about the contestants helps develop what he calls an "authentication" narrative. Music reality shows use "bio- and autobiographical vignettes" where contestants "are typically placed in highly scripted contexts in which they are expected to perform themselves."[36] By placing the contestants in normal/everyday situations with relatable backgrounds, Stahl contends authentication narratives help to make fans connect with idols.[37] Authentication narratives can be found in human-interest stories for sporting events, as well. In order to reach more viewers, television producers for sporting events, most notably the Olympics, go to great lengths to construct narratives that allow the events to reach a broader audience. To develop these narratives, part of *The Voice* audition process includes a 10-page questionnaire with 56 questions.[38] These questions include banal informative questions ("What genre of music do you sing?"), probing personal questions ("What obstacles, if any, have you overcome to pursue your love of singing?" "Are you in a serious romantic relationship? … If no, why not? … If yes, please tell us about it …"), occupational questions ("What do you do for a living?"), and attitudinal questions ("Why are you the one to beat?" "How do you deal with harsh criticism?"). While most of the 56 questions could lead to developing authentication narratives, those questions relating to their personal lives and occupations provide the richest authenticating content. For instance, much has been written about Kelly Clarkson's rise from waitress to American Idol—on the other hand, working as a well-paid white-collar employee would not have the same Horatio Alger story. Earlier, I mentioned KJ, who could not decide whether to go to the next round of *America's Got Talent*. His story would make the perfect human-interest story for *The Voice*. He coaches a nonprofit basketball team for at-risk youth. The kids mean so much to KJ that he would be willing to miss his dreams of being a celebrity to work with these kids. As I heard this story, I could imagine *The Voice* directors cutting to a clip of him coaching, and then having the kids wishing him luck as he goes on stage to perform. These stories are made for TV moments that can allow audience members to bond with the contestant in a way that can proffer votes throughout the contest. Former contestant, Ddendyl, described to *The Washington Post* that producers loved her dad, so the show flew her parents to the audition, and made her dad bring his bagpipes. While Ddendyl's dad's bagpipe skills are unrelated to Ddendyl's talent to win the show, his performance (both in his personality and bagpiping) contained the potential to increase viewership. The questionnaire provides opportunities for early round judges to establish reasons beyond a singer's voice to advance them to the next stages.

However, *The Voice*'s questionnaire not only produces content to increase viewership, but also questions potential contestants about their belief in the ideology of getting signed. In the questionnaire, the most relevant question to this project asks: "How would a record deal change your life?" This question is significant for two reasons. First, it implies that contestants think record deals can change their lives (who would answer, "It won't"?). Producers do not inquire whether contestants think a record contract *could* change their lives, but rather they assume that record contracts *will* change contestants' lives. Furthermore, the underlying assumption is that contestants will respond that record contracts will *affirmatively* change their lives. There is no context for how record contracts will change contestants' lives; producers do not provide a picture of what record contracts do for/to recording artists. It is unclear how producers use this information. Are contestants disqualified if they say that a record contract will ruin their lives? Probably not because in order for a contestant to audition, they already believe that the prize of the show (a record contract) is the ultimate goal for an aspiring singer.

Second, the question about how a record deal will change their lives makes these contestants vocal proponents of the ideology of getting signed, which creates a force to propagate the ideology. By having contestants describe on paper how a record contract will affect their lives, producers begin the process of allowing contestants to shape their message about record contracts. "The contestant who sells his or her voice … for the chance at a 'break,' instead of perhaps financially satisfying remuneration, must believe in the value of fame itself as a commodity. It is fame as a reified concept, and not the labor that leads to it, whose value appears to have been naturalized by the hopeful singers."[39] The question sends a signal to contestants that they are expected to think and articulate a reason why they *need* a record contract. Incorporating a narrative about their desire for a record contract into their self-authenticating narratives allows the record contract to be at the forefront of their minds when they speak on camera. The question is a way for contestants to speak, seemingly unprompted, about record contracts because one goal of reality television is to create scripted dialogue without a script.[40] As I interviewed aspiring singers and their friends and family, it was clear that the main reason why they wanted to audition was to receive a contract. Not many people I spoke with understood how record contracts work, but the desire for a record contract was deep seeded. Two singers mentioned that record contracts would bring them "financial stability." They believe that record contracts are a means to wealth, and they obtain this belief from what they see on television. Ensuring that current contestants believe in record contracts ensures that they can construct that belief among the next generation of aspiring singers watching at home.

People do more than watch the show for pure entertainment value because future singing competition show contestants watch as well. While some singers may watch because they already have the dream of signing a record contract, others may develop the dream from watching the show. As they watch, they learn what it means to be a recording artist. Not only do aspiring singers watching at home learn the affective aspects of musical performance taught by the coaches, but they also learn the ultimate goal is signing a record contract. Furthermore, Wei spoke with early round contestants of *American Idol* and found that many of them were encouraged to pursue music through watching the show. "Contestants' friends and family did not simply tell them to audition, but also helped them imagine themselves succeeding in the competition and gave them confidence when they had doubts."[41] I observed this when I attended *The Voice* auditions. In one instance, I spoke with the sister and cousin of a singer. The sister told me that they always watched the show, but her brother had never watched it. He has a degree in music, and they encouraged him to audition. They told him that an easy way to receive a record contract would be to audition and win. *The Voice*'s plot inscribes the ideology of getting signed to a record contract into the minds of viewers, but this inscription is effective because most viewers already know that a record contract is the marker of success for musicians.

While coaches actively teach contestants about performance, they neglect to teach contestants about the music business. Coaches teach contestants in two main areas: voice and presence. Voice involves giving contestants vocal lessons: i.e., instructing pitch, timbre, range, breathing, etc. Presence consists of teaching contestants how to look on stage: dance, position of microphone, posture, clothing style, hairstyle, etc. These mechanisms are about the performance affect that the contestants present on stage, and they are the types of instruction that viewers at home can understand because whether they are aspiring singers or not, the audience wants to watch the performance. The mother of one auditionee mentioned that this role of the coach was the specific reason her daughter, Jacquelyn, decided to audition. She possessed the hope that the coaches could teach Jacquelyn to be a star. In this hope, she meant these two affective points of training. However, what contestants and viewers could learn most from coaches would be the conditions under which music is produced; this is the aspect that they do not mention on the show. Coaches do not teach what is in a record contract, what a contract does, the role of support personnel in their careers, how to manage their support personnel, how to get gigs, when to seek a lawyer, etc. These may seem like disconnected concepts to becoming a pop star, but they are quintessential things that any pop star would have to know to negotiate their everyday lived reality—especially if they want to avoid being taken advantage of by others in the music business. Coaches hold a pivotal position of authority on these issues because they undoubtedly "made it," and their perspectives would be valuable to the contestants and viewers at home. However, the absence of instruction on the music *business* demonstrates the ideological role *The Voice* plays in creating the desire for a record contract.

Discussing ideology is only useful insofar as we think about what ideology conceals. By watching *The Voice*, viewers consume the ideology of getting signed, but they do not see the social relations of production. Not only are discussions about contracts with lawyers that happen behind the scenes absent from the show, the contestants sign a legal contract stating that they will not disclose business matters. In the "Grant of Rights, Release, Confidentiality and Arbitration Agreement," contestants agree that they will not disclose "Producer's business methods and practices" because such disclosure would cause "substantial and irreparable injury" to the producer of *The Voice*. A disclosure would result in "**liquidated damages, and not as a penalty, the sum of Five Hundred Thousand United States Dollars (US $500,000.00) per breach**" (emphasis in original).[42] While teaching contestants about music and television business practices could be one of the most enlightening aspects of *The Voice*, the void of such practices is not a product of oversight or a perception that audiences will tune out, but rather, it is a decision made by the producer of the show to hide business practices. If contestants, who work without pay, disclose the very work conditions they labor under, they will be fined $500,000 per offense. Ideology works to obscure the real conditions under which people labor.

Furthermore, the ideology of getting signed becomes embedded in the American Dream because the show awards winners with glitz and glamor for the "hard work" that they put into their craft. Here, the American Dream is the idea that anyone can pick themselves up by their bootstraps and become rich and famous. In Katherine Meizel's account of *American Idol*, she establishes that both the successful and the unsuccessful contestants fulfill the American Dream by achieving fame through the show.

> American understandings of fame intertwine perceptions of ordinariness and extraordinariness. This dichotomy is typically imploded in American Dream discourses of possibility, of the potential mutability of identity and status, but is simultaneously reinforced in the social distance implicit between the star and the fan. During the course of an *American Idol*

> season, that distance is ostensibly narrowed as the boundaries that separate producer, consumer, and product/star are blurred. Anyone (within a certain age group) may audition, anyone may make the transition from the living room couch to the living rooms of millions ... In this apparent democratic redistribution of cultural power, the ordinary and the extraordinary, failure and success, can be assigned comparable value.[43]

Contestants must be ordinary, they could be any of us, at the same time that their performance ability has to far exceed the capabilities of everyday Americans. Scholars variously describe this as "democratization of opportunities"[44] or "democratic authenticity"[45] because anyone has the ability to compete on television talent shows. Contestants do not have to be the children of rich and/or famous people to have a chance at winning the show—unless that will help with the show's ratings.[46] This sends the message to viewers that they too could audition and become famous. Even when *The Voice* viewers are not singers, they receive the message that the American Dream is alive and well. Audience members and music consumers advance the ideology of getting signed because of its affinity to the American Dream. People watching *The Voice* at home understand that hard work and determination are supposed to bring success. Being able to observe the American Dream when a contestant wins reaffirms a belief that the American Dream exists. Discourse about the American Dream places the ideology of signing record contracts within a broader dominant ideology within American society.

Conclusion

What young aspiring singers learn from *The Voice* is that it is okay to work hard for no pay for the chance to earn less than the value they create. While contestants work long hours for no pay, viewers believe they do so for the ultimate chance of success in the recording industry: a record contract. At no time in the show does the dominant view become disturbed, but rather, *The Voice* acts as an echo chamber for the importance of record contracts. However, record contracts remain the mechanism through which record labels exploit musicians. *The*

Voice articulates and reifies the ideology of getting signed to a national audience.

On the one hand, this is what Hollywood does: sells glitz and glamor to an audience. People watch *The Voice* to shut out their everyday toil. As Adorno and Horkheimer contend, the Culture Industry takes the role of deadening our senses to the mind-numbing work we do in the "factory."[47] On the other hand, our alienation from Hollywood workers blinds us to the fact that they work under the same conditions as everyone else. However, we take enjoyment from their exploitation, so we further blind ourselves to the conditions under which they work. In fact, their exploitation becomes unavoidable for dream fulfillment. Even when people become aware of the working conditions, they think the exploitation still provides tangible benefits. People say things like, "It is okay that the show doesn't pay contestants because they get publicity" or "contestants are nobodies, so they are interchangeable." These are the comments I hear when I speak with people about my research. People develop this rationalization on their own; the show's host, Carson Daly, does not say this on the show because it does not need to be said to the audience.

The Voice is the perfect vessel of the ideology of getting signed. Contestants believe that signing a record contract will change their life for the better. When they appear on the show, this ideology exudes their presence. People consume this ideology at home while producers conceal the reality of the show's labor circumstances. More specifically, a non-disclosure agreement that contestants sign to be on the show conceals the labor practices. Viewers can imagine their dream of performing on television and winning a contract without realizing the nature of the contestants' exploitation.

Notes

1. Trust, "Auditioning for 'The Voice.'"
2. According to The Voice's website accessed 10:10 a.m. September 18, 2017.
3. Yahr, "'The Voice' Star Ddendyl on Life after Reality TV, and How the NBC Singing Show Really Operates."

4. Melnick, "Reality Radio."
5. Here, there is a class difference between types of contestants. Not all contestants attend the Open Call Auditions because the show's producers invite some contestants to the first round in Los Angeles through recruitment efforts. I discuss this more below.
6. Gill and Pratt, "Precarity and Cultural Work: In the Social Factory? Immaterial Labour, Precariousness and Cultural Work," 3.
7. Culture Industry is a term developed by Max Horkheimer and Theodor Adorno that signifies the industrial character of the modern production of music and film. They use the term to distinguish the production of culture from the term "mass culture." They resist the term mass culture because it connotes a relationship to the masses as if it emerges from the masses. Rather, mass culture emerges from the corporate boardroom, and Horkheimer and Adorno desired to emphasize this side of cultural production. Horkheimer and Adorno, "The Culture Industry: Enlightenment as Mass Deception."
8. Chandler, "All Work and No Pay."
9. Chandler.
10. Coincidentally, most musicians are freelance, even superstars, because of the structure of record contracts.
11. Peterson, *Creating Country Music: Fabricating Authenticity.*
12. Ross, "The New Geography of Work Power to the Precarious?" 34.
13. Marx, *Capital.*
14. Marx.
15. Grazian, "Neoliberalism and the Realities of Reality Television."
16. Jian and Liu, "'Democratic Entertainment' Commodity and Unpaid Labor of Reality TV," 532.
17. Hardt and Negri, *Multitude: War and Democracy in the Age of Empire*, 131.
18. Marx, "The German Ideology."
19. Skinner, "Life After NBC's The Voice Can Be a Lonely Reality for Its Contestants"; Yahr, "'The Voice' Star Ddendyl on Life after Reality TV, and How the NBC Singing Show Really Operates."
20. Stahl, "A Moment Like This: American Idol and Narratives of Meritocracy."
21. http://www1.salary.com/CA/Los-Angeles/Camera-Operator-Salary.html accessed September 21, 2017.
22. Jian and Liu, "'Democratic Entertainment' Commodity and Unpaid Labor of Reality TV," 533.
23. Arditi, "Downloading Is Killing Music"; Arditi, *ITake-Over.*

24. Flanagan, "Grammys 2015."
25. van Es, "Social TV and the Participation Dilemma in NBC's The Voice," 112.
26. "Participant Agreement, Release and Arbitration Provision" from Season 9 of *The Voice.*
27. van Es, "Social TV and the Participation Dilemma in NBC's The Voice," 113.
28. Skinner, "Life After NBC's The Voice Can Be a Lonely Reality for Its Contestants."
29. Turner, "The Mass Production of Celebrity," 155.
30. "Life After NBC's The Voice Can Be a Lonely Reality for Its Contestants."
31. Clawson, "Masculinity and Skill Acquisition in the Adolescent Rock Band," 104.
32. Jian and Liu, "'Democratic Entertainment' Commodity and Unpaid Labor of Reality TV," 525.
33. Jian and Liu, 525.
34. Meizel, "Making the Dream a Reality (Show)," 484.
35. Wei, "I'm the Next American Idol," 9.
36. Stahl, "A Moment Like This: American Idol and Narratives of Meritocracy," 218.
37. Stahl, 219.
38. "Participant Agreement, Release and Arbitration Provision" from Season 9 of *The Voice.*
39. Meizel, "Making the Dream a Reality (Show)," 483–84.
40. Kellner, *Media Spectacle*; Grazian, "Neoliberalism and the Realities of Reality Television."
41. Wei, "I'm the Next American Idol," 10.
42. From "Participant Agreement, Release and Arbitration Provision" from Season 9 of *The Voice.* "I understand that, in connection with my participation in the casting selection process and potential participation in connection with the Program, information may be disclosed to or obtained by me, pursuant to my communications with Producer or otherwise, including, without limitation, information regarding the Program's selection process, identities of potential or actual participants or other on-air talent participating in the Program, Producer's personnel, the content of the Program, Producer's business methods and practices, and other confidential and/or proprietary information of Producer and Distribution Entities (collectively, the "Confidential Information"). I agree that I will not, directly or indirectly, verbally or otherwise, at anytime [sic] (whether

or not I ultimately participate in the Program) disclose, reveal, publish, disseminate or cause to be disclosed, revealed, published or disseminated ("Disclosure"), any Confidential Information to any individual or entity. I understand that Disclosure of the Confidential Information constitutes a material breach of this Agreement and will cause Producer, and the Distribution Entities substantial and irreparable injury and accordingly, **I agree that in the event of any Disclosure by me, I will be liable to Producer and Distribution Entities, and must pay to Producer and the Distribution Entities collectively, as liquidated damages, and not as a penalty, the sum of Five Hundred Thousand United States Dollars (US $500,000.00) per breach, which amount represents the result of a reasonable endeavor by Producer and the Distribution Entities and me to ascertain the fair average compensation for any harm that Producer and the Distribution Entities will sustain as the result of such Disclosure.**"

43. Meizel, "Making the Dream a Reality (Show)," 482–83.
44. Jian and Liu, "'Democratic Entertainment' Commodity and Unpaid Labor of Reality TV," 530.
45. Meizel, "Making the Dream a Reality (Show)," 483.
46. Walsh, "Watch Candace Cameron Bure's Daughter Audition for The Voice."
47. Horkheimer and Adorno, *Dialectic of Enlightenment*.

Bibliography

Arditi, David. "Downloading Is Killing Music: The Recording Industry's Piracy Panic Narrative." Edited by Victor Sarafian and Rosemary Findley. *Civilisations*, The State of the Music Industry, 63, no. 1 (July 2014): 13–32.

———. *ITake-Over: The Recording Industry in the Digital Era*. Lanham, MD: Rowman & Littlefield Publishers, 2014.

Chandler, David. "All Work and No Pay: Creative Industries Freelancers Are Exploited." *The Guardian*, May 18, 2017, sec. Guardian Small Business Network. http://www.theguardian.com/small-business-network/2017/may/18/all-work-and-no-pay-creative-industries-freelancers-are-exploited.

Clawson, Mary Ann. "Masculinity and Skill Acquisition in the Adolescent Rock Band." *Popular Music* 18, no. 1 (1999): 99–114.

Es, Karin van. "Social TV and the Participation Dilemma in NBC's The Voice." *Television & New Media* 17, no. 2 (February 1, 2016): 108–23. https://doi.org/10.1177/1527476415616191.

Flanagan, Andrew. "Grammys 2015: Recording Academy's Neil Portnow Uses Speech to Lobby on Streaming Payouts." *Billboard*, February 8, 2015. http://www.billboard.com/articles/events/grammys-2015/6465670/grammys-2015-neil-portnow-streaming-payouts.

Gill, Rosalind, and Andy Pratt. "Precarity and Cultural Work: In the Social Factory? Immaterial Labour, Precariousness and Cultural Work." *Theory, Culture & Society* 25, no. 7–8 (2008): 1–30.

Grazian, David. "Neoliberalism and the Realities of Reality Television." *Contexts* 9, no. 2 (2010): 68–71. https://doi.org/10.2307/41960112.

Hardt, Michael, and Antonio Negri. *Multitude: War and Democracy in the Age of Empire*. New York: The Penguin Press, 2004.

Horkheimer, Max, and Theodor W. Adorno. *Dialectic of Enlightenment*. New York: Herder and Herder, 1972.

———. "The Culture Industry: Enlightenment as Mass Deception." In *Dialectic of Enlightenment*, xvii, 258. New York: Herder and Herder, 1972.

Jian, Miaoju, and Chang-de Liu. "'Democratic Entertainment' Commodity and Unpaid Labor of Reality TV: A Preliminary Analysis of China's Supergirl." *Inter-Asia Cultural Studies* 10, no. 4 (December 2009): 524–43. https://doi.org/10.1080/14649370903166382.

Kellner, Douglas. *Media Spectacle*. 1 edition. London ; New York: Routledge, 2003.

Marx, Karl. *Capital: Volume 1: A Critique of Political Economy*. New York, NY: Penguin Classics, 1992.

———. "The German Ideology." In *Karl Marx: Selected Writings*, edited by David McLellan, 2nd ed., 175–208. Oxford and New York: Oxford University Press, 2000.

Meizel, Katherine. "Making the Dream a Reality (Show): The Celebration of Failure in American Idol." *Popular Music & Society* 32, no. 4 (October 2009): 475–88. https://doi.org/10.1080/03007760802217725.

Melnick, Ross. "Reality Radio: Remediating the Radio Contest Genre in Major Bowes' Amateur Hour Films." *Film History* 23, no. 3 (2011): 331–47. https://doi.org/10.2979/filmhistory.23.3.331.

Peterson, Richard A. *Creating Country Music: Fabricating Authenticity*. Chicago: University of Chicago Press, 1997.

Ross, Andrew. "The New Geography of Work Power to the Precarious?" *Theory, Culture & Society* 25, no. 7–8 (December 1, 2008): 31–49.
Skinner, Paige. "Life After NBC's The Voice Can Be a Lonely Reality for Its Contestants." *Dallas Observer*, January 26, 2016. http://www.dallasobserver.com/music/life-after-nbcs-the-voice-can-be-a-lonely-reality-for-its-contestants-7963258.
Trust, Gary. "Auditioning for 'The Voice': One Contestant's Experience." *Billboard*, May 8, 2012. http://www.billboard.com/biz/articles/news/tv-film/1097035/auditioning-for-the-voice-one-contestants-experience.
Turner, Graeme. "The Mass Production of Celebrity: 'Celetoids', Reality TV and the 'Demotic Turn.'" *International Journal of Cultural Studies* 9, no. 2 (June 1, 2006): 153–65. https://doi.org/10.1177/1367877906064028.
Walsh, Lara. "Watch Candace Cameron Bure's Daughter Audition for The Voice." *InStyle.Com*, October 4, 2016. http://www.instyle.com/news/candace-cameron-bure-daughter-natasha-voice-audition.
Wei, Junhow. "'I'm the Next American Idol': Cooling Out, Accounts, and Perseverance at Reality Talent Show Auditions." *Symbolic Interaction* 39, no. 1 (February 1, 2016): 3–25. https://doi.org/10.1002/symb.206.
Yahr, Emily. "'The Voice' Star Ddendyl on Life after Reality TV, and How the NBC Singing Show Really Operates." *Washington Post*, May 20, 2014, Digital edition, sec. Arts and Entertainment. https://www.washingtonpost.com/news/arts-and-entertainment/wp/2014/05/20/the-voice-star-ddendyl-on-life-after-reality-tv-and-how-the-nbc-singing-show-really-operates/.

8

Conning the Dream: Musical Showcase as Confidence Game

Record labels are not the only entities that actively exploit the ideology of getting signed. The recording industry is saturated with companies and people who aim to make money from musicians' dreams. A few schemes exist that appeal to aspiring musicians' dreams to sign record contracts, and they come in varying degrees of legitimacy. From shady agents who take fees without delivering results to companies that help artists distribute their music online, from managers charging high rates with little return to *The Voice* (discussed in Chapter 7), people and businesses populate the recording industry who utilize capitalism to extract a profit from the labor of musicians. At times, these shady practices often resemble a confidence game.

A long tradition exists in describing sociological phenomena as confidence games (or con games).[1] As Erving Goffman defines a confidence game, "the con, as its practitioners call it—is a way of obtaining money under false pretenses by the exercise of fraud and deceit."[2] In "The Production of Popular Music as Confidence Game: The Case of the Chicago Blues," David Grazian applies the theory of the con game to the Chicago blues scene.[3] He maintains "the confidence game has long served as a metaphor for impression management and other types of

D. Arditi, *Getting Signed*,
https://doi.org/10.1007/978-3-030-44587-4_8

deceptive interaction rituals."[4] Grazian presents the blues music performance aesthetic in Chicago as one that stretches beyond a well-crafted performance to a con game. Selling each blues performance as authentic, Grazian argues, requires a system of social relations that ultimately satisfies the unwitting tourist (i.e., mark). Ultimately, the successfully conned mark becomes an accomplice in the system when they return home and tell stories about the authenticity of blues to their friends and families. While Grazian's case study of authenticity in the Chicago blues scene demonstrates the way a system cons tourists into believing they experienced authentic Chicago blues, these low-stake con games ultimately deliver the feeling of experiencing "real" Chicago blues to the victims. To experience authentic blues, Grazian says, there is a "desire among victims to be swayed by the production."[5] This desire to be swayed translated into the aspiring musician's side of the music industry is the ideology of getting signed; aspiring musicians want to sign record contracts, so they willingly believe the unbelievable for the chance to make it in music. Whereas the Chicago blues case does little harm and functions as an analogy, the artist showcase system that I describe in this chapter victimizes aspiring musicians by enticing them to spend significant cash for a dream that has little material reward for the winner.

In this chapter, I present the example of a musician's showcase and the way this specific showcase provides a con game for willing marks. However, these marks are not tourists who are willing to be taken for a ride in the interest of experiencing "authentic" blues, but rather the marks are the aspiring musicians themselves. Their willingness to pursue the dream of signing record label contracts opens them to forms of exploitation. This chapter proceeds with a description of a musical showcase I attended in Dallas, Texas. Second, I provide a brief analysis of the performers that I observed at the showcase. Third, I explore how the competition aspect of Coast 2 Coast LIVE helps hook aspiring musicians through the ideology of getting signed. Finally, I provide connections between this specific musical showcase and other forms of exploitation in the music industry and capitalism.

The Music Showcase

By happenchance I stumbled upon a confidence game that directly exploits the dream of young musicians who want record labels to notice and to sign them. Throughout my research, I attended a number of showcases and competitions that provided opportunities for musicians to perform in front of label Artist & Repertoire (A&R), booking agents, managers, talent scouts, and the general public. To find these events, I would search Google for "showcases" in various locations that I would visit. Some of these showcases, such as those for the Association for Performing Arts Professionals, the Folk Alliance International, and the National Association for Campus Activities, charge acts a registration fee to perform or have a table at their conferences. However, people who do booking at venues across the country attend these events, looking for up-and-coming talent to book at their venues. They hold auditions (usually acts submit press packages complete with audio and video recordings) to decide who to invite to perform, and these participants know they will be in front of people who can provide them with gigs. Since this is a typical arrangement, charging acts to perform at a showcase does not surprise me, even though I still find the practice exploitative and punitive (in the sense that it is aimed at limiting entrants). In this chapter, I explore an event that I attended in Dallas, Texas, where a company (Coast 2 Coast LIVE) charged artists to perform with no tangible benefits to the performers.

When I ran a search for "artist showcase Dallas, TX," I was very happy to find an event in my area. The event was "Coast 2 Coast Live Artist Showcase," which bills itself as the "largest artist showcase in the world."[6] The website claims that "celebrity judges" would judge aspiring artists, and throughout the website, they claim that this is a chance for artists to perform in front of label personnel, DJs, producers, and other music industry gatekeepers. I purchased a ticket online, and I looked forward to the event at Struggling Joe's Bar in Dallas, Texas. After receiving the ticket, I did no further research on "Coast 2 Coast LIVE"[7] until after the show, aside from a brief skim through the website. All that I discovered ahead of time was that artists registered, which included submitting a recording to attend the event. However, I found there is far more than meets the eye on the website hidden behind an elaborate system in which you receive more details after you submit audio materials.

When I attended the event, it was a hot summer evening in Dallas. The show was supposed to start at 9 p.m. I arrived at 8:30 p.m. thinking that I could go in early and begin speaking with aspiring artists. However, when I arrived there were only a handful of people standing around outside, waiting to get into the locked venue. There was a cast of characters waiting outside with one person, Jordan, promoting his cousin's music by stuffing a phone in his hat at his forehead, so everyone could hear and see his cousin's SoundCloud page. Jordan would later announce that the "Coast 2 Coast models" would arrive at 10 p.m.—"the most beautiful girls you've seen, and they're working girls" (no models arrived). Some people were tailgating across the street listening to music while they waited. At 9 p.m., Little M&M, the host, came out to ask everyone to line up, with artists in the front of the line. This was a surprise to me because I assumed that performers would have earlier access to the venue, as is the case for every show I have ever played or watched. At that point, there was a crowd, and they made us wait an additional five minutes before they began permitting people to enter the venue.

While waiting in line, I spoke with people around me, all of which were there to support friends and family. They seemed genuinely excited that their aspiring musician had a chance to be discovered at this show. People waiting to be audience members talked about their aspiring vocalists with other people. There was comradery as many of them were in the same position hoping that someone would notice their own aspiring musician. This contrasted with the uncomfortable club feel where organizers intentionally created a line to appear as if Struggling Joe's Bar was the happening place in town. Inside, the props discussed below and the DJs fronting (to put up a façade)[8] made people feel like they needed to be quiet. Outside, everyone talked to each other about how they were excited to see their friends/family perform. As we waited, someone began taking pictures and video of the line outside the venue. Later I would figure out the photographer was the evening's DJ. It turned out that the line had less to do with passersby than for online marketing about the showcases.

As the bouncer finally allowed the crowd to enter, he took our printed tickets or acknowledged our tickets on our phones. It surprised me that they did not scan tickets. Audience members could have printed any number of copies of tickets, and no one would have noticed. Then again, I do not think they were concerned about the $10 cover charge, which offered multiple ways of circumventing on the website (e.g., anyone could have registered as "Media" or "DJ" for a free ticket). I would later learn that the admittance cover was a pittance to the revenue they would earn from the aspiring artists. The atmosphere at the door was a cog in the confidence game, where the bouncer and the line of paying audience members unconsciously acted as ropers who helped to encourage marks of the game's legitimacy.

Upon entering, I noticed that artists lined up to register with Little M&M on stage. The stage itself had a table with a black tablecloth where Little M&M sat in front of a laptop. Behind the table was a backdrop with dozens of "Coast 2 Coast LIVE" logos and a large one centered. Three microphones lined the front of the stage, and a makeshift DJ booth on a table with a black tablecloth sat next to the backdrop. The aesthetics of the event had an air of cheap professionalism that was enough to look like a legitimate operation to the unwitting mark, but still looked like the faux decorations you would see at a cheap prom after party. In the corner to the right of the stage, "Coast 2 Coast LIVE" set up a media backdrop with professional lights and photography equipment to interview performers following their performances—a façade to make the event look better for social media pictures and videos. After the artists registered, Little M&M gave them a lanyard with a badge. While these badges provided the vocalists with credentials to perform, more importantly they signified importance for the aspiring stars. The materiality of the badges added legitimacy to the operation by connoting an established business like all-access passes for artists at large concerts and festivals. Performers treasured these badges as a marker that they "made it." The badge gave performers elite status, but no one once asked a performer for their badges when it was their turn to perform; this struck me as a mechanism to pull the marks in with an aesthetic of professionalism.

It took me a while to realize that, along with their CDs, the artists were handing the host (Little M&M) money as part of the registration process. This struck me as strange to exchange money at registration on stage in front of the audience, but not out of the ordinary because the practice of pay-to-play is common in the music industry. However, I was unable to tell how much money was changing hands. While artists registered, DJ Lose, the evening's DJ, played popular music and took pictures of the artists and crowd. Registration lasted until 9:20 p.m., but the host did not rush to get the show started. The lethargy paid off as one more artist showed up at 9:40 p.m. to register to perform and, most importantly, to pay. Still, the show that was supposed to hit (i.e., start) at 9 p.m. did not begin until after 10 p.m. During the interlude between registration and performance, DJ Lose tried to "turn up" the crowd—hearing the 40-something DJ use contemporary slang struck me as odd. DJ Lose punctuated his beats with exhortations for "21 and up hit that bar, get that drink, leave that tip… if you're underage, get that soda and water … If you livin', put your hands in the air." At this point, I felt as though I was at some weird middle school dance with a struggling DJ trying to be cool as everyone compulsorily put their hands in the air, but no one seemed ready to turn up.

As 10 p.m. approached, DJ Tang, one of the night's judges, arrived in head-to-toe high-end Dallas Cowboys gear. His demeanor gave an air of importance like the one an important person in the music industry may display. However, judging by his own social media presence, his only gig is his monthly jaunts as a judge for Coast 2 Coast, sometimes DJing the event himself. At the point when DJ Tang and Little M&M sat on stage waiting to start the show, I began having a strong feeling that this was a confidence game. Finally, the second judge, DJ Lift, arrived just before 10 p.m. Again, DJ Lift's social media and web presence do not show him to be actively gigging. In fact, the website links on his social media pages no longer worked. The DJs were part of the confidence game and played the part of a "shill."[9] While Coast 2 Coast LIVE sold these judges as music industry powerbrokers, they too operated from a marginalized position in the recording industry as likely musicians with grandiose dreams who all but achieved a record contract.

When Little M&M started the showcase, he laid out some rules. He rattled off his four rules like a seasoned professional—a skill, I learned later, he developed from explaining the rules three to five times per week.

First, Little M&M wants artists to be ready when it is their turn. Despite the fact that these aspiring artists just handed over cash to perform, they only receive one shot at performing in the specified lineup. The rigidity with which he runs the show demonstrates a lack of empathy for musicians who dream of making it big. They provide him with a paycheck, but he will not wait. This contempt for the performers does not translate into his larger point below about networking because networking and mentorship require the people in positions of authority to recognize the varied needs of performers and help instruct them.

Second, Little M&M adamantly told the artists they could only perform one song—"if the beat changes, your song is over. We know what one song sounds like. Don't do some long acapella intro," he urged. I find this highly problematic as those who know about music know that music changes can be aesthetic tools in popular music songs: from the Latin dance break in Will Smith's "Welcome to Miami" to the key change in Michael Jackson's "Man in the Mirror" or Kendrick Lamar's movement-esque tracks like "XXX" to the Bossa Nova/Jazz transition in "On Green Dolphin Street." His reductive view of music embraced the lack of creativity Adorno and Horkheimer derided as "ready-made clichés to be slotted in anywhere."[10] They go on to claim that with pop music, "once the trained ear has the first notes of the hit song, it can guess what is coming and feel flattered when it does come."[11] This is Little M&M's point, he knows what popular music is supposed to sound like, and he will not accept deviations from the norm. Since this is a showcase competition, it also means that the Culture Industry's norms (i.e., conventions) must be advanced if the contestants would like to win. Rachel Skaggs observed similar rules in her analysis of aspiring songwriters at Nashville's Song Club where songwriters could only perform one chorus and one verse.[12] As Skaggs observed, the standardization helps establish routine and rhythm among participants. By asking contestants to stick to his rules, M&M demonstrates to the crowd that he is a veteran of this game and he has seen these attempts to gain more time on stage. While I do not mean to overstate the role that Little M&M and Coast 2 Coast LIVE play as gatekeepers, every incantation of a set of rules helps to socially construct norms and discipline the mark[13]—people at these showcases internalize a limited view of the form of a popular music song.

Next, Little M&M was concerned especially with entourages insisting that "if they not on the record, keep their ass off the stage [laughing]." His derision inhibits creativity among the contestants because they cannot change what they do from what they recorded. It also may keep everyone from discovering the next star if they can't access the stage. This point seems to compound the previous point about song changes. The best performers bring spontaneity to their performances, but the Coast 2 Coast LIVE crew demonstrates little desire to discover the best performers under such rigid rules.

Finally, Little M&M linked networking to egos by stating, "If you're here, you want to make it and you haven't yet. Check your egos at the door. Be supportive of others. They tryin' to do the same thing you are." This was his strongest plea for the passion of performers. However, it is delivered with a certain irony because those on stage possess outsized egos. In a way, Little M&M articulates a logic that says that people that make it in the music industry can have a large ego (e.g., Kanye West), but those who pursue the ideology of getting signed must demonstrate humility. Everyone performing at the showcase must demonstrate humbleness and support each other, but the authorities running the show can demonstrate their self-admiration. The admonition to network was a theme throughout the night, but no one demonstrated that the means of networking leads to any perceived goals of the performers. At the end of the night, Little M&M returned to the theme of networking:

> If you're here, you want to make it. You need to network. Meet the other artists. Add me on twitter. Send me an email – my email is … If you don't email me, you're not serious and you don't take yourself seriously. Get at me.

While Little M&M berates the performers to network to demonstrate their seriousness, the event itself demonstrates an utter lack of empathy. Rather, Coast 2 Coast LIVE cultivates an elaborate confidence game to entice willing marks (aspiring artists) to be professionals and be discovered by professionals while knowing that no one is at the showcase venue to discover acts.

Little M&M's exhortation to network runs counter to the overall aims and position of the showcase, but it also runs counter to other areas of performance that favor mentorship. While musicians, especially men musicians, resist acknowledging mentorship, mentorship is an important part of a musician's development.[14] For instance, Jooyoung Lee discusses in *Blowin' Up* the role of mentors at the open mic sessions at Project Blowed in Los Angeles, California. While Project Blowed possesses strict rules about open mic performances, organizers use these rules to give emcees a positive platform on which to hone their rhyming skills. Those rules, as outlined by Lee, include:

> Rappers were expected to perform a polished piece of music. This was where you got critical feedback on original music. And this crowd, which was mostly other rappers, should be critical of performers. Nobody should get a free pass. This was part of Project Blowed's legacy as a tough training ground in the underground hip hop world. Before turning to the next performer, Trenseta asked us again, "How do you expect to get better if nobody tells you that you wack?"[15]

Specifically, if the crowd thinks a particular performer is wack at Project Blowed, they respectfully chant, "Please pass the mic!" This struck me as a more gracious way to inform performers they need to work than the tradition at Amateur Night at the Apollo Theater in New York City where the crowd boos talent that they do not like—bad acts even get a siren and a clown drags them off with a cane at the Apollo. In contrast, Little M&M had a rule that you should not boo the performers because he said that he wanted to foster respect and collegiality. However, the only feedback given to performers at Coast 2 Coast LIVE is the raw score they receive at the end of the night, which does not provide information on specific categories, like a rubric. In Skaggs' account of rejection for songwriters, there is a similar disdain for explaining why the music publisher "passed" on a song.[16] Coast 2 Coast LIVE is not a venue where performers develop their craft for future growth, but rather the showcase creates an atmosphere of competition, posturing (i.e., fronting), unsubstantiated hope, and exploitation.

The Performers

The musicians performing at Coast 2 Coast LIVE could benefit from the mentorship experienced at places such as Project Blowed because in my observation, none of the performers struck me as having any potential to succeed in the music industry. Everyone universally rapped or sang over their own vocals. Partly, this is a product of the venue, where the performer is expected to provide the DJ with their backing track. However, experienced performers know that they should provide the DJ with a recording of the song without their vocals. While this says nothing about their capacities as performers, it speaks volumes to their preparedness to "make it," or even win the showcase. Every emcee also sang despite the fact that only one or two of them could carry a tune. I thought that there would be a lot to discuss with regard to the performers, but their performances did not demonstrate much potential or talent—from the rappers who could not keep up with their tracks to the performers who cussed every-other word without a message. Judges gave no performer any indication that their performance could be improved nor how they could improve it. In fact, there was not much communication between performers in the crowd, nonetheless between performers and the Coast 2 Coast crew.

The only singer who I thought could really perform and whose song had a conscious theme (i.e., fighting racism) did not make the top five at the end of the night. Despite her obvious talent, the judges were clearly laughing at her appearance during her performance (she was overweight wearing a tight spandex one-piece low-cut gold sequenced jumpsuit). She was also the only woman who performed that evening. Her absence from the top five points to larger patterns of patriarchy that were present that night. This demonstrates Tricia Rose's argument about the music industry's tendency to profit "handsomely from highly vulgar and explicit forms of sexism specifically targeting black women—a fact that only encourages other up-and-coming artists to follow in their misogynist footsteps to get famous and rich."[17] The other performers and audience members could read and internalize the ridicule and misogyny of the judges toward this particular performer even though she could not see them. Because she could sing, rap, and dance, her exclusion from the top five was a notable void.

While the performers did not impress me, I heard an overall message of a dire reality that they would use music to lift themselves out of poverty. Most of the performers appeared to be from lower socioeconomic status. Racially, nine performers were African American, seven were Latino, and one was white. Many performers expressed a desire to use music to bring themselves money and fame. One emcee claimed, "One way or another, my family is going to eat." He implied that he would "make it" through his music. Money was a dominant theme despite the fact that performers were spending more money to perform than they likely had made for a gig before. One performer's t-shirt stated "Money Never Sleeps, Stay on your grind"—a t-shirt available on Amazon for $16.99. This t-shirt summarized Theodor Adorno and Max Horkheimer's contention that leisure is an extension of the workday; workers create value even in their time off from work. Another emcee kept yelling "Gucci," but he was not wearing any Gucci[18] or other high-end apparel. While conspicuous consumption is a predominant theme in commercial hip-hop, the celebration of conspicuous consumption was a dominant theme at Coast 2 Coast LIVE without the demonstration of conspicuous consumption, but rather, the celebration of conspicuous consumption stands as a potential and desire for the performers.

As I watched these performers, I reflected on Tricia Rose's book *The Hip Hop Wars* and her perception of "commercial hip hop." In the book, Rose states: "'Mainstream' white America, black youth, black moguls (existing and aspiring), and big mass-media corporations together created hip hop's tragic trinity, the black gangsta, pimp, and ho—the cash cow that drove the big mainstream crossover for hip hop."[19] Rose places the blame of commercial hip-hop on the pursuit of profits by large corporations. Whereas her earlier book *Black Noise* argued that hip-hop could never be commodified,[20] *The Hip Hop Wars* reflexively addresses the genre's commodification. In the tradition of other scholars,[21] Rose identifies the SoundScan era as the harbinger of commercial hip-hop. With the implementation of SoundScan's point-of-sale measurement system, recording industry personnel recognized that the largest consumers of hip-hop music were white suburban teenagers.[22] The result has been a disturbing trend where corporations attempt to profit from racist stereotypes held by white consumers. This creates a weird cultural tourist mentality. It is weird because white consumers think they understand what it means to be from "the hood," but the music they consume merely creates the very fantasy that they already believe. In turn, aspiring emcees internalize the music that they hear and attempt to reproduce what hits—a strategy repeated throughout the Culture Industry.[23] This strategy becomes adopted by more aspiring musicians as industry executives claim that it is a "reflection of reality … as more profits are generated from various 'takes' on the black gangsta, hustler, and pimp, more artists are encouraged to redefine themselves to fit those molds."[24] As Byron Hurt's documentary *Hip-Hop: Beyond Beats and Rhymes* highlights, aspiring artists are willing to reinforce these themes as a means to sign record contracts and improve their class position.[25] The performers also can't be blamed for taking these positions, as many who feed these fantasies are better off for it. Through the commercial hip-hop norms and expectations, the "tragic trinity" becomes the route to success for aspiring emcees.

The most frustrating part of the event was when I heard a performer talking to a friend near the bar. This performer stated, "I gotta win this. It cost me two weeks' pay to enter." At this point in the night, I really began to wonder how much musicians pay to perform. My assumption was that they paid $20–50 for a chance to compete, but that wouldn't add up to two weeks' pay for anyone. The next day, I began to do research on Coast 2 Coast LIVE. On the surface level of the website, nothing appears to cost money. To enter, musicians send the company a demo. Coast 2 Coast LIVE never responded to my inquiry about how much it costs to enter the showcase. Their only response to a question about how much it costs to compete in a showcase was essentially "Submit to get the details just like everyone else."[26] Since I was curious about how much Coast 2 Coast LIVE charges to compete, I began to search online for my answers. The tactics that Coast 2 Coast LIVE deploys caused several bloggers to write about their practices.[27] After bloggers began writing about Coast 2 Coast LIVE as a "scam" and "scheme," Coast 2 Coast threatened defamation lawsuits, but never went through with them.[28] It turns out that after musicians submit their demo, Coast 2 Coast LIVE contacts them back to inform them that they are interested in having them compete in the showcase. This creates an affective response for the musicians who internalize their dreams that they might someday make it in the music industry.[29] Somebody noticed them, took interest in their work, and invited them to perform. At this point, musicians must place a deposit online for half the cost to perform at a showcase. The cost to perform is $300, so they need to pay $150 upfront online and $150 at the show. After someone is on the rope for $150, there is an obligation to continue playing the confidence game. Whereas $300 may be too high for a mark (i.e., the musician) to pay in one shot, Coast 2 Coast found a strategy to make the buy-in seem smaller at the same time that they hook the mark ahead of time. It also ensures that the marks will follow through and perform. The confidence game would not work if musicians did not show up at the showcases. Part of the foundation work is the promotional materials, which Coast 2 Coast LIVE uses online to demonstrate that the showcase is legit. If no one showed up, Coast 2 Coast would not have the promotional videos and testimonials on their website that lure aspiring musicians to the showcase. This foundational work creates a situation in which the company can build an emotional response from potential contestants. In Lauren Berlant's terminology, Coast 2 Coast LIVE produces "cruel optimism"[30] among contestants because they think the showcase will allow them to live their dream while it acts as a threat to their existence.

Winning/Losing

As with any confidence game, artist showcase schemes "are built entirely on hoaxes and false promises that leave their victims empty-handed."[31] The contestants buy into a complicated prize system in which they think there is much to gain from paying the $300 entrance fee. Two temptations exist concurrently that lure unwitting musicians to the showcase, but both ultimately hinge on the ideology of getting signed. First, Coast 2 Coast LIVE proclaims that industry professionals (specifically, A&R staff) attend the events to find talent. Second, Coast 2 Coast LIVE gives the top five contestants a prize each night that helps them promote their music and image. However, neither case allows fruitful opportunities for contestants to fulfill their dream of becoming famous musicians.

The main prize that Coast 2 Coast LIVE gives winners of every event is the opportunity to compete at another event—the annual Coast 2 Coast Music Convention on Labor Day Weekend in Miami. Aside from the chance to compete in Miami, everything they win derives from Coast 2 Coast's own pyramid schemes. According to their website, Coast 2 Coast awards the following to the first-place winner of each showcase.

- Spot in 2019 World Championship to Compete for the Grand Prize of $50,000 Cash;
- 1 Free VIP Pass to the Coast 2 Coast Music Conference 2019 ($400 Value);
- 1 Spot in Direct 2 Exec Meeting with Major Record Label A&R ($300 Value);
- Premium PR Promotion Package ($1000 Value);
- 1 Spot on an upcoming Coast 2 Coast Mixtape Hosted by Major Artist ($400 value);
- 250 Spins on Coast 2 Coast Radio ($600 Value);
- Featured Artist Performance at Upcoming Coast 2 Coast LIVE Showcase ($600 Value);
- Track Placed on the Official Coast 2 Coast Winner's Circle Spotify Playlist.

The main prize that any winner receives is the chance to compete in Miami. Note that all of the values correspond to the price associated with purchasing these services on the Coast 2 Coast websites. The Direct 2 Exec prize is a service where artists pay to perform in front of an executive (discussed below). They do not list prices for any of their promotional services on their website, but rather just like submitting to perform at a Coast 2 Coast LIVE showcase, artists must submit information to receive an email. The Premium PR Package is a mixtape package that they value at $1000, but many of the services are either free or available cheaply.[32] Again, Cost 2 Coast Mixtape is another one of their products/services. Coast 2 Coast Radio is a streaming radio app on which artists can pay to have spins, but the radio is difficult to find and it is not apparent how many people listen to this radio station. If Coast 2 Coast Radio is as anemic as their Spotify playlist, where songs receive less than 1000 plays, then there is no value for artists to pay $600 for 250 spins. A Featured Artist Performance consists of playing at a Coast 2 Coast LIVE showcase at the end of the night after the host announces the winners. The host does not mention what it means to be a featured performer and it is opaque as to whether these performers paid to perform or won a previous showcase. The idea that any of these prizes represent something of value is a deception built upon false promises. However, without the allusion of prizes, no marks would pay the $300 to participate in the showcase.

Underlying the prizes is the illusion of publicity because ultimately these musicians want to be seen, heard, and noticed by industry professionals. The website proclaims that every showcase presents artists with the chance to "Perform for Industry Judges including A&R's, Radio DJs, Platinum and Grammy Winning Producers!" When I attended, there wasn't a single person in the crowd that could do anything for their careers. By contending that industry professionals will be at the show, Coast 2 Coast LIVE creates an illusion of publicity for unsuspecting marks.

Publicity motivates every aspect of Coast 2 Coast's services and the Direct 2 Exec service epitomizes an exhibitionist ethos whereby being seen and heard is the route to being signed. As I mentioned above, the only apparent claim to fame that the judges have in Dallas is that they are judges for Coast 2 Coast LIVE. This charade is matched by their Direct 2 Exec services. With Direct 2 Exec,[33] musicians pay $199/month to have the opportunity to perform one on one with a music industry executive. I spent some time analyzing over 70 Direct 2 Exec recap videos that Coast 2 Coast posts to their website. In each video, vocalists line up and receive the chance to perform one song for this "executive" (really just anybody in the industry they could convince to participate) in a small room or studio. The website states that these "executives" provide written feedback and a five-minute session to discuss the performance, along with a photo to promote on the artist's website. However, clicking through the website demonstrates that the term executive is loose here because most of them are low-level industry personnel. Furthermore, Gaetano contends that Coast 2 Coast pays industry personnel to judge for these events.[34] Strikingly, the judges look bored as they watch artists perform for them while they sit behind their tablets and laptops with the Direct 2 Exec app in front of them.

Since Direct 2 Exec is a subscription, the website states that Direct 2 Exec automatically bills the artists' credit cards each month until they stop the payments. It is not clear what musicians receive with their subscription other than the one-on-one session. While it is a subscription for this once a month opportunity, it is not clear where or when this opportunity happens. The recap videos only provide a limited glimpse into the attendance and circulation of the service. As of December 2018, there are 72 recap videos dating back to February 2016. Yet, there are exponentially more events that do not include recap videos. For instance, the Direct 2 Exec events page lists 17 events for February 2019, and with most events including 20–30 artists, my analysis only scratches the surface. In 61 videos, the page lists the showcase artists for the show. From this limited sample, it demonstrates that Direct 2 Exec has had a minimum of 1600 performances. In my analysis of these videos that listed the showcase performers, 104 artists performed at more than one Direct 2 Exec event, and one artist performed at least six times (spending $1200). However, there is no information on the website about how many artists signed with labels as a result of these events even though this is the goal sold to artists established in the service's first blog post written by Coast 2 Coast's president Nick Hiersche entitled "How to Get a Record Deal."[35] Of course, the only advice given by Hiersche about how to get a record deal is to attend a Direct 2 Exec event. While Coast 2 Coast feeds on the ideology of getting signed, there is no evidence that a subscription to Direct 2 Exec provides the means to sign a record contract (nor does the company provide any information about the pros and cons involved in signing a deal).

Publicity saturates every stage of the confidence game from the Coast 2 Coast LIVE website to the line outside the venue because publicity is the strongest pull for young musicians who dream of signing a record contract into the Coast 2 Coast orbit. Direct 2 Exec exemplifies the twofold nature of performance-as-publicity opportunity because contemporary culture thrives on being seen—one of the prizes that the first-place showcase winners win at each event. Following each event,

Coast 2 Coast LIVE posts a recap on the website. Every part of the show from the line created outside to the backdrop for photographs was for this video to make it look like a hot event. Again, this presents an air of professionalism to lure marks into the con game. At the end of each video, the tagline is "Get Seen, Get Discovered, Get Heard." We could add to the end of this "Get Signed" in the theme of this book. This is the goal of each showcase over and above the idea that they could potentially win serious cash in Miami. Ben Agger calls this environment of narcissistic overexposure "a pornographic culture … a culture of self-exposers, of people who watch themselves."[36] These artists dream of getting signed, but they also want to be seen by others—in an interesting turn of the ideology of getting signed, signing a record contract is a means to be seen. Coast 2 Coast provides aspiring recording artists with the platform, both digital and material, to be seen by other people, but not a route to success.

Conclusion

According to Coast 2 Coast LIVE's website, the biggest prize seems legitimate: the winner in Miami receives $50,000 cash. In a way, while it costs a fee to enter, performers probably have a smoother (i.e., less expensive) route to and better odds of winning the Coast 2 Coast Conference than they would have at winning the $100,000 grand prize on *The Voice*. While contestants on *The Voice* do not pay to perform (though people do need to make it to the initial audition, and at least in Arlington, TX, the stadium charged for parking), they do forgo up to 8 months of pay. In *The Protestant Ethic and the "Spirit" of Capitalism*, Max Weber establishes the protestant work ethic by quoting Benjamin Franklin.

> Remember, that time is money. He that can earn ten shillings a day by his labor, and goes abroad, or sits idle, one half of that day, though he spends but sixpence during his diversion or idleness, ought not to reckon that the only expense; he has really spent, or rather thrown away, five shillings besides.[37]

Weber's point, by way of Franklin, is that not working is equivalent to wasting that amount of money under capitalism. While I find this claim heavily ideological (as does Weber), the underlying concept identifies that *The Voice* contestants spend far more than $300 for a chance to win the show. By forgoing work for up to 8 months and giving up their means to produce value through their music, *The Voice* contestants lose that value, the same as paying it. This approach highlights the speciousness between the two ways of reaching the dream of making it in the music industry.

In American society, the American Dream of pulling oneself up from one's bootstraps creates the environment where people open themselves up to exploitation. Part of the reason is that exploitation is endemic under capitalism—not least because the way capitalism generates surplus value is through the exploitation of labor. People look for quick ways to garner celebrity and capital to participate in conspicuous consumption. What we often do not notice is that the schemes that promise the most, ultimately further ensnare us and everyone else in systems of exploitation, what Berlant calls "cruel optimism."[38]

When Coast 2 Coast offers the opportunity to be seen, heard, and signed by record label A&R representatives, they tap into the ideology of getting signed held by willing marks. The confidence game does not work without the willing mark. By offering aspiring artists with the opportunity to see themselves as Beyoncé, Drake, Taylor Swift, or Kanye West, Coast 2 Coast appeals to a sentiment contained within the musicians. These singers and emcees think they have what it takes to dominate the recording industry and voluntarily expose themselves to the confidence game. Whether as contestants on *The Voice* or showcase participants, sidewalk buskers, or local guitar heroes, the music industry encourages people to dream because often that provides the only opportunity to access obscene wealth, even though the opportunity is false. The specific confidence game is a symptom of a much larger confidence game: capitalism. We all become willing marks when we labor at our jobs with the thought of advancing our careers or saving enough money for a vacation. Antonio Gramsci described how we consent to hegemony in his prison notebooks,[39] and Coast 2 Coast LIVE provides one example of this consent. Capitalism is one big confidence game that we consent to as willing marks as we struggle to meet our needs and receive a larger piece of the pie.

Notes

1. Zorbaugh, *The Gold Coast and the Slum: A Sociological Study of Chicago's Near North Side*; Cressey, *The Taxi-Dance Hall*.
2. Goffman, "On Cooling the Mark Out," 451.
3. Grazian, "The Production of Popular Music as a Confidence Game."
4. Grazian, "The Production of Popular Music as a Confidence Game," 139.
5. Grazian, "The Production of Popular Music as a Confidence Game," 140.
6. "Coast 2 Coast LIVE."
7. I am not using pseudonyms for "Coast 2 Coast LIVE." During my ethnography, I did not interview or speak with anyone associated with the organization. I think it is important to describe and publicize the scheme that they run. In fact, Coast 2 Coast's parent company, Lil Fats, Inc., threatened litigation against websites that have been critical of their practices (Resnikoff, "Coast 2 Coast Threatens Litigation Against DMN for Calling It a 'Scheme,'" March 21, 2016.). However, I do anonymize the artists and their supporters for their protection.
8. Goffman, *The Presentation of Self in Everyday Life*.
9. Grazian, "The Production of Popular Music as a Confidence Game," 145.
10. Horkheimer and Adorno, "The Culture Industry: Enlightenment as Mass Deception," 125.
11. Horkheimer and Adorno, "The Culture Industry: Enlightenment as Mass Deception," 125.
12. Skaggs, "Socializing Rejection and Failure in Artistic Occupational Communities."
13. Goffman, "On Cooling the Mark Out."
14. Ramirez, *Destined for Greatness*.
15. Lee, *Blowin' Up*, 50.
16. Skaggs, "Socializing Rejection and Failure in Artistic Occupational Communities."
17. Rose, *The Hip Hop Wars*, 151.
18. While "gucci" has become a slang reference to good, cool, okay, and chill, it still speaks to a larger obsession with high-end conspicuous consumption that people use the brand this way.

19. Rose, *The Hip Hop Wars*, 25.
20. Rose, *Black Noise: Rap Music and Black Culture in Contemporary America*.
21. Watkins, *Hip Hop Matters: Politics, Pop Culture, and the Struggle for the Soul of a Movement*.
22. Rose, *The Hip Hop Wars*, 15.
23. Grazian, *Mix It Up*, chap. 6.
24. Rose, *The Hip Hop Wars*, 143.
25. Hurt, *Hip-Hop: Beyond Beats and Rhymes*.
26. Email exchange—

    Me: How much does it cost to perform at one of the showcases?
    C2C: Please submit your music for our artist opportunities, thanks!
    Me: How much do I have to pay to perform?
    C2C: Sign up to get all the details!
    Me: Wouldn't it be easier to answer my question?
    C2C: Would be better if you signed up and went through the process to get the information like everyone else.

    When I responded that I am a serious musician and like to know information before I send my copyrighted music, they ceased responding.

27. Resnikoff, "5 Music Industry Schemes That Still Exploit Artists"; "Music Industry Exposed—Coast 2 Coast Mixtapes."
28. Resnikoff, "Coast 2 Coast Threatens Litigation Against DMN for Calling It a 'Scheme,'" March 21, 2016.
29. Berlant, *Cruel Optimism*.
30. Berlant, *Cruel Optimism*.
31. Grazian, "The Production of Popular Music as a Confidence Game," 142.
32. **Premium Mixtape Promotion Includes:**

    - Upload to MyMixtapez App
    - Sponsored Mixtape on Datpiff.com
    - 300,000 Email Blast
    - 5000 Artist Discovery Ad Views
    - 100,000 300x100 Banner Impressions
    - 10x Twitter Campaign
    - Facebook Campaign
    - Instagram Promo Ad/Post
    - Promotion Status Report
    - Listener Demographic Report

- 150 Spins on Coast 2 Coast Radio
- 3 Days Homepage Takeover Ad on Coast 2 Coast
- 2 Days Featured Mixtape on Coast 2 Coast
- Cover Design
- 1 Day Website Takeover Skin
- Press Release Written & Distributed
- 2 Songs Mixtape Release Party

33. "Direct 2 Exec."
34. "Music Industry Exposed—Coast 2 Coast Mixtapes."
35. Hiersche, "How to Get a Record Deal."
36. Agger, *Oversharing*.
37. Weber, *The Protestant Ethic and the Spirit of Capitalism*, 9.
38. Berlant, *Cruel Optimism*.
39. Gramsci, *Selections from the Prison Notebooks of Antonio Gramsci*.

Bibliography

Agger, Ben. *Oversharing: Presentations of Self in the Internet Age*. New York, NY: Routledge, 2011.

Berlant, Lauren. *Cruel Optimism*. Durham, NC: Duke University Press Books, 2011.

"Coast 2 Coast LIVE." Business Website. *Coast 2 Coast Live*, July 18, 2018. http://coast2coastlive.com/about.aspx.

Cressey, Paul Goalby. *The Taxi-Dance Hall: A Sociological Study in Commercialized Recreation and City Life*. New edition. Chicago, IL: University of Chicago Press, 2008.

"Direct 2 Exec." *Direct 2 Exec*. Accessed December 10, 2018. http://direct2exec.net/.

Gaetano. "Music Industry Exposed—Coast 2 Coast Mixtapes: Yes, They Are A F*cking Scam." Blog. *Gaetano*, August 16, 2017. https://officialgaetano.com/music-industry/exposed/coast-2-coast-mixtapes-reviews-scam/.

Goffman, Erving. "On Cooling the Mark Out." *Psychiatry* 15, no. 4 (November 1, 1952): 451–63. https://doi.org/10.1080/00332747.1952.11022896.

———. *The Presentation of Self in Everyday Life*. 1st ed. New York, NY: Anchor, 1959.
Gramsci, Antonio. *Selections from the Prison Notebooks of Antonio Gramsci*. Edited by Quintin Hoare and Geoffrey Nowell-Smith. London: Lawrence & Wishart, 1971.
Grazian, David. *Mix It Up: Popular Culture, Mass Media, and Society*. 2nd ed. W. W. Norton, Incorporated, 2017.
———. "The Production of Popular Music as a Confidence Game: The Case of the Chicago Blues." *Qualitative Sociology* 27, no. 2 (June 1, 2004): 137–58. https://doi.org/10.1023/b:quas.0000020690.48033.00.
Hiersche, Nick. "How to Get a Record Deal." *Direct 2 Exec*, August 15, 2014. http://direct2exec.net/2014/08/15/how-to-get-a-record-deal/.
Horkheimer, Max, and Theodor W. Adorno. "The Culture Industry: Enlightenment as Mass Deception." In *Dialectic of Enlightenment*, xvii, 258p. New York: Herder and Herder, 1972.
Hurt, Byron. *Hip-Hop: Beyond Beats and Rhymes*. DVD, Documentary. Media Education Foundation, 2006.
Lee, Jooyoung. *Blowin' Up: Rap Dreams in South Central*. Chicago: University of Chicago Press, 2016.
Ramirez, Michael. *Destined for Greatness: Passions, Dreams, and Aspirations in a College Music Town*. Rutgers University Press, 2018. https://www.jstor.org/stable/j.ctt1vgw7xj.
Resnikoff, Paul. "5 Music Industry Schemes That Still Exploit Artists." *Digital Music News*, January 21, 2016. https://www.digitalmusicnews.com/2016/01/21/70725/.
———. "Coast 2 Coast Threatens Litigation Against DMN for Calling It a 'Scheme.'" *Digital Music News*, March 21, 2016. https://www.digitalmusicnews.com/2016/03/21/coast-2-coast-threatens-legal-action-against-digital-music-news-for-calling-it-a-scheme/.
Rose, Tricia. *Black Noise: Rap Music and Black Culture in Contemporary America*. Music/Culture. Hanover, NH: University Press of New England, 1994.
———. *The Hip Hop Wars: What We Talk About When We Talk About Hip Hop—And Why It Matters*. 2nd ed. New York: Civitas Books, 2008.
Skaggs, Rachel. "Socializing Rejection and Failure in Artistic Occupational Communities." *Work and Occupations* 46, no. 2 (May 1, 2019): 149–75. https://doi.org/10.1177/0730888418796546.
Watkins, S. Craig. *Hip Hop Matters: Politics, Pop Culture, and the Struggle for the Soul of a Movement*. Boston: Beacon Press, 2005.

Weber, Max. *The Protestant Ethic and the Spirit of Capitalism: And Other Writings*. Edited by Peter Baehr and Gordon C. Wells. New York, NY: Penguin Classics, 2002.

Zorbaugh, Harvey Warren. *The Gold Coast and the Slum: A Sociological Study of Chicago's Near North Side*. Chicago, IL, 1976. http://www.press.uchicago.edu/ucp/books/book/chicago/G/bo3640349.html.

9

Conclusion

In 2018, the recording industry spent a reported $4.1 billion to develop new artists through their Artist & Repertoire (A&R) departments—around a quarter of the recording industry's reported revenue, and more than double what they spent a couple years ago.[1] This is a product of record labels' renewed interest in developing new acts. Recent history saw a decline in A&R spending before streaming's meteoric rise. At one point in my research, I spoke with a music publisher, Stan, who runs a songwriting house. Stan claimed that music publishers now do the bulk of the work "breaking" an artist because record labels don't put money into artist development. Instead, Stan worked with a number of songwriters who went on to have blockbuster careers after they put in time at his songwriting house. Furthermore, he said songwriters are "using their experience as songwriters to leverage a record contract." Even when record labels weren't spending much on artist development, this points to the desire among musicians to sign a record deal. However, Stan noticed the industry shifting again because streaming was changing the recording industry's business model. Now, record labels see value in developing new artists, more than doubling their investments from a few years ago, and

D. Arditi, *Getting Signed*,
https://doi.org/10.1007/978-3-030-44587-4_9

they have plenty of unsigned artists to choose from who believe in the ideology of getting signed.

While $4.1 billion is a lot of money, this doesn't mean that the money goes into musicians' pockets. In fact, the idea that record labels have billions of dollars to spend on new artists further obscures the livelihoods of newly signed musicians. Whether or not record labels put money into A&R or actively sign large numbers of artists, the ideology of getting signed lives on. The ideology of getting signed makes us think that when a musician signs a record contract they become immersed in instant fame, success, and wealth. However, record contracts provide advance money on sales that an artist must pay back on their portion of recording sales (i.e., royalties). Musicians and non-musicians are surrounded by the ideology when they watch television, movies, read the news, and listen to music. In some ways, record contracts are seen as a get-rich-quick scheme—i.e., a quick way out of poverty. People think that if their favorite artist can pull themselves up by the bootstraps and succeed in the music industry, they (or their musician friends) can follow a similar path. What we miss is the intimate details of our favorite artists' lives. Yes, there may be a singer whose music is ubiquitous, but that does not mean that they make any money nor does it mean that their career will have longevity. Through public relations and marketing campaigns, these artists become larger than life and aspiring musicians observe their behavior and emulate their careers as a path to success. But the alienated nature of the recording industry means that aspiring artists don't know how to emulate an artist's career because they don't have access to it. How many people have seen Jay-Z's record deal? Better yet, how many people have seen a one-hit wonder's record contract? How big is an artist's advance? What is their recoup rate? Royalty rate? Do we know if and when a band recoups their advance? While these are rhetorical questions, they point to the absence of shared knowledge about the recording industry—a product of our alienated relationship from the production of music. Everyone wants to sign a record contract without realizing that a record contract forces a musician to relinquish most artistic control to record labels at the same to that it registers them as in debt to their labels.

After two decades of digital music production, distribution, and consumption, the recurrence of a common theme of digital disruption in the music industry keeps the prospect for an alternative to major record labels alive—an alternative that does not exist in material reality. Musicians hope that digital media can bypass traditional distribution/circulation barriers to allow unsigned and low-level signed acts to interface directly with their fans. This hope is a persistent feature of digital media (and emerging media more generally), a part of the digital dialectic—the idea that new media will save us admits to the inequalities, inequities, and lack of democracy and freedom that exist in society.[2] However, the hope for a more equitable music system continues to fail. The problem is that alternatives remain embedded in the desires created through the ideology of getting signed. Musicians not only want to be successful, but rather, they define signing a record contract *as* success. This circular logic is apparent in the rise of SoundCloud. Artists from Billie Eilish to Juice WRLD distribute their music on SoundCloud—a web application that allows musicians to upload and distribute music. While Billie Eilish and Juice WRLD became famous for topping the SoundCloud charts, they used their popularity to sign record contracts. At the same time, SoundCloud GO pays more than other platforms,[3] and if these artists remained independent, they would earn revenue directly without sharing with record labels. Yet, time and again, musicians choose to sign record contracts. Below I discuss the way artists do benefit from signing a record contract, even though they lose revenue by signing record contracts.

Techno-Utopian Mantras

Through my research, two mantras emerged that I heard would make independent artists viable in a digital music system. Both mantras caught on among musicians, but they originate from editors of *Wired* magazine. First, throughout my interviews with musicians, the most prevalent belief is in the idea of the "long tail" developed by former *Wired* editor Chris Anderson.[4] These musicians believe that while major label artists may benefit the most from digital media, the reduced cost and expanded access to the same means of distribution (e.g., iTunes, Spotify, etc.) allows them to sell music that they would otherwise be unable to sell. Second, several artists discussed establishing "1000 true fans" as an alternative model, which unknown to me at the time was developed by another *Wired* editor, Kevin Kelly.[5] These musicians believe that 1000 "true" fans can produce the equivalent of $100,000 per year. Neither mantra comes from someone familiar with the day-to-day grind of being a gigging musician, but nevertheless many musicians believe this is their best way to financial success outside of a major label. While the belief in either mantra provides a seemingly rational way out of poverty for musicians, neither idea deals with the hard facts of the recording industry: stardom comes through major record labels, and most musicians who sign a record contract will end up for the worse from the deal.

Thinking back to my conversation with Connor, discussed in Chapter 4, about how "serious" musicians pay the $30 to CD Baby[6] to distribute on other platforms, he provided a somewhat militant account of the "long tail" rhetoric. According to Chris Anderson, "it's clear that the story of the Long Tail [sic] is really about the economics of abundance—what happens when the bottlenecks that stand between supply and demand in our culture start to disappear and everything becomes available to everyone."[7] Anderson thinks that money can be made on the margins and those who previously would have been unable to sell albums can now be heard online. In Connor's account, he averages $800 per month through sales of his band's music. The Internet provides a great leveling for musicians as anyone can pay this "low" cost and start bringing in revenue, according to Connor. While it is true that a band could theoretically be heard by a larger audience thanks to the Internet, there is little evidence to suggest that independents flourish online—in fact there is plenty of evidence of the opposite.[8]

In other conversations I had with musicians, some claimed that Bandcamp and SoundCloud provide the perfect place for musicians to upload their music and be heard by people across the world. Bandcamp allows anyone to upload their music and distribute it for whatever cost they want to set. This has a democratizing effect on music because it allows anyone to distribute their music at whatever price they want to sell it. A musician in Dallas, Texas, could sell their music to someone in Japan for

$1, earning them about $0.80 for the sale through Bandcamp. However, there is so much music on Bandcamp that unless you are looking for a particular band, you will not find much of anything. SoundCloud provides musicians with up to 3 hours of uploaded music for free or unlimited uploads for a fee. Again, this means that anyone can upload their music and be heard. But how do music listeners find music when it is free and ubiquitous? It turns out that we have to be told what to listen to through different curation models (playlists, front-page placement, etc.).[9]

The main problem with the "long tail" argument is that digital distribution tends toward infinite options, and when we have infinite options, we don't know what to pick. I experience this every time I open Spotify because I am old school enough to want to listen to a band/artist instead of a playlist. As a result, I open Spotify and stare blankly at my options. When it comes time for me to search, I end up searching for that which I already know (and probably own). Even for people who don't hunt for a single artist, the options can be overwhelming.

> Even someone like Matt, who wholeheartedly loves Spotify-pop, agrees that it's an environment that devalues music: "It's disposable AF. It's too disposable. New Music Friday has seventy-plus songs every week. Who is actually supposed to hang on to any of those songs? There's too much!" This is a symptom of the attention-driven platform economy as well: the churning stomach of the content machine constantly demands new stuff. In such an economy, music that doesn't take off is dropped once it has outlived its usefulness—either as a brand prop or as playlist-filler.[10]

The music industry's economy here is to offer a ton of music, see what hits, and push it harder. Those songs that don't hit won't stick around long. To think that the "long tail" helps an artist by providing a platform obscures the fact that the platform has different heights, metaphorically speaking. Those with record label support receive a higher platform that is visible to users while most musicians are stuck on ground-level platforms, which are obscured from view by the taller platforms. The varied heights of the respective platforms alter the availability of music.

In one surreal conversation I had with Solace (the band discussed at length in Chapter 6), I thought the band members were onto something when they discussed "1000 True Fans." It turns out that Kevin Kelly, Chris Anderson's successor as editor at *Wired* magazine, developed the idea of 1000 true fans as a way for artists to support themselves without dealing with major corporations.[11] In my conversation with Solace, they explained it like this:

Rick: I mean, a [record] deal is one way to make a living, but there are alternatives.
Me: What are the alternative business models to major record labels?
John: The business model is to have 1000 fans who are willing to pay $100 per year per band member. [4000 fans for a 4 piece band]. So if you are a solo artists and you show up with your laptop, acoustic guitar, and loop pedal or whatever. Then you can make 100 k a year and you can make a living. You can pay for your website, pay for your recording, and you can do your own YouTube videos and totally be an artist and have fans. Then maybe if you have 10 k fans a year you can go look for partners like labels or publicists or Mountain Dew and work from there.
Me: How do you get that $100/year from a fan?
Jake: Just like any other business. You release a product. You release a product every year for them to buy.
John: If you find a way to spend 50 grand to make that 100 grand then you walk away with 50 grand to live off of. And again, as a musician, you get put into so many positions where someone will pay you to do something and give you freebies (i.e. clothes, shoes, rad boots, killer shades). So yeah, you just have to be smart like any other business person. And figure out how not to spend money in a stupid way. And do whatever you can with free resources. And then just like any other business you have to improve the quality of your product and you have to be consistent. And it sounds shitty but you have to maximize profit and minimize expenditures.

The logic is crystal clear: a band needs to find people who are willing to spend $100 per year on their music, tickets to their shows, and merchandise. Then, all they have to do is add up the number of fans they need to make what they consider a comfortable living per band member (and true fans bring their friends to shows, which is icing on the cake). The smaller the group, the fewer fans they need. What I didn't understand was how do you know how many true fans you have? What happens if they stop being a "true" fan and become tepid fans?

The problem is that as a mantra, "1000 true fans" makes perfect sense, but when faced with reality, it quickly falls apart. There is nowhere for a fan to sign up as a true fan. "Finding fans is not simply the same as finding an audience to purchase your tickets for your concerts and downloads."[12] In other words, a "true fan" is as ephemeral as anything else. Adding up the number of true fans a band has doesn't establish a steady income. It is just as strange to say that a band needs to play 7 days a week for $200 per night per person to make $70 k per year. The logic of the goal of 1000 true fans is admirable because it attempts to solve the question of how to earn a living from making music. However, the out-of-touch nature of the idea to the concrete demands of earning a living playing music becomes an ideology upon which more musicians' dreams can die.

When *Wired* editors and other techno-utopians dream of the potential impact that the Internet can have on creative communities, they do so without actual experience making a living as a creator. Pipe dreams can produce hypothetical and seemingly rational scenarios to make a living from creative practice, but it doesn't mean they can come true. While these mantras provide alternatives to the record labels, they don't provide paths for musicians around record labels. In fact, there are perfectly rational reasons why musicians do sign record contracts; in the next section, I explore some of those rationales.

Label Resources

When I started this project, I wanted to study *why* musicians desired to sign record contracts. As I researched the subject, the ubiquity of the dream and its ideological trappings became more interesting to me. As I argued in Chapter 6, one concrete reason that a band may sign a record contract relates to the solidarity of the contract forms. Signing a record deal forces those signed to it to honor in a legally binding way. Here, I explore some of the other material and immaterial reasons why musicians sign record contracts. Rather than being unwitting dupes, musicians negotiate a complex political economic system in which they establish their identities as musicians.

First, record labels have national and international teams/networks that can push an artist's album after release. A band could have the money to release an album, but without the right contacts, spending that money is inefficient. A label's employees help grease the wheels of a band's album. This is quintessentially important for an artist to get on radio. "For a record to become a hit it had to be played on national [UK] radio but competition for such airplay was enormous and unless the recording was of a very high standard and had a record company to promote it, it would never be played."[13] While Sara Cohen discussed the situation for local rock musicians in Liverpool, England, this is even more the case in the United States. Without the force of a record label behind an act, it is nearly impossible to get on the radio—especially national radio in the United States. With the concentration of radio ownership, it has become even more difficult because iHeartMedia will not talk to local or independent acts. In the past, there was some ability for local bands to receive spins at local radio stations.

The support that labels provide to receive airplay continues into the digital era and streaming. With the popularity of streaming music, the industry works with new industry intermediaries to enable a system that works for them. A 2017 article in *Billboard* entitled "The Playlist Bandwidth Problem" describes a new challenge that major record labels face saturating the 4500 editorially owned and curated playlists on Spotify.[14] As a result of the unstructured system in place for adopting music on these playlists, "Spotify has been scrambling to launch an official channel for labels and artists to submit music for playlist consideration."[15] Spotify calls the large number of songs available through its service "the bandwidth problem," which is akin to the problem with the so-called long tail[16]—because so much music is available, people do not necessarily know where to look for music. When Apple's iTunes was the dominant player, labels had a centralized authority that could funnel users to specific music using iTunes' front page and chart system.[17] The way Spotify initially dealt with this problem was to develop curated playlists based on Beats Music's original playlist concept.[18] However, creating these playlists created more work for record label employees who now doggedly contact playlist curators to promote their songs. Now, Spotify has the bandwidth problem—"how to cope with the onslaught of label reps, managers and promoters trying to work their songs up Spotify's charts by any means necessary."[19] Record labels are valuable in this chaotic situation for the same reason they were valuable for artists to receive radio airplay. Payola is the practice where record labels pay radio stations to play a specific song. This was how labels got songs on the radio for decades, but it was outlawed in 1960. Even though payola is illegal, labels have a number of workarounds to continue paying for radio spins, including paying an intermediary to pay radio stations. Now, record labels and artists pay for inclusion on Spotify and Apple Music playlists.[20] Without a record label, it is difficult for musicians to access radio and playlists.

Second, bands have a difficult time booking gigs without a record contract. When I spoke with Solace, Charlotte, a former band member who dropped in during my interview, explained, "I used to be in the band and handle the booking. If people haven't heard of the band or the manager, they won't even talk to you. I had such a hard time even talking to people early on. But I think a booking agent would be more valuable [than a manager]." Most bands like to perform, and they want to play on bigger and bigger stages through their career. However, as Charlotte states, it is difficult to get gigs at many venues without the credential of being signed to a record label. Some festivals and venues only book signed acts. Signing a record contract opens doors for artists that would be otherwise locked shut to play gigs.

Third, record contracts give artists the space, time, and support to work full time playing music. One lap steel guitarist told me, "When major labels dedicate money to artist development, people have the time to create, develop their craft." Her perspective reinforced the idea I developed in Chapter 6 that performance becomes a signed artist's full-time job. She continued, "Big record labels give artists the opportunity to create—not to have to work a day job." The contract may not give artists wealth, but they do receive a (small) stipend and the contract covers different incidentals while on the label's time. After they sign, artists can quit their day job. While they do have to pay everything back on their portion of the proceeds, it is not a loan that has to be paid back, but rather future loans are contingent on these initial loans. In other words, record contracts provide signed artists with the resources to dedicate 100% of their time to music and many musicians are attracted to this idea.

Fourth, the marketing networks and power of major record labels are unrivaled for musicians trying to receive mass promotion. "No matter how a recording is funded or distributed, there is always the problem of creating a fan base of people willing to purchase the recording. The function of major labels has become… more and more that of marketers: they produce less and hope to continue to make profits by selling more, and selling more means spending more on advertising."[21] In many ways, record labels provide more to artists in marketing during the digital era than they provide in distribution. Even aspects that do not seem like marketing are in fact marketing. For instance, choosing a big name producer has less to do with producing a particular sound than attaching the producer's name to the project—only big labels have the reach to contract these producers. Similarly, labels can bring other performers on to a song. As I discussed in Chapter 4, these collaborative projects allow audiences to merge, which increases the overall audience size. This is a big consideration for music in the streaming era. People who follow Taylor Swift on Spotify will be taken to her 2012 collaboration with rapper B.o.B, which exposes both artists' fans to each other's music. This can have the power to boost an unknown artist and lift an established artist to the top of the charts. All of this is marketing and rarely relates back to the music. "Musicians, especially those starting out, need a platform to make their music known. Spotify and other streaming services can help, but since they don't pay well, most musicians still need to find support somewhere so they can build an audience and name recognition."[22] Labels provide the marketing power to launch new artists' careers.

Nothing compares to the full weight of record labels supporting a band. As a result, "plenty of today's talents are still willing to sign long-term deals at traditional royalty rates of less than 20% in exchange for a big advance and the ability to harness a major label's full power."[23] The "full power" of major record labels came up in a number of my interviews. In a conversation I had with a veteran band manager, she asserted,

"When the full force of a major record label is behind an artist, there is no limit to success. They have access and resources that grease the wheels of the machine. An artist can't contact radio stations, streaming services, retailers on their own. But even signed bands rarely receive that backing." In an interview I had with a singer/songwriter, Jack, at a booking showcase he expressed that he is not a fan of the terms of record contracts. Since Jack grew up on the road with his parents, he knew how to make a living playing music. However, he said that while there is "a lot you can do to kick-start your own career, there is no way to get big without a label." He continued, "Labels are the only way to get huge, to be in the 1%." As opposed to most musicians that I spoke with, Jack had a strong understanding of the music business. He told me that before he would begin speaking with a label, he would "have to be in the right place." Jack described the right place as having leverage to create better terms on the contract. However, it was very clear that Jack saw no alternative to record labels for a musician who desired fame and wealth.

The material resources associated with major label support were not the only reasons why musicians desire contracts. More often, musicians described certain abstract, less tangible aspects of a record contract that they found seductive. For instance, John from Solace expounded on the possible benefits of a bad record contract, "Maybe it would have been cool for us, maybe we would have gotten on Jimmy Fallon or whatever." As a non-celebrity, it's hard to imagine what it feels like to go on *The Tonight Show Starring Jimmy Fallon,* but as John points out, record labels can open the door to performing on late night shows. This is part of their marketing prowess because they have the connections to make promoting a recording on talk shows a reality. Notice that John didn't say that labels could get his band on Jimmy Fallon's show to help promote the album. Instead, John sees going on *The Tonight Show* as an experience itself disconnected from the promotional aspect. These experiences are difficult to obtain without the backing of a label.

Record contracts also mean celebrity even when they don't bring the artists money. Another member of Solace, Rick, explained a situation where he would sign a contract:

> If I were a solo artist, I've thought if I was approached by a record label, and they basically wanted to take all my money, but you're gonna be big. You're going to be a $30k/year famous person. I don't know, maybe I would take it. If it were me, maybe I would take it. You know 30k for just me, and I'd get sponsorships, and I'd go on *Dancing with the Stars*, and whatever else goes with it. But that's also the right contract and situation. I wouldn't do that for anything under the big record labels.

There is this dream among many musicians that they will be famous from performing their music, and the fame itself keeps them pursuing a contract. Part of this is a deep-seated narcissism that exists among many people who pursue music, especially as a lead singer or other featured instrumentalist. These musicians want to be seen, and as I describe in Chapter 5, they want to be seen as "the best." Rick's reference to *Dancing with the Stars* relates to other mechanisms of celebrity. He sees a record contract as a means to other forms of celebrity, like reality TV shows. Through my fieldwork, I spoke with or observed dozens of performers who pointed to their experience on reality TV as a resume builder. Fame and celebrity have their own attraction for aspiring musicians, and record labels are a means to their attainment.

When musicians sign record contracts, it gives them valuable working experience that becomes marketable skills in their own right. Both Ross Haenfler[24] and Jooyoung Lee[25] discuss the acquisition of skills through performance. While they discuss the DIY punk aesthetic and the hustle hip-hop aesthetic for unsigned acts, respectively, these skills can ultimately lead to record contracts. Even when record contracts fail to enrich artists, or even allow them to subsist, they do develop skills through the process. Some of the skills they learn relate to copyright, record contracts, the recording process, distribution, marketing, radio airplay, public speaking, public relations, promotion, booking large gigs, managing bands, etc. These skills easily convert to jobs in the music industry following their time as artists, but they also land musicians in other careers. I spoke with several people who did not recoup, but who nonetheless established careers outside of music because of the skills they learned—from someone who runs a successful digital marketing firm to a real estate agent. Additionally, college music industry programs like to hire people who have "real-world" experience to teach their students about careers in the music industry.[26] Navigating the recording industry with a record contract allows signed artists to develop a myriad of skills, which hold their own value.

The list goes on for all the benefits that musicians accrue from signing a record contract. I hope this shows that I don't think musicians who pursue a contract are dupes, but it does not negate their exploitation. Exploitation in this context is underpayment for one's labor. Even if musicians receive benefits from signing a record contract, record labels still underpay them for their work creating and promoting their music. Often, when we desire something, it provides the means to exploit us.[27] We need a more equitable system for compensating musicians' work, and I turn now to a possible alternative.

Thinking of an Alternative

After this lengthy critique of record contracts and the recording industry, you might think that the system is too entrenched to provide musicians with a way to make a living from making music. In fact, musicians themselves seem most hung up on record contracts because they believe in the value of copyright. Overthrowing the copyright regime is a scary path that may seem unfair to some musicians because they believe in the value of being paid for their music. Throughout my study, I heard time and again from musicians some iteration of "I deserve to be compensated for music I produce." To that I wholeheartedly agree, but their reasoning almost always includes a romantic ideal of the product of their labor and not the labor itself. Copyright is the law through which record labels exploit musician's labor and a record contract is the mechanism that allows them to do so. What is a more equitable model of music production for musicians? To answer this question, musicians need to give up their hope and belief in copyright and demand rights as workers and as human beings.

Obviously, the first step is overcoming the romanticized notion that copyrights have anything to do with musicians. Copyright is not about providing payment to musicians for their labor, it is about exploiting their labor. It "is a widely used instrument allowing individuals and organizations to monopolize creative expression."[28] Record labels buy the rights to musicians' music on the hope that they can make money from that bargain in the future. Musicians fear that giving up their rights to their music will mean that their record label will make money down the road and that they should be entitled to it. However, the current condition of the recording industry is one in which a tiny percentage of artists benefit from that system, while most never recoup their advance and never make money from the sale of music. As I discussed in Chapter 3, copyright is akin to land enclosure. Copyright created the system through which companies could exploit musicians' labor.

Instead, we need a system that pays musicians for their labor, full stop. At a record label, executives, A&R staff, administrative assistants, and janitors all receive salaries and benefits from the labels, but musicians, the group that creates the product to pay everyone else, don't earn a salary. How is this possible with labor laws in the United States? Simply, contract law supersedes labor law. If a musician says they are willing to work under these conditions because they are "contractors," then labels do not have to pay them. However, musicians never receive an option to sign a contract on other terms. Even if they were given other terms, I fear that the strength of the ideology of getting signed would allow them to still take the bet on copyright. This is why it is so pervasive of an ideology in American society.

Since record labels increasingly use 360 deals that take a cut out of all aspects of a musician's income streams, this provides a unique opportunity to reimagine record contracts. If labels already take revenue from all of the musicians' streams of income, then this centralizes all of the processes in the label or other entity. Record labels or Apple or managers can create arrangements with artists that pay them for their work instead of on the remuneration of royalties. As in other parts of the Culture Industry, the recording industry can create what are known as "joint works"[29] in which the musicians become workers instead of contractors. In the film industry, game industry, and software industry, dozens of workers help to create the cultural commodity, and no one has copyright control other than the company. Here is my plan. Musicians can become full-time **salaried employees**. They sign an employee contract that provides terms of their employment. As such, they become a "worker for hire." As employees, they should earn benefits and a salary. If they do their jobs, they should be able to receive raises. A yearly contract could entitle them to a raise or they can leave at any time, the same way that any worker can leave their job. Of course, as a worker for hire, the label would own the copyrights to the music produced by any musician on their label, but musicians could move on to another label/entity to earn a higher income. Furthermore, this creates more bargaining room for musicians. If a musician is successful, they could negotiate for a share of their work's revenue. Most importantly, if the label doesn't do anything with their music, they can leave like any other employee.

I suspect that many musicians would balk at the idea of relinquishing control of all their copyrights, but this would be a step forward. Notice the plan is not even utopian in the sense of the workers owning/controlling the means of production. In order for musicians to push through to collective ownership, they must first be viewed as workers. The ideology of getting signed to record contracts keeps musicians from moving out of earlier craft production eras. However, this is a necessary step toward musicians ensuring that they receive a wage for their work. Until musicians overcome the ideology of getting signed, they will continue to be stuck as contractors. As contractors, labels do not owe anything to recording artists that is not in the contract. By believing that record contracts allow musicians to flourish, the ideology of getting signed ensures their exploitation.

Notes

1. Ingham, "Why Spend $4.1bn on A&R?".
2. Arditi and Miller, *The Dialectic of Digital Culture.*
3. Paul Resnikoff, "What Your Favorite Streaming Service is Actually Paying Artists…"
4. *The Long Tail.*
5. "1000 True Fans."

6. Note: The $30 figure was provided by my informant. There are different tiers of pay for different services, and the current formula does not include anything that costs $30.
7. Anderson, *The Long Tail*, 11.
8. Andrejevic, *Infoglut*; Arditi, "ITunes"; Elberse, *Blockbusters*; Vaidhyanathan, *The Googlization of Everything*.
9. Arditi, "ITunes"; Arditi, "Digital Subscriptions."
10. Pelly, "Streambait Pop."
11. Kelly, "1000 True Fans."
12. Anderson, *Popular Music in a Digital Music Economy*, 175.
13. Cohen, *Rock Culture in Liverpool*, 57.
14. Gensler, "The Playlist Bandwidth Problem."
15. Gensler, 11.
16. Anderson, *The Long Tail*.
17. Arditi, "ITunes."
18. Arditi, "Digital Subscriptions."
19. Gensler, "The Playlist Bandwidth Problem," 11.
20. Sanchez, "Will Spotify's New 'Playlist Consideration' Feature Kill Playlist Payola?"
21. Taylor, *Music and Capitalism*, 126.
22. Taylor, 126.
23. Karp, "The Wild West of Record Deals," 13.
24. Haenfler, "The Entrepreneurial (Straight) Edge."
25. Lee, *Blowin' Up*.
26. This is a strange phenomenon to me. For instance, I recently read that the guitarist from Hootie and the Blowfish teaches at a college in South Carolina, and I know of dozens of musicians who now teach at colleges. Though note that this is one of the only fields where universities hire industry professionals to teach students.
27. Berlant, *Cruel Optimism*.
28. Sinnreich, *The Essential Guide to Intellectual Property*, 8.
29. Sinnreich, 83.

Bibliography

Anderson, Chris. *The Long Tail: Why the Future of Business is Selling Less of More*. 1st ed. New York: Hyperion, 2006.

Anderson, Tim J. *Popular Music in a Digital Music Economy: Problems and Practices for an Emerging Service Industry*. New York: Routledge, 2014.

Andrejevic, Mark. *Infoglut: How Too Much Information is Changing the Way We Think and Know*. 1st ed. New York, NY: Routledge, 2013.

Arditi, David. "ITunes: Breaking Barriers and Building Walls." *Popular Music and Society* 37, no. 4 (2014): 408–24.

———. "Digital Subscriptions: The Unending Consumption of Music in the Digital Era." *Popular Music and Society* 41, no. 3 (2018): 302–18. https://doi.org/10.1080/03007766.2016.1264101.

Arditi, David, and Jennifer Miller, eds. *The Dialectic of Digital Culture*. Lanham, MD: Lexington Books, 2019.

Berlant, Lauren. *Cruel Optimism*. Durham, NC: Duke University Press Books, 2011.

Cohen, Sara. *Rock Culture in Liverpool: Popular Music in the Making*. New York: Oxford University Press, 1991.

Elberse, Anita. *Blockbusters: Hit-Making, Risk-Taking, and the Big Business of Entertainment*. New York: Henry Holt and Co., 2013.

Gensler, Andy. "The Playlist Bandwidth Problem." *Billboard*, July 22, 2017.

Haenfler, Ross. "The Entrepreneurial (Straight) Edge: How Participation in DIY Music Cultures Translates to Work and Careers." *Cultural Sociology*, June 27, 2017, 1749975517700774. https://doi.org/10.1177/1749975517700774.

Ingham, Tim. "Why Spend $4.1bn on A&R? Because New Artists are Accelerating Streaming's Growth." *Music Business Worldwide* (blog), June 6, 2019. https://www.musicbusinessworldwide.com/why-spend-4-1bn-on-ar-new-artists-are-accelerating-streamings-growth/.

Karp, Hannah. "The Wild West of Record Deals." *Billboard*, July 1, 2016.

Kelly, Kevin. "1,000 True Fans." *The Technium* (blog), March 4, 2008. http://kk.org/thetechnium/1000-true-fans/.

Lee, Jooyoung. *Blowin' Up: Rap Dreams in South Central*. Chicago: University Of Chicago Press, 2016.

Paul Resnikoff. "What Your Favorite Streaming Service is Actually Paying Artists..." *Digital Music News* (blog), February 21, 2014. http://www.digitalmusicnews.com/permalink/2014/02/21/favoritepays.

Pelly, Liz. "Streambait Pop." *The Baffler*, December 11, 2018. https://thebaffler.com/downstream/streambait-pop-pelly.

Sanchez, Daniel. "Will Spotify's New 'Playlist Consideration' Feature Kill Playlist Payola?" *Digital Music News* (blog), July 19, 2018. https://www.digitalmusicnews.com/2018/07/19/spotify-playlist-consideration-payola/.

Sinnreich, Aram. *The Essential Guide to Intellectual Property*. New Haven, CT: Yale University Press, 2019. https://www.worldcat.org/title/essential-guide-to-intellectual-property/oclc/1055252885.

Taylor, Timothy D. *Music and Capitalism: A History of the Present*. Chicago, IL: University of Chicago Press, 2015.

Vaidhyanathan, Siva. *The Googlization of Everything*. Berkeley: University of California Press, 2011.

Index

Numbers

A

D. Arditi, *Getting Signed*,
https://doi.org/10.1007/978-3-030-44587-4

CPSIA information can be obtained
at www.ICGtesting.com
Printed in the USA
LVHW091357031020
667792LV00001B/44